PEOPLE
in Time and Place

INDIANA
HOOSIER HERITAGE

AUTHORS

Dr. Claudia Crump
Professor of Elementary
Social Studies Education
Indiana University Southeast
New Albany, IN

Dr. Norman J.G. Pounds
Former University Professor of
History and Geography
Indiana University
Bloomington, IN

SERIES CONSULTANTS

Dr. James F. Baumann
Professor and Head of the Department of
Reading Education, College of Education
The University of Georgia
Athens, GA

Dr. Theodore Kaltsounis
Professor of Social Studies Education
University of Washington
Seattle, WA

LITERATURE CONSULTANTS

Dr. Ben A. Smith
Assistant Professor of Social Studies Education
Kansas State University
Manhattan, KS

Dr. John C. Davis
Professor of Elementary Education
University of Southern Mississippi
Hattiesburg, MS

Dr. Jesse Palmer
Assistant Professor, Department of Curriculum and Instruction
University of Southern Mississippi
Hattiesburg, MS

SILVER BURDETT & GINN

MORRISTOWN, NJ • NEEDHAM, MA
Atlanta, GA • Cincinnati, OH • Dallas, TX • Deerfield, IL • Menlo Park, CA

SERIES AUTHORS

Dr. W. Frank Ainsley, Professor of Geography, University of North Carolina, Wilmington, NC

Dr. Herbert J. Bass, Professor of History, Temple University, Philadelphia, PA

Dr. Kenneth S. Cooper, Professor of History, Emeritus, George Peabody College for Teachers, Vanderbilt University, Nashville, TN

Dr. Claudia Crump, Professor of Elementary Social Studies Education, Indiana University Southeast, New Albany, IN

Dr. Gary S. Elbow, Professor of Geography, Texas Tech University, Lubbock, TX

Roy Erickson, Program Specialist, K–12 Social Studies and Multicultural Education San Juan Unified School District, Carmichael, CA

Dr. Daniel B. Fleming, Professor of Social Studies Education, Virginia Polytechnic Institute and State University, Blacksburg, VA

Dr. Gerald Michael Greenfield, Professor and Director, Center for International Studies, University of Wisconsin — Parkside, Kenosha, WI

Dr. Linda Greenow, Assistant Professor of Geography, SUNY — The College at New Paltz, New York, NY

Dr. William W. Joyce, Professor of Education, Michigan State University, East Lansing, MI

Dr. Gail S. Ludwig, Geographer-in-Residence, National Geographic Society, Geography Education Program, Washington, D.C.

Dr. Michael B. Petrovich, Professor Emeritus of History, University of Wisconsin, Kenosha, WI

Dr. Norman J.G. Pounds, Former University Professor of History and Geography, Indiana University, Bloomington, IN

Dr. Arthur Roberts, Professor of Education, University of Connecticut, Storrs, CT

Dr. Christine L. Roberts, Professor of Education, University of Connecticut, Storrs, CT

Parke Rouse, Jr., Virginia Historian and Retired Executive Director of the Jamestown-Yorktown Foundation, Williamsburg, VA

Dr. Paul C. Slayton, Jr., Distinguished Professor of Education, Mary Washington College, Fredericksburg, VA

Dr. Edgar A. Toppin, Professor of History and Dean of the Graduate School, Virginia State University, Petersburg, VA

GRADE-LEVEL WRITERS/CONSULTANTS

LuAnna Whaley Carmichael, Fourth Grade Teacher, Grandview Elementary School, Bloomington, Indiana

Andrew Joshua Hendrickson, Fourth Grade Teacher, Tekoppel Elementary School, Evansville, Indiana

Claudia J. Hoone, Fourth Grade Teacher, R.W. Emerson School #58, Indianapolis Public Schools, Indianapolis, Indiana

Mary Reeder, Fourth Grade Teacher, Caze Elementary School, Evansville, Indiana

ACKNOWLEDGMENTS

Grateful acknowledgement is made to the following publishers, authors, and agents for their permission to reprint copyrighted material. Any errors or omissions in copyright notice are inadvertent and will be corrected in future printings as they are discovered.

Moving Hills of Sand by Julian May. Copyright © 1969 by Julian May Dikty and John Hawkinson. A Hawthorn Book. Reprinted by permission of E.P. Dutton, a division of Penguin Books USA Inc.

"Swift Thunder of the Prairie" from *Indians, Indians, Indians: Stories of Tepees and Tomahawks Wampum Belts and War Bonnets, Peace Pipes and Papooses* as told by Lois Maloy.

Tecumseh: Destiny's Warrior by David C. Cooke. Copyright © 1959 by Julian Messner Inc. Used by permission of the publisher.

Abraham Lincoln: An Initial Biography by Genevieve Foster. Reprinted with permission of Charles Scribner's Sons, an imprint of Macmillan Publishing Company. Copyright 1950 Genevieve Foster; copyright renewed © 1978 Genevieve Foster.

The Amish School by Sara E. Fisher and Rachel K. Stahl. Copyright © 1986 by Good Books, Main Street, Intercourse, PA 17534. All rights reserved. Used by permission.

Hoosier Farm Boy. Copyright © 1971 Nancy Niblack Baxter. Guild Press of Indiana, Indianapolis, IN. Used by permission.

Alexandra Gripenberg's "A Half Year in the New World": Miscellaneous Sketches of Travel in the United States (1888). Translated and edited by Ernest J. Moyne (Newark: University of Delaware Press, 1954, 83–84).

Raggedy Ann depiction herein is the Trademark of Macmillan Inc. © 1990. All rights reserved. Used with permission.

Garfield comic strip reprinted by permission of UFS, Inc.

CONTENTS

UNIT 4 INDIANA TODAY AND TOMORROW

RESOURCE SECTION

MAPS

ATLAS

TIME LINES

GRAPHS

TABLES

CHARTS

DIAGRAMS

SKILLBUILDER

SPECIAL FEATURES

USING SOURCE MATERIAL

LITERATURE

CITIZENSHIP AND AMERICAN VALUES

LET'S TAKE A LOOK AT INDIANA

Many people come to my hometown of Indianapolis to see the Indy 500. Maybe someday I will drive a car in the race. *Joey*

My family lives in Michigan City in northern Indiana. My parents own a restaurant near the water. I like living so close to Lake Michigan.

Rich

I live near historic Conner Prairie. When I am older, I want to dress like the pioneers did and tell visitors about this famous place. *Lisa*

Indianapolis is the capital of Indiana. There is much to do here. My family enjoys going to see some of the many different shows and performances.

Margaret

Gary is a very large and important city. Many people here, including my father, work in the steel industry.

Julio

There are many fun things to do in Fort Wayne. Every year, my family goes to the raft race at the Three Rivers Festival.

Christie

I love basketball. I like to watch college basketball games and cheer for my favorite team. Maybe when I am in college, I will be a great Indiana athlete.

Marcus

Southern Indiana is very pretty.
I like to spend a lot of time
outdoors. I enjoy riding my
bike and taking walks.

Barbara

Dear Hoosier Student,

Let us introduce ourselves to you. We are the authors of your textbook. I am Claudia Crump, and I especially like the study of history. I am Norman J. G. Pounds, and my special area is geography. Together we wrote your book, even though we live far, far apart—in Indiana and in England. But we share many interests and experiences. Both of us are teachers who have lived in Indiana a long time. We both think Indiana is a very special state. We are proud to be called Indianans or Hoosiers.

Why is Indiana a special place to live? Nature has been good to Indiana. Our state has rolling hills, rich flatlands, and shifting dunes. Rimming the state are large lakes and rivers for moving goods. Scattered throughout are many smaller lakes and streams, which are especially good for boating and fishing. The state is famous for its many forested parks. Mineral resources provide jobs and goods for many people.

Indiana also has a rich heritage of history. Long, long, long ago—as long as 400 million years—the land was covered by warm seas and then by grinding, cold glaciers. Dinosaurs and mammoths appeared, followed by different families of Indians who gave their name to the state. Next, Indiana was explored and settled by people from different countries. Today we can learn about the past by visiting history parks and living museums, where the past is repeated. We can also be part of festivals where Indianans celebrate their heritage— what they treasure most from their past.

Both of us travel a great deal. We ask what other people know about Indiana. Many have heard of the fast race cars of the Indianapolis 500. Most know about basketball and the wild "Hoosier Hysteria" of fans during games. People admire our leaders, explorers, authors, songwriters, and movie stars. They point to famous buildings made of Indiana limestone. They depend on medicines and many other products shipped from Indiana. Living around the world are students who have been educated in Indiana's famous universities.

When you finish this textbook, you will know much about Indiana's past and present. But what will you know about its future? Remember that you are the future Hoosiers. What are you going to do for your special state?

Sincerely,

Claudia Crump   Norman J Pounds

INDIANA: A SPECIAL PLACE

Each region of Indiana has its own special features. There are many beautiful sights to see and things to do throughout the state.

▲ Dairy farms are a common sight throughout the countryside in Indiana.

The Wabash River flows across the state and forms part of Indiana's border with Illinois. ▶

Many people visit Indiana Dunes
State Park on the shores of
Lake Michigan. ▶

◀ The peony, Indiana's official
state flower, is found throughout
the state.

▲ The Market Square Arena in
Indianapolis is where the Pacers
play basketball.

MAP SKILLS HANDBOOK

Knowing how to work with maps is a social studies skill that everyone must have. You can't learn history and geography without being able to read maps. Maps, however, have many uses that go beyond the material that you are learning in school.

Watch the nightly news. How many times are maps used? The next time you are in the library, take a copy of a weekly newsmagazine and count the number of maps that accompany the articles. Are maps used in any of the advertisements in the magazine? Keep a record over a week of all the times you see or use a map.

As you study United States history this year, you will be using map skills that you already have. You will also be learning some new map skills. All the map skills you will need appear in this Map Skills Handbook. Study the table of contents on these pages to see what you will learn.

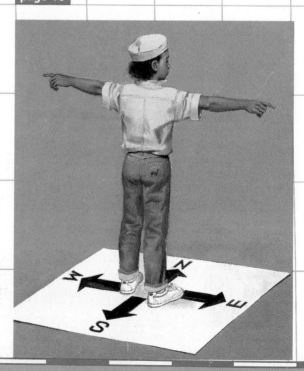

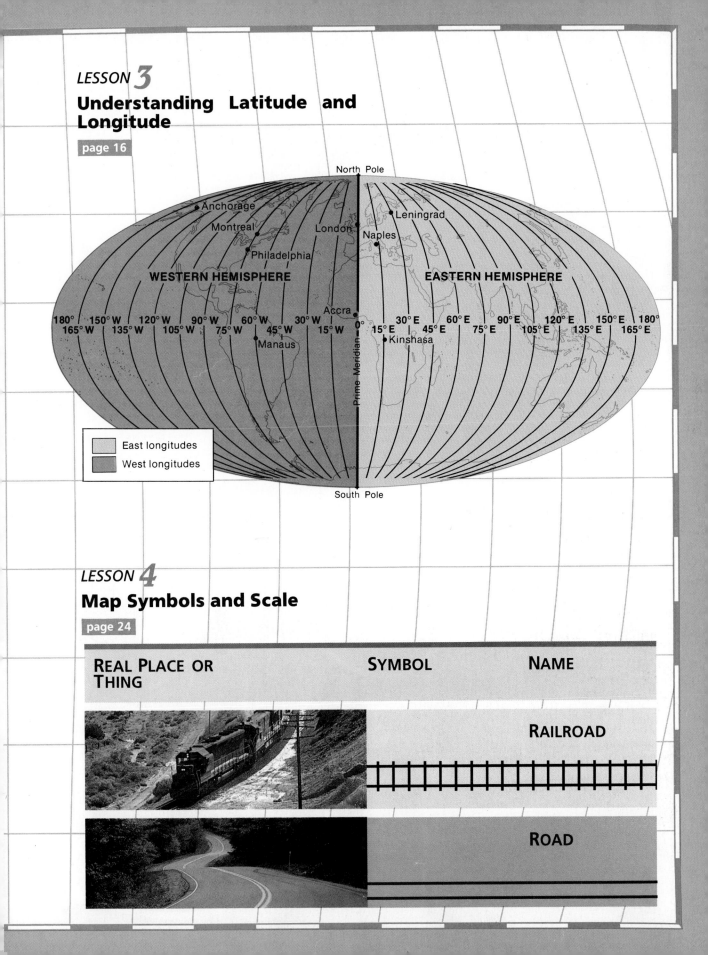

North Pole

Anchorage
Montreal
London
Leningrad
Naples
Philadelphia
WESTERN HEMISPHERE
EASTERN HEMISPHERE
Accra
180° | 150° W | 120° W | 90° W | 60° W | 30° W | 15° W | 0° | 30° E | 60° E | 90° E | 120° E | 150° E | 180°
165° W | 135° W | 105° W | 75° W | 45° W | 15° W | 15° E | 45° E | 75° E | 105° E | 135° E | 165° E
Manaus
Kinshasa
Prime Meridian

East longitudes
West longitudes

South Pole

REAL PLACE OR THING	SYMBOL	NAME
		RAILROAD
		ROAD

Describing Where Places Are

Make a list of any states you have visited outside of Indiana. Then make a list of any countries you have visited outside the United States.

location	ocean
map	continent
sphere	history
globe	geography

What must we know to study the geography of Indiana?

A. Looking at the Earth

Locating Places on a Map "Hey, Dad!" Ben called as he burst through the kitchen door. "I got my first letter from my pen pal!"

This year Ben's teacher, Miss Rivera, had told her class that each student would get the name and address of a child who lived in another country—a pen pal. The students and their pen pals would get to know each other by writing letters.

Ben's pen pal lived in Sweden. His name was Erik Johannson. In his letter, Erik told about his family.

He also explained the **location** of Sweden and of his hometown. A place's location is where it is compared with other places around it. Here is part of his letter:

Hello, Ben. My name is Erik, and I live in Sweden. Sweden is part of Europe. It is across the Atlantic Ocean from the United States. I live in Stockholm, the largest city in Sweden. My hometown is on the coast.

"Can you please show me where those places are, Dad?" Ben asked eagerly.

"Of course, Ben," his dad said with a smile. Ben's dad brought out a book with many **maps** in it. A map is a kind of drawing that shows the world or a part of the world on a flat surface. The cover of the book had a picture like the one on page 6.

Ben's pen pal lives in Sweden. Ben looked at a map to find Sweden's location.
▶ Why do people use maps?

"Let's look at this picture on the cover first, Ben," his dad said. "It shows what the earth would look like if you were an astronaut, flying very high above the earth. You would be looking down on it," Ben's dad continued.

A Model of the Earth "The earth looks round, Dad," said Ben.

"Yes, it is. The earth is shaped like a sphere. That means it is round." Ben's dad picked up an orange from a bowl on the kitchen table. He held it up. "How much of this orange can you see at one time?" he asked.

"Only half," Ben answered.

Ben's dad turned the orange around. "Now you see the other half.

The earth is the same. Even from outer space — even in the picture — you can look at only half of the earth at one time."

"Come on, Ben," his father said. "Let's go into the living room. Bring the orange along. We might be needing it."

Land and Water On the way to the living room, Ben's father explained that the earth is made up of land and water. He steered Ben to the shelf where the globe was kept. A globe is a model of the earth. A model is a small copy of a real thing. The picture below shows a globe like the one Ben's family owned. The globe showed Ben the shape of the earth's land and water.

These are two ways of looking at the earth. One is a photograph taken from space. The other is a model of the earth.
▶ What can you see in these two pictures?

6

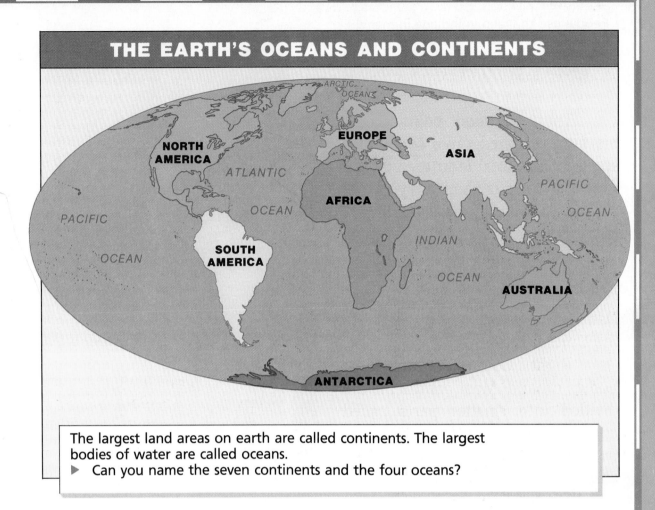

THE EARTH'S OCEANS AND CONTINENTS

The largest land areas on earth are called continents. The largest bodies of water are called oceans.

▶ Can you name the seven continents and the four oceans?

B. Oceans and Continents

The globe helped Ben's father explain many things. He said that about two thirds of the earth's surface is covered by water. The largest bodies of water are called **oceans.** There are four oceans. They are the Atlantic, Arctic, Indian, and Pacific oceans. Ben could see that the Arctic Ocean is the smallest. He could also see that the largest ocean, the Pacific Ocean, is enormous.

Ben's dad pointed out that one third of the earth is made up of land areas. These land areas are divided into **continents.** Continents are the largest areas of land on the earth. There are seven continents. Ben's father turned the globe slowly and called out the names as he pointed to them: "Africa, Antarctica, Europe, Asia, Australia, North America, and South America. Asia is the largest continent, and Australia is the smallest."

"But Dad," said Ben with a puzzled frown, "Europe and Asia are really part of the same land area."

"That's a good point, Ben," his father replied. "We sometimes speak of the total land area of Europe and Asia as Eurasia (yoo RAY zhuh). That word combines letters from the words *Europe* and *Asia*."

C. Countries

"Sweden isn't a continent, is it, Dad?" Ben asked. "And neither is the United States, right?"

"Right. Continents are large bodies of land. Most continents are divided into smaller parts called countries. There are over 170 countries in the world. Here's Sweden, above Germany and Poland."

Ben's dad pointed out that not all continents are divided into countries. For example, Antarctica is not. This continent lies around the South Pole. It is covered with ice and is very cold. People visit it, but no one lives there all the time.

"Australia, though, is both a continent and a country," continued Ben's father.

"You can tell Erik that our country, the United States, is on the continent of North America," said Ben's dad. "It is the second largest country on the continent. Only Canada is larger."

D. States

"Most countries are divided into even smaller regions. Our country is divided into parts called states," said Ben's dad.

"Right! The United States is divided into 50 states. And Indiana is one of them," said Ben proudly.

"Now when I write to Erik, I can tell him that I live in the state of Indiana. And I can tell him that Indiana is in the United States.

"I also want to tell him about the rich and colorful **history** of the state. I know from my social studies class that history is the study of the past," said Ben.

"I can tell Erik interesting stories about Indiana's people and events. Events are what happens in the state. And, of course, I can tell him about the **geography** of Indiana. Geography is the study of the earth and how people use it." Ben was happy that he had so much to write about to his new pen pal. He sat down to begin his letter.

LESSON *1* REVIEW

THINK AND WRITE

A. In what ways is a map different from a globe?
B. What are the seven continents?
C. Which continent is also a country?
D. Why is it important to study the geography of Indiana?

SKILLS CHECK

MAP SKILL

Locate the following places on the map on page 7: Asia, Africa, Antarctica, and the Atlantic Ocean. Which one does not belong in this group, and why?

Learning the Language of Maps

THINK ABOUT WHAT YOU KNOW

Describe a time when you saw someone use a map. What did the person want to know? How did the map help?

STUDY THE VOCABULARY

boundary   compass
compass rose   rotate

FOCUS YOUR READING

How do we describe where places are on a map?

A. Using Maps to Get Around

Help for Travelers "And there we are unloading the car. That was on the day we got back from Kentucky," Mr. Montgomery said. "Please turn on the lights, Kenisha!"

Kenisha's family liked to look at slides from their past vacations. They had just finished viewing pictures from a trip they had made in August to Lexington.

Kenisha's mother began to smile. "Do you remember the time we got lost going to Richmond—right here in Indiana?"

That was just after the Montgomerys had moved to Muncie from the state of Oregon. They did not know their way around Indiana very well. From Muncie to Richmond should have been an easy trip of about 40 miles. But it did not turn out that way.

"How did we ever end up in Ohio?" Kenisha's mother asked, shaking her head. "Oh, yes—I remember. Your father said he knew *exactly* where he was going."

Mr. Montgomery gave an embarrassed grin. "Oh, yes. I said I didn't need to look at a map."

Paying attention to a map would have helped. Maps show

Looking at a map will help you get where you want to go.
▶ What are some of the things that maps show?

INDIANA: ONE OF 50 STATES

Indiana is one of the 50 states of the United States.
▶ Which states touch Indiana?

where places are. They help people get to the places they want to go. They can even tell how far places are from one another.

Kenisha got out a map of the United States like the one shown above. "On this map," she said, "it's easy to see where one state ends and the next one begins."

Boundary Lines Notice that lines on the map are used to separate one state from the next. These lines are called **boundary** lines. A boundary is a line that separates one state or one country from another. A boundary can also be called a border.

"But I don't remember going over a line like this when we went into Ohio," Kenisha said. "I didn't see any marking at all."

"Those boundary lines are only on maps. They are not really marked on the land," her mother replied.

B. Using Directions

Which Way to Go Kenisha's parents decided this might be a good time for her to learn more about maps. Her parents explained that to use a map she needed to know something about directions.

"There are four important direction words that you can use to locate places on a map," her father said. "These main words are *north, south, east,* and *west.*"

Kenisha's father got out a very large piece of white paper. On it he drew a diagram like the one shown below. He asked Kenisha to stand in the middle of the diagram and face toward the letter *N*.

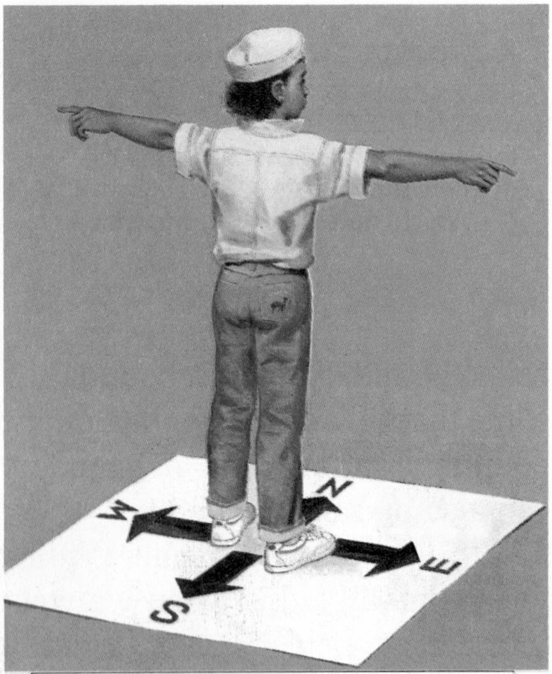

If you face north, south is behind you.
▶ Which direction is on your left, and which is on your right?

"OK, Kenisha, the letters *N*, *S*, *E*, and *W* stand for north, south, east, and west. What direction is to your right?"

Kenisha looked to her right side. "East is on my right."

"What direction is to your left?" her dad asked.

Kenisha looked to her left side. "West is on my left," she said.

Now Kenisha's father asked her to turn and face toward the letter *W*. "OK, Kenisha, now tell me where the other three directions are."

"East is behind me now. And north is to my right and south to my left," Kenisha said.

A Special Rose Kenisha's father explained that many maps have a drawing like this to show directions on the map. The drawing is called a compass rose. Some people call it a direction finder. A compass is a tool for finding directions. The diagram of the earth on page 13 contains a compass rose.

Zoo Map Next Mr. Montgomery dug out a map of the new Indianapolis Zoo. There is one like it on the facing page. Kenisha's father asked her to look at the map of the zoo. He showed Kenisha the direction finder in the upper right corner.

This compass rose shows all of the directions.
▶ Which direction is between north and west?

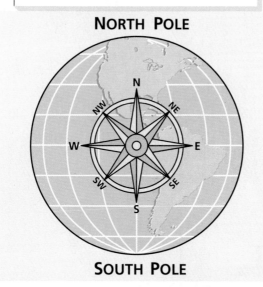

NORTH POLE

SOUTH POLE

"Imagine that you are standing right here." Mr. Montgomery pointed to a spot that was halfway between the Souvenirs building and the Hoosierfest building. "Now use a direction word to tell me where the Administration building is found."

Kenisha said, "That building is to the south."

"Good. Now tell me, where is the Cafe on the Commons?" Kenisha's dad asked.

This map shows fun things to see and do at the Indianapolis Zoo.
▶ In what direction would you travel to get from the forests to the plains?

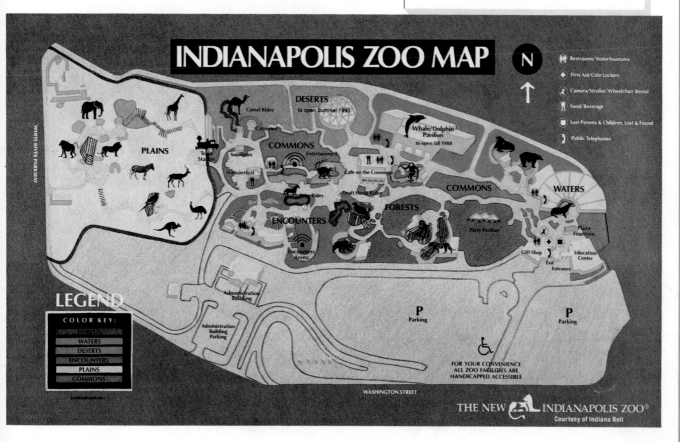

"It is to the east," Kenisha replied promptly.

"And where is the place where you can get a pony ride?" Kenisha's dad asked next.

Kenisha looked puzzled. "Well, it's *between* south and east."

Kenisha's father explained that sometimes the four main direction words are not enough. To be clear, Kenisha would have to say that the area for pony rides lies to the southeast. Something that lies between north and west is northwest. In what direction would you need to go to find the Deserts?

C. Understanding Directions

"I see how to use the direction words," Kenisha said. "But I'm not sure what they really mean. How did someone figure out where north is? Or south?"

Kenisha's mother explained that north is the direction toward the North Pole. The location of the North Pole is shown in the diagram on page 13. If Kenisha were to travel north a very long way, she would come to the North Pole. Part of this long and difficult journey would be across the Arctic Ocean.

Actually, the North Pole is just a point on the map. In that sense, it is like a boundary between states. It

The North Pole and the South Pole are found at opposite ends of the earth.
▶ Which is the most northern place on the earth?

does not really exist on the surface of the earth.

Then Kenisha's mother said: "Imagine that you are going south from Indiana. You would cross Kentucky, then Tennessee and Alabama. If you went on for a very long distance, you would at last get to the continent of Antarctica. Then if you trekked across that continent, you would reach the South Pole."

The North and South poles are always in the same place. The earth rotates around them.
▶ What does *rotate* mean?

Kenisha's dad brought over their globe. He pointed to the North Pole and the South Pole on the globe as well. Then he took the globe off its stand and put one finger on the North Pole and another on the South Pole. He asked Kenisha's mother to slowly **rotate**, or turn, the globe. "My fingers are like the North and South poles," he explained. "They do not move. The earth just turns around them."

LESSON 2 *REVIEW*

THINK AND WRITE

A. What is a boundary?
B. What are the eight directions that could be shown on a compass rose on a map?
C. In what way are the North and South poles like boundary lines between states?

SKILLS CHECK

MAP SKILL

Look at the map of the United States on pages 354–355. For each of the following states, use a direction word to give the state's location in relation to Indiana: Alabama, Wisconsin, Maine, Illinois.

15

Understanding Latitude and Longitude

THINK ABOUT WHAT YOU KNOW

Suppose you are trying to find a building on a town map. Someone tells you that it is at the corner of Main Street and 10th Street. How does this information help you find the building on the map?

STUDY THE VOCABULARY

hemisphere	Prime Meridian
Equator	grid
latitude	estimate
longitude	time zone

FOCUS YOUR READING

How can we say where a place is located on the earth?

A. The Equator

"Are you *sure* you have to move away, Nicole?" Amanda sighed and looked glum. Nicole was Amanda's best friend.

"I'm sure. My father is being transferred by his company," Nicole said. "It won't be so bad. I'll still be living in Indiana!"

"Oh, stop it! There's nothing good about this move. I'll be here in Fort Wayne, and you'll be far away in Evansville. You might just as well be on the other side of the earth," Amanda complained.

Amanda sometimes exaggerates. Nicole is *not* moving to the other side of the earth. Let's take a look at what that would really mean. Nicole would have to be moving to a different **hemisphere** (HEM ih sfihr). A hemisphere is one half of the earth. Indiana is in the Northern Hemisphere. The Northern Hemisphere is separated from the Southern Hemisphere by an imaginary line. This line runs completely around the earth. It is called the **Equator.** The Equator is halfway between the North Pole and the South Pole. Can you find the Equator on the map on the facing page? What color is the Northern Hemisphere?

The girls found Fort Wayne and Evansville on a map of Indiana.
▶ What are the lines that run across a map called?

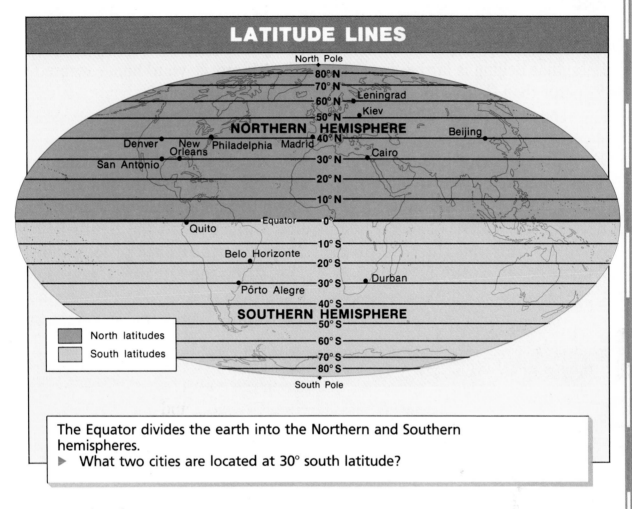

LATITUDE LINES

North Pole

80° N
70° N
60° N — Leningrad
50° N — Kiev

NORTHERN HEMISPHERE
40° N   Beijing

Denver • New   Philadelphia Madrid
Orleans   Cairo
                        30° N
San Antonio
20° N

10° N

Quito   Equator — 0°

10° S
Belo Horizonte
20° S
                        Durban
                        30° S
Pôrto Alegre
40° S
SOUTHERN HEMISPHERE
50° S

North latitudes   60° S
South latitudes   70° S
80° S

South Pole

The Equator divides the earth into the Northern and Southern hemispheres.

▶ What two cities are located at 30° south latitude?

B. Latitude

Amanda and Nicole decided to find out more about the location of Evansville. They thought that might help Nicole get ready for her move. They got out a map of Indiana like the one on page 20. They noticed a lot of lines running across the map.

All lines that run across a map are called lines of **latitude.** The Equator is a line of latitude. The lines between the Equator and the North Pole are lines of north latitude. Those that lie between the

Equator and the South Pole are lines of south latitude.

Amanda studied the map. She noticed that the lines of latitude were numbered. These numbers are called degrees of latitude. The symbol for degree is °. These numbers run from 0° at the Equator to 90° at the North Pole.

We use the number of degrees of latitude to tell us how far a place is from the Equator. The larger the number, the farther from the Equator a place is. For example, Cairo is at 30° north and Beijing is at 40° north. We know, from these numbers, that Beijing is farther from the Equator than Cairo.

The two girls decided to use degrees of latitude to compare where Fort Wayne and Evansville are. They noticed on the Indiana map that a line of latitude labeled 41° north runs just south of Fort Wayne. Another line runs just north of Evansville. It is 38° north. "Only three degrees of latitude between us!" Nicole exclaimed with a grin.

"That makes the two cities seem a *little* closer together!"

Where is your home located? What is its latitude?

C. Longitude

Nicole pointed out to Amanda that lines were also running up and down the map. These lines run from the North Pole to the South Pole. They are called lines of **longitude.** They cross the Equator. If you look at the map below, you will notice an interesting thing. The greatest

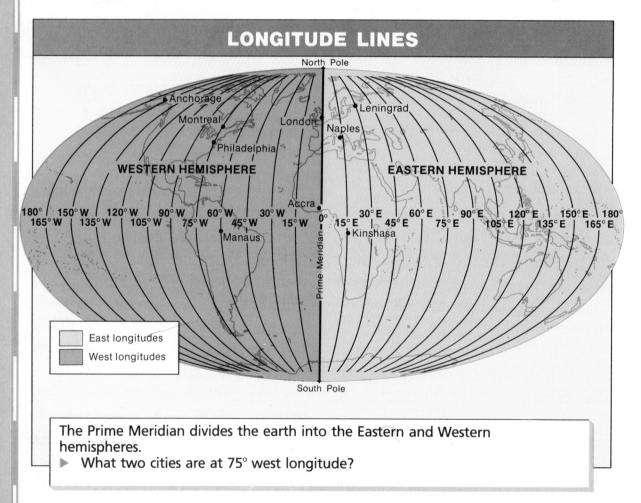

LONGITUDE LINES

The Prime Meridian divides the earth into the Eastern and Western hemispheres.
► What two cities are at 75° west longitude?

amount of space between the lines of longitude occurs at the Equator. But the lines of longitude come together at the North and South poles. That is because the earth is a sphere.

The Equator is the special imaginary latitude line that divides the Northern and Southern hemispheres. There is also a special line of longitude. It runs from pole to pole. It passes through Greenwich, England. This line of longitude is called the **Prime Meridian.** The Prime Meridian is 0° longitude. All other lines of longitude measure distances east or west of it.

The half of the earth that lies west of the Prime Meridian is called the Western Hemisphere. The half that lies to the east is called the Eastern Hemisphere. Besides being in the Northern Hemisphere, Indiana is in the Western Hemisphere.

Look again at the map on page 18. Put your finger on the line marked 30°E. *E* stands for east. Move your finger along the line until you come to Leningrad. Can you see that Leningrad lies at 30° east longitude? Look back at the map on page 17. Leningrad also lies at 60° north latitude. You can say that Leningrad is 60° north and 30° east.

Philadelphia is also shown on both maps. This city is on the line of latitude of 40° north and the line of

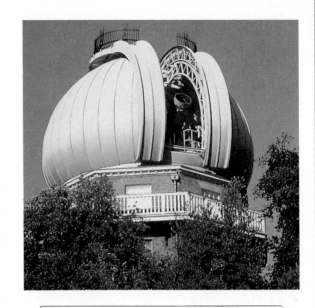

Longitude measurements are made from this observatory in Greenwich, England.
▶ What is longitude?

longitude of 75° west. It is most important to be able to say just where a place is on the earth.

D. Using a Grid

The lines of latitude and longitude on the map form a **grid.** A grid is a system of lines that cross and form squares or boxes. We can also use this grid to say where a place is. For example, as the girls were looking at the map of Indiana, they saw that neither Fort Wayne nor Evansville lies just where the lines cross. When this happens you have to **estimate,** or figure out *about,* where a place is.

They saw from the map that Fort Wayne is at nearly 41° north

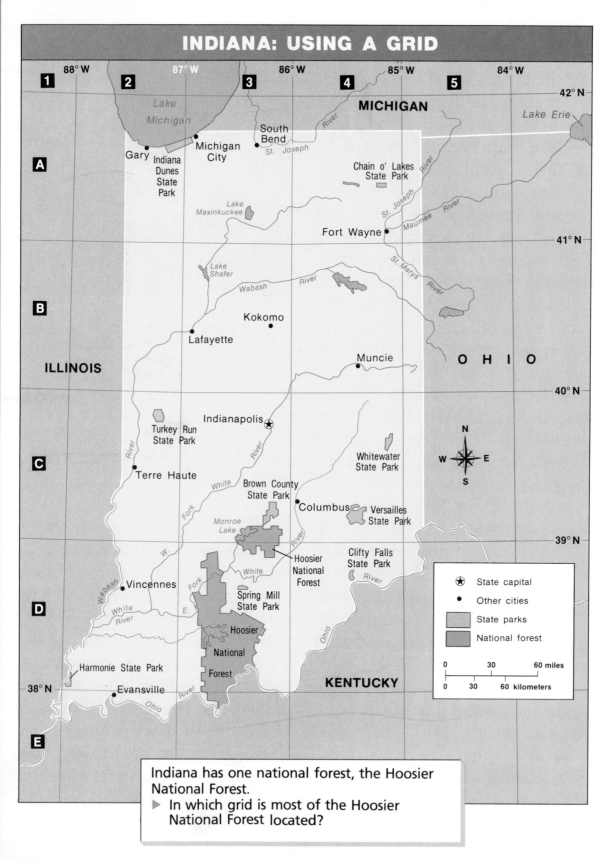

INDIANA: USING A GRID

Indiana has one national forest, the Hoosier National Forest.

▶ In which grid is most of the Hoosier National Forest located?

and very close to 85° west. Evansville was a little more difficult. It is clearly at about 38° north. Yet it is almost exactly halfway between 87° west and 88° west. That made deciding between the two hard.

But this problem actually helped the girls. They discovered that there is an easier way of saying where a place is. They noticed that the boxes on their map were numbered across the top of the map from 1 to 5, just as they are on your map. They are also lettered from A to E on the side of the map. Fort Wayne lies in the fourth box from the left in row A. It is in box A-4. Evansville is in box E-2. Where is Vincennes? Where is Lafayette? Where is Muncie? Grids are often used to locate places.

Long ago, people told time by the sun. The shadow on this sundial tells the time.
▶ What time is shown here?

E. The Time of Day

Time Differences "You know what the strangest thing about your moving will be, Amanda?" Nicole asked mysteriously.

"No. What?" Amanda said.

"It will be a different time in Evansville than it is here."

"Hold on, Nicole. What do you mean?" Amanda protested.

Have you ever traveled to a place where you had to change your watch or clock to match the local time where you were visiting? Why did that happen?

You know that the earth moves around the sun. But to us, it looks as if the sun moves across the sky from east to west. That is the reason why we say the sun rises in the east and sets in the west.

What time of day is it by your school clock? Is it before noon or after noon? Noon is when the sun is highest in the sky. But the sun reaches its highest point in the sky in Ohio before it reaches its highest point in Indiana. (Indiana is farther west, so the sun "gets there" later.)

On the other hand, it is highest in the sky in Indiana before it is highest in the sky in most of Illinois.

Look again at the map of Indiana. Imagine that everyone in Indiana told time only by the sun. First it would be noon in Fort Wayne and a few minutes later noon in Muncie. It would be noon in Kokomo just shortly before it was noon in Lafayette. When you traveled east or west, you would have to adjust your watch every few miles.

About a hundred years ago, the clocks in all these places showed different times. All the times were correct by the sun. But it was confusing that the time in one city was a little bit different from the time in a neighboring city.

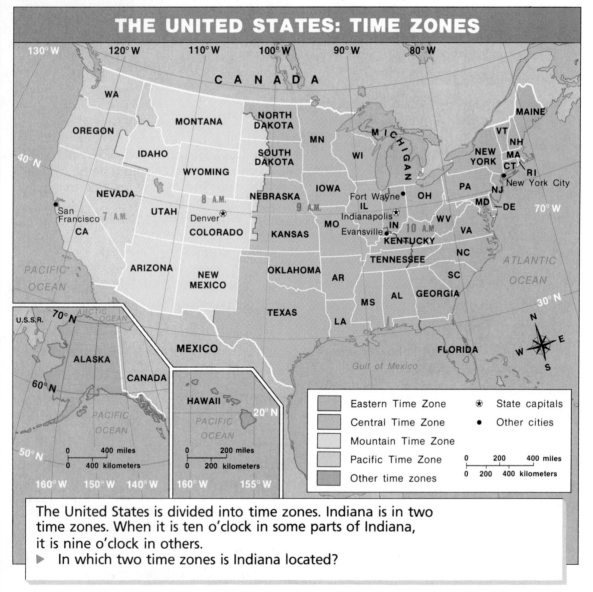

THE UNITED STATES: TIME ZONES

Eastern Time Zone
Central Time Zone
Mountain Time Zone
Pacific Time Zone
Other time zones

⊛ State capitals
• Other cities

The United States is divided into time zones. Indiana is in two time zones. When it is ten o'clock in some parts of Indiana, it is nine o'clock in others.
▶ In which two time zones is Indiana located?

Time Zones Fortunately, our country has been divided into **time zones.** Within each of these large areas, all the clocks show the same time. Look at the time zone map on page 22. Most of Indiana is in the Eastern Time Zone. Some of the state, including Evansville, is in the Central Time Zone. To the west of the Central Time Zone is the Mountain Time Zone. Beyond that is the Pacific Time Zone. When it is nine o'clock in the morning in Evansville, it is ten o'clock in the morning in Fort Wayne — and also in New York City. What time is it then in Denver, Colorado? What time is it in San Francisco, California?

"So, Nicole," said Amanda, "you'll be in the Central Time Zone, and I'll be in the Eastern Time Zone. Your time will be an hour earlier than mine. Sometime when you're

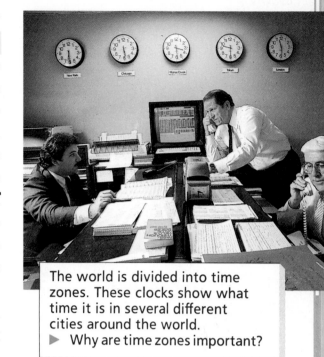

The world is divided into time zones. These clocks show what time it is in several different cities around the world.
▶ Why are time zones important?

taking a test at 11 o'clock in the morning, think of me. At that moment, I'll just be sitting down to a delicious lunch." Amanda smiled playfully. "You know, I guess there *is* something good about your moving to Evansville after all!"

LESSON **3** *REVIEW*

THINK AND WRITE

A. What line runs around the earth midway between the North and South poles?
B. What does it mean to say that a place is at a latitude of 50° north?
C. From what special line do we measure longitude?
D. How do you use the grid on a map to tell where a place is?

E. Is it later by the sun in a city on the East Coast of the United States or in Indianapolis?

SKILLS CHECK

MAP SKILL

Use the map on page 20 to estimate the latitude and longitude for the following places: Columbus, Turkey Run State Park, Lake Shafer.

Map Symbols and Scale

THINK ABOUT WHAT YOU KNOW

You have studied maps of the world and a map of the Indianapolis Zoo. List three other places that you could use a map to find out about.

STUDY THE VOCABULARY

symbol   **scale**
key

FOCUS YOUR READING

What must we know to read a map correctly?

A. Pictures and Maps

It was show-and-tell day. Kevin was excited about the two things he had brought. One was a picture of a recreation center where his father had taken him. The picture had been taken from an airplane. You can see a picture like it on page 25. In this picture you see fields, bleachers, a running track, houses, trees, and even a few cars. There are also many other things in the picture. You can see some of them clearly. Others are not so clear.

Kevin had also brought a drawing. It is shown below the picture on page 25. This is a map of the place seen in the photo. What differences can you find between the photo and the map? One important difference is that the map leaves out a lot of things that appear in the picture. The map shows only the things that are important, such as the fields, the bleachers, and the running track. Most maps leave out details such as cars and single trees.

THE METRIC SYSTEM

On page 30 you will see that the measurement of a map is given in inches and centimeters. Later you will find bigger measurements given in miles and kilometers. Centimeters and kilometers are units of measure in the metric system.

The metric system is a way of measuring area, distance, weight, capacity, and temperature. This system is used in all major countries except the United States. Plans are being made to "go metric" here also.

To get you ready for this change, both American and metric measurements are given in this book. Each measurement used in our country is followed by the metric measurement that is about equal to it. Miles are changed to kilometers (km), inches to centimeters (cm), feet or yards to meters (m), acres to hectares (ha), pounds to kilograms (kg), and degrees Fahrenheit (°F) to degrees Celsius (°C).

Bleachers	Road	Baseball field	Soccer field
Houses	Running track	Football field	Other land

1 inch stands for 130 feet.

The places and things shown in the photograph are shown by symbols on the map.

▶ Find the running track in the photograph and on the map.
Describe the symbol on the map for the baseball field.

B. Symbols

Mr. Hart, Kevin's teacher, was excited about Kevin's show and tell. Mr. Hart said that it would be an interesting way for the class to learn about maps and **symbols.** A symbol is something that stands for the real thing. Before you can use a map, you need to find out what the symbols on the map mean.

The part of the map that tells what the symbols stand for is called the **key.** It is also called a legend. A map key may contain many different symbols. Look at Kevin's map on page 25. At the bottom of the map is the map key.

Mr. Hart explained that in the key on Kevin's map, the orange symbol stands for houses. Yellow shows the running track, and dark green stands for a football field.

On page 27 you can see some of these map symbols. A river is shown by a wavy blue line. A railroad is a black line with short lines across it. The symbol looks like an actual railroad track.

C. Scale

The picture and the map on page 25 measure only about 8 inches (25 centimeters) across. But how big is the recreation center? How far would Kevin have to walk to get from the baseball field to the soccer field? To answer these questions, you need to know the **scale** of the map. Scale tells us how much bigger the real place is than the map.

Both of these models show the same train. But each model was built to a different scale.
▶ What is scale?

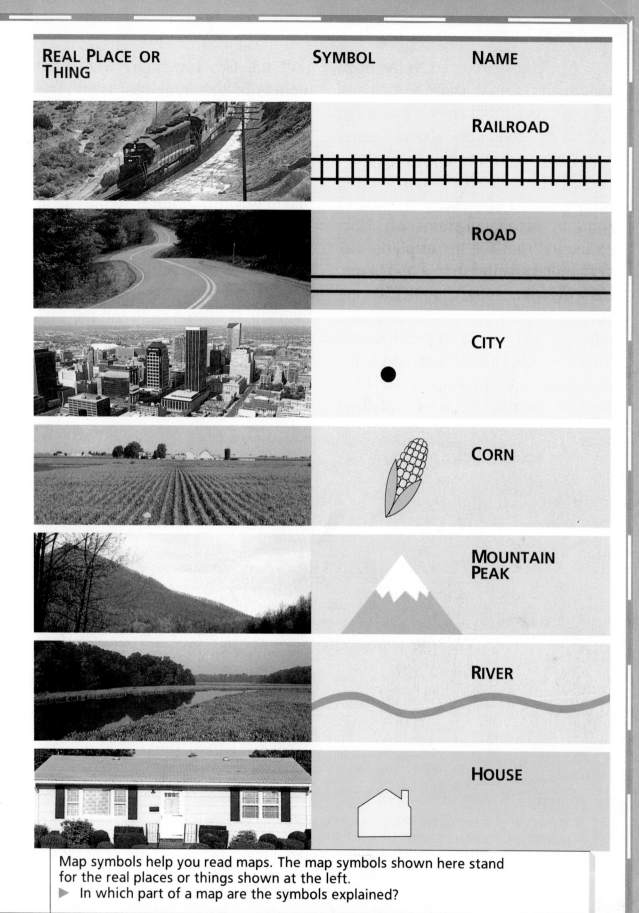

REAL PLACE OR THING	SYMBOL	NAME
		RAILROAD
		ROAD
	●	CITY
		CORN
		MOUNTAIN PEAK
		RIVER
		HOUSE

Map symbols help you read maps. The map symbols shown here stand for the real places or things shown at the left.
▶ In which part of a map are the symbols explained?

Mr. Hart explained to the class that maps cannot show places and things in their real sizes. Places and distances must be shown many times smaller than they really are.

Mr. Hart asked Melanie to bring up her model airplane and Scott to bring up his model trains. Mr. Hart explained that the toy airplane was very much smaller than a real plane. Its wings measured 1 foot (30 cm) across. A real plane like it would measure 100 feet (3,048 cm) across its wings. "In this toy airplane," Mr. Hart said, "1 foot stands for 100 feet. That is its scale." Mr. Hart explained that the two toy trains were both models of the same real train. The models were different sizes because they were built at different scales.

On a map, a certain number of inches stand for a certain number of feet or yards or miles on the earth. When we show size or distance in this way, we say that the map is drawn to a certain scale. The map scale is often shown in a corner of the map. It allows us to tell the real distance from one place to another.

Mr. Hart asked his class to pretend that they were high above a football field. He drew a picture on

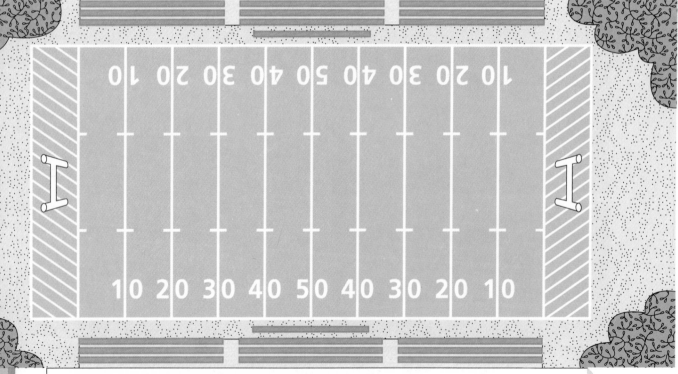

This picture of a football field is drawn to scale. The picture is much smaller than the real football field would be.
▶ Why could this field not be drawn to its real size?

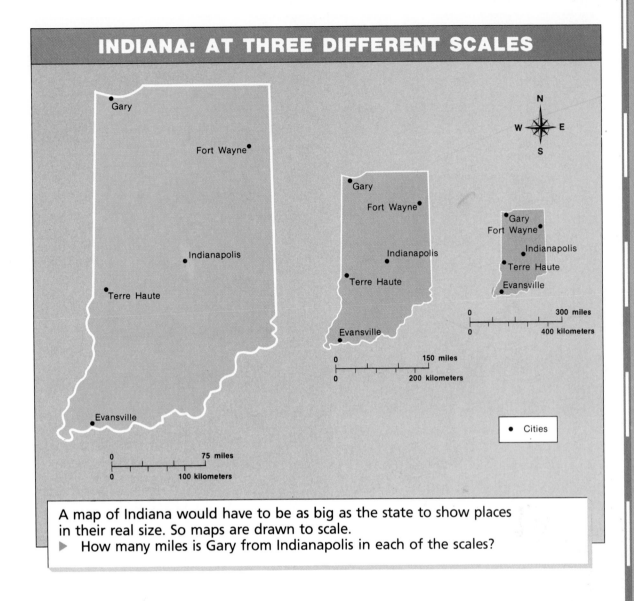

INDIANA: AT THREE DIFFERENT SCALES

Gary
Fort Wayne
Indianapolis
Terre Haute
Evansville

0   75 miles
0   100 kilometers

Gary
Fort Wayne
Indianapolis
Terre Haute
Evansville

0   150 miles
0   200 kilometers

N
W   E
S

Gary
Fort Wayne
Indianapolis
Terre Haute
Evansville

0   300 miles
0   400 kilometers

• Cities

A map of Indiana would have to be as big as the state to show places in their real size. So maps are drawn to scale.
▶ How many miles is Gary from Indianapolis in each of the scales?

the chalkboard that looked like the drawing on page 28. This drawing was made to a scale in which 1 inch stands for 20 yards. The drawing is 6 inches long. So the total length of the real football field is 120 yards, or six groups of 20 yards. Use a ruler to measure the width of the football field in inches. How many yards does this represent?

D. Indiana and Scale

The scale line on a map shows what distance an inch (or a centimeter) on the map stands for. Maps can be drawn to many different scales. Look at the three maps of Indiana on this page. Each map is drawn to a different scale.

Put a ruler under the scale line of the map on the left. You will see

that 1 inch stands for about 75 miles. (One centimeter stands for about 50 kilometers.) On this map, how many inches (centimeters) is it in a straight line from Terre Haute to Gary? If you measure correctly, your answer should be 2 inches (5 cm). To find out how many miles 2 inches stands for, you would multiply 2 by 75. The answer is 150 miles. To find out how many kilometers 5 centimeters stands for, multiply 5 by 50.

Do the same on the other two maps. If you measure carefully and use the correct scale, you always find that the distance from Terre Haute to Gary stays the same.

E. What a Map Shows

Mr. Hart explained that Kevin's photograph made clear an important point about maps. The photograph let the class look down on the land. So does a map. You will be using many maps as you study the geography and history of Indiana. But each time you look at a map, you must ask what its scale is, what symbols it has, and what the symbols mean.

You will find maps that show the whole world and maps that show only our own country or our own state of Indiana. They differ in scale. How much they can show you depends on their scale.

about it. In the column called *Area Rank,* the county that is number 1 is the largest in area. It is Allen County. To find out which county has the largest population, look in the column called "Population Rank." Marion County is number 1. That means it has more people than any other county.

C. Reading a Bar Graph

Indiana is not one of the largest of the 50 states. In fact, 37 states are larger. Look again at the map of the United States. Name some states that are larger than Indiana and some that are smaller. You can show these different sizes on a special drawing called a bar graph. Look at the bar graph below. It shows the

This bar graph shows the size of Indiana and its neighbors.
▶ What is the size of Indiana in square miles?

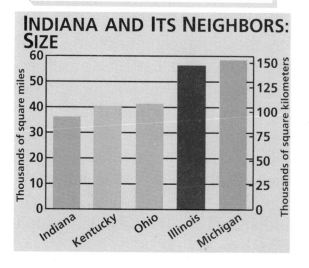

INDIANA AND ITS NEIGHBORS: SIZE

Thousands of square miles / *Thousands of square kilometers*

Indiana, Kentucky, Ohio, Illinois, Michigan

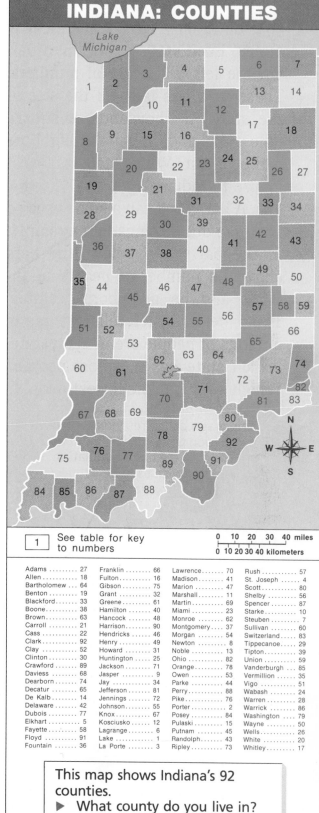

INDIANA: COUNTIES

Lake Michigan

| 1 | See table for key to numbers |

0 10 20 30 40 miles
0 10 20 30 40 kilometers

Adams 27	Franklin 66	Lawrence....... 70	Rush 57
Allen 18	Fulton 16	Madison 41	St. Joseph 4
Bartholomew ... 64	Gibson 75	Marion 47	Scott 80
Benton 19	Grant 32	Marshall 11	Shelby 56
Blackford 33	Greene 61	Martin 69	Spencer 87
Boone 38	Hamilton 40	Miami 23	Starke 10
Brown 63	Hancock 48	Monroe 62	Steuben 7
Carroll 21	Harrison 90	Montgomery... 37	Sullivan 60
Cass 22	Hendricks 46	Morgan 54	Switzerland..... 83
Clark 92	Henry 49	Newton 8	Tippecanoe..... 29
Clay 52	Howard 31	Noble 13	Tipton 39
Clinton 30	Huntington ... 25	Ohio 82	Union 59
Crawford 89	Jackson 71	Orange 78	Vanderburgh ... 85
Daviess 68	Jasper 9	Owen 53	Vermillion 35
Dearborn 74	Jay 34	Parke 44	Vigo 51
Decatur 65	Jefferson 81	Perry........... 88	Wabash 24
De Kalb 14	Jennings 72	Pike........... 76	Warren 28
Delaware 42	Johnson........ 55	Porter 2	Warrick 86
Dubois 77	Knox........... 67	Posey 84	Washington ... 79
Elkhart 5	Kosciusko 12	Pulaski 15	Wayne 50
Fayette 58	Lagrange........ 6	Putnam 45	Wells........... 26
Floyd 91	Lake 1	Randolph...... 43	White 20
Fountain 36	La Porte 3	Ripley.......... 73	Whitley........ 17

This map shows Indiana's 92 counties.
▶ What county do you live in?

size of Indiana and some nearby states. Each state has its own bar. On the left is a scale of numbers. These numbers tell you the size of the states in thousands of square miles. Which of Indiana's neighbors is the largest? Which state is closest in size to Indiana?

A bar graph can also be used to compare other things. For example, in the bar graph below, the bars show the number of people in Indiana and its neighboring states. The scale on the left tells how many millions of people are in each state. Which state has the most people? Which state has the fewest people?

> This graph compares Indiana's population to that of its neighbors.
> ▶ Which state has a population almost twice as large as Indiana's population?

INDIANA AND ITS NEIGHBORS: POPULATION

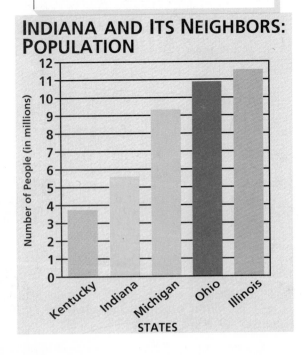

D. Population Density

The bar graphs have shown you the size of Indiana and the number of people who live in the state. You can use this information to find out its **population density.** Population density tells how crowded a place is. To find the population density, you must divide the number of people who live in a place by the size of the land in that place.

As the population bar graph shows, about 5,600,000 people live in Indiana. The size of the state is 36,185 square miles. If you divide 5,600,000 by 36,185, you get about 155. So the population density of Indiana is 155 people per square mile. The population density of Ohio is about 266 people per square mile. Ohio is more crowded than Indiana.

E. Cities, Towns, and Farms

The map on page 39 shows the population density for each Indiana county. With the map is a table listing the 25 largest cities in the state. Which counties have the most people per square mile? The counties that are most crowded are those that contain large cities. In fact, one of the two counties with the most people per square mile contains the largest city in Indiana— Indianapolis. Over 700,000 people live there.

INDIANA: POPULATION DENSITY

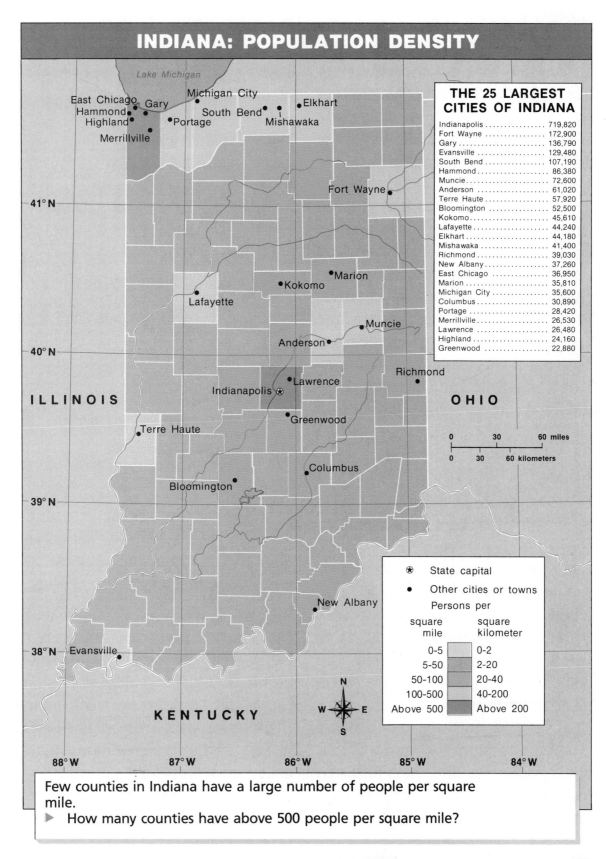

Lake Michigan

East Chicago Gary
Hammond
Highland
Merrillville
Portage
Michigan City
South Bend Elkhart
Mishawaka

Fort Wayne

41° N

ILLINOIS

Lafayette
Kokomo Marion

Muncie

Anderson

40° N

Indianapolis Lawrence

Richmond

OHIO

Terre Haute

Greenwood

Columbus

39° N

Bloomington

New Albany

38° N Evansville

KENTUCKY

88° W   87° W   86° W   85° W   84° W

THE 25 LARGEST CITIES OF INDIANA

City	Population
Indianapolis	719,820
Fort Wayne	172,900
Gary	136,790
Evansville	129,480
South Bend	107,190
Hammond	86,380
Muncie	72,600
Anderson	61,020
Terre Haute	57,920
Bloomington	52,500
Kokomo	45,610
Lafayette	44,240
Elkhart	44,180
Mishawaka	41,400
Richmond	39,030
New Albany	37,260
East Chicago	36,950
Marion	35,810
Michigan City	35,600
Columbus	30,890
Portage	28,420
Merrillville	26,530
Lawrence	26,480
Highland	24,160
Greenwood	22,880

⊛   State capital

•   Other cities or towns

Persons per

square mile	square kilometer
0-5	0-2
5-50	2-20
50-100	20-40
100-500	40-200
Above 500	Above 200

N W E S

0   30   60 miles
0   30   60 kilometers

Few counties in Indiana have a large number of people per square mile.

▶   How many counties have above 500 people per square mile?

39

Look again at the population density map on page 39. You will also notice that much of the state has a low number of people per square mile. You will see that these areas with low population density do not contain any large cities.

Knowing these facts, you can generalize. That means that you can sum up this information in a short statement. Counties that have many people per square mile have large cities, or urban areas. The counties that have few people per square mile are rural. Rural areas are made up of farms and very small communities. Later, you will find out why these differences occur within Indiana.

F. Drawings That Help Explain Things

Learning from Drawings Do you remember Ben, who used a map to see where his pen pal, Erik, lived? Ben's father helped Ben learn how to use a map to find out exactly where Sweden and other places were located. Maps, of course, show where things are. They help you compare places. They also help you measure distance.

But you can use many other drawings to study geography. You just used tables and bar graphs to find out about the places, the size, and the population of Indiana.

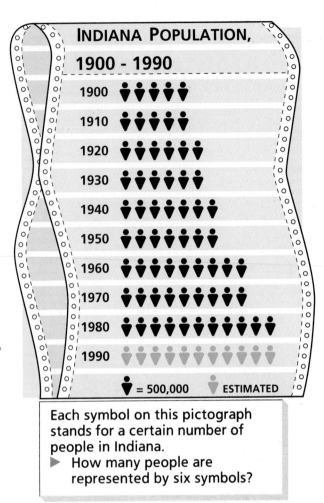

INDIANA POPULATION, 1900 - 1990

1900	♟♟♟♟♟
1910	♟♟♟♟♟
1920	♟♟♟♟♟♟
1930	♟♟♟♟♟♟
1940	♟♟♟♟♟♟
1950	♟♟♟♟♟♟
1960	♟♟♟♟♟♟♟
1970	♟♟♟♟♟♟♟
1980	♟♟♟♟♟♟♟♟
1990	♟♟♟♟♟♟♟♟

♟ = 500,000   ▮ ESTIMATED

Each symbol on this pictograph stands for a certain number of people in Indiana.
► How many people are represented by six symbols?

You can also use pictures, lines, and circles to help explain facts about people and places and to compare different things.

Picture Symbols For instance, in the last hundred years, there have been great increases in Indiana's population. How could you show this? You could show each year's population with little drawings of people. This type of drawing is called a **pictograph.**

Look at the pictograph above. Each drawing stands for a half million (500,000) people. The numbers on the left show the years. For example, there are five drawings of people to show the population of Indiana in 1900. By multiplying $5 \times 500,000$, we find out that 2,500,000 people lived in Indiana in 1900. Count the symbols to find out how many people were living in Indiana in 1940. There are seven symbols, so 3,500,000 people were living in Indiana in 1940. How many people were living there in 1980?

Changes over Time Another way you could show this information is with a **line graph.** People often use line graphs to show how something changes over the years. Below is a line graph that shows the change in Indiana's population between 1900 and 1990. The scale on the left shows the number of people in

millions. Along the bottom of the graph, the years are shown. This graph can show you when the population of Indiana grew most rapidly. That would be when the line from one year to the next year on the graph is the steepest. In what period of time did this happen?

Piece of the Whole There is one more kind of graph. Have you ever cut a pie into slices? That is how a **pie graph,** or circle graph, works. It shows the parts of a whole.

A pie graph consists of a circle divided into slices of differing sizes. Each slice stands for part of the whole thing.

This line graph shows how Indiana's population has changed over time.
► What was Indiana's population when you were born?

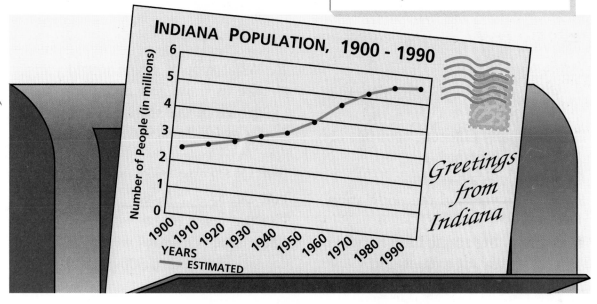

INDIANA POPULATION, 1900 - 1990

Number of People (in millions)

YEARS
—— ESTIMATED

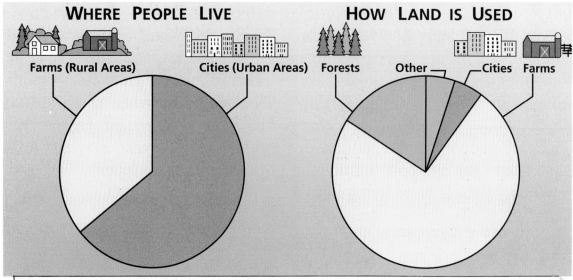

WHERE PEOPLE LIVE

Farms (Rural Areas)   Cities (Urban Areas)

HOW LAND IS USED

Forests   Other   Cities   Farms

Most Indianans live in the urban areas of the state. Most of the land, however, is used for farming.
▶ In which area do the farmers live?

Look at the two pie graphs above. The one on the left shows where the people of Indiana live. It shows how many people live in farming areas and how many live in cities. You can see that many more people live in cities than in farming areas. The pie graph on the right shows how the land in Indiana is used. The largest slice stands for farmland. More land is used for farming than for any other activity.

LESSON 1 REVIEW

THINK AND WRITE

A. What is one explanation for the word *Hoosier*?

B. How many different counties are there in Indiana?

C. What does a bar graph do?

D. How do you find the population density of an area?

E. What is the connection between areas with large cities and population density?

F. What type of graph would you use to show how much corn was grown in the state of Indiana from 1950 to 1980?

SKILLS CHECK

MAP SKILL

Use the maps on pages 37 and 39 to name three counties with population densities of 100 to 500 persons per square mile.

A Picture of the Land

THINK ABOUT WHAT YOU KNOW

Think about some trips you have taken in Indiana. How would you describe the land in each area? Is it flat? Are there gentle hills? Are there lots of small lakes?

STUDY THE VOCABULARY

relief map   **contour**
elevation   **line**

FOCUS YOUR READING

How do we describe the surface of the land?

A. Relief Maps

You have already studied several maps in this book. Would any of them be able to tell you how high or low a certain place is? No. For that, you would need a special kind of map. You would need a **relief map.** Relief maps show how high or how low places are. The map on page 45 shows the heights of the different parts of Indiana. But from what point is the height of a place measured? Every valley, hill, and mountain is measured from the same base. That base is the level of the sea. The distance of a place above the level of the sea is called **elevation.** Sea level is 0 feet or 0 meters. We say that a place is so many feet (or meters) above sea level. For example, the highest point in Indiana is in Wayne County. It is 1,257 feet (383 m) above sea level.

Unlike most of Indiana, Brown County has many rolling hills.
► What is the land like in most of Indiana?

B. Contour Lines

The relief map on page 45 shows heights by the use of different colors. The lines that separate one height from another are called **contour lines**. A contour line is a line drawn through all the places having the same height.

Look at the drawing of an island on this page. The island rises to more than 300 feet (91 m) above sea level. The line marked "100 ft (30 m)" connects all the points on the island that are 100 feet (30 m) above sea level. This line marks the 100-foot (30-meter) contour. The next line connects all the points that are 200 feet (61 m) above sea level. This line marks the 200-foot (61-meter) contour.

Below the drawing is a sketch of the contour lines as they would appear from directly overhead. This drawing also shows the elevations of places that fall between the contour lines. These places are marked by individual dots. This type of map can be used to find the height of any place above sea level.

In the third drawing, color is used to make contour lines clearer. All the land that is below 100 feet (30 m) is shaded green. The land that is between 100 feet (30 m) and 200 feet (61 m) is colored orange, and so on.

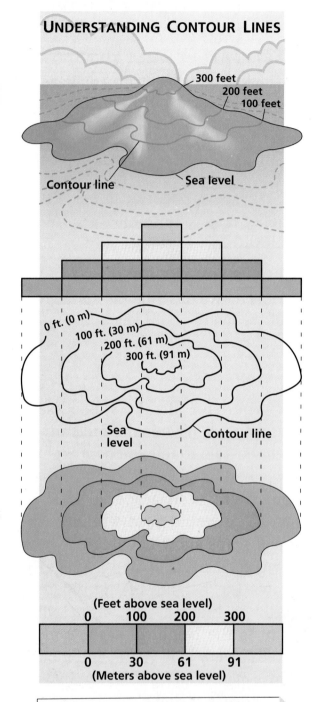

UNDERSTANDING CONTOUR LINES

300 feet
200 feet
100 feet

Contour line   Sea level

0 ft. (0 m)
100 ft. (30 m)
200 ft. (61 m)
300 ft. (91 m)

Sea level   Contour line

(Feet above sea level)
0   100   200   300

0   30   61   91
(Meters above sea level)

Contour lines show the height of the land. All points along one contour line are exactly the same distance above sea level.
► What does the red color show?

C. Relief of Indiana

Look at the relief map of Indiana on this page. Study the key as well as the map. Where is the lowest land in the state? What is its color? How high above sea level is this area of land? You will find the lowest land in southwest Indiana. It lies beside the Ohio and Wabash rivers in Posey and Vanderburgh counties. This land is slightly lower than 325 feet (99 m) above sea level.

Where is the highest land in Indiana? The highest land is located in the eastern part of the state. This land is found close to the boundary with Ohio. Most of Indiana is between 600 and 1,000 feet (200–300 m) above sea level. What is the elevation of your hometown?

What is the difference between the highest point in Indiana and the lowest point in Indiana? The highest point is 1,257 feet (383 m). The lowest point is 324 feet (99 m). The difference between the two is only 933 feet (284 m).

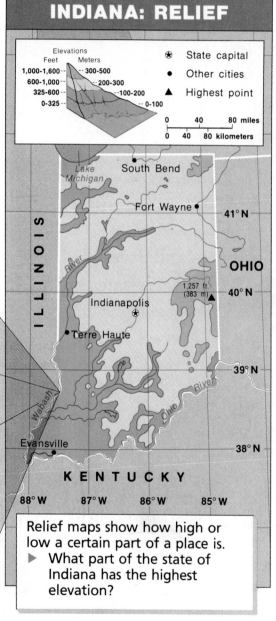

Wabash River Valley

Relief maps show how high or low a certain part of a place is.
▶ What part of the state of Indiana has the highest elevation?

45

The elevation of these mountains starts at sea level.
► If you made a drawing of this picture, would the contour lines be close together or far apart?

D. Gentle and Steep

Suppose you wanted to climb to the top of the island shown in the drawing on page 44. There are two possible ways to the top. One way is to go up the left side. The other way is to go up the right side. Which side will you take?

The way on the left looks shorter. You might want to take that one. But first you should look more closely at the contour lines.

When you look at the contour lines of the island as seen from overhead, you notice that the contour lines on the left lie close together. That means the land gets higher quickly. The climb on this side of the island would be very steep. The contour lines are much farther apart on the right. The land rises more slowly. That would make this climb a very gentle one. Which do you think is better: a short, steep climb, or a longer and more gentle one? That depends on you!

LESSON **2** *REVIEW*

THINK AND WRITE

A. What information can you get from relief maps?
B. What is the main purpose of contour lines?
C. Where is the highest land in Indiana located?
D. If contour lines are close together, does it mean that the slope is gentle or steep?

SKILLS CHECK

WRITING SKILL

Look at the relief map of Indiana on page 45. Write a sentence describing where you would expect to find the greatest area of flat land. Write another sentence telling where you would expect to find an area of steep hills.

The Regions of Indiana

THINK ABOUT WHAT YOU KNOW
Find two pictures in this book that show very different-looking parts of Indiana.

STUDY THE VOCABULARY

glaciation	till
deposit	route center
gravel	silt
moraine	delta

FOCUS YOUR READING
How do different parts of Indiana compare with one another?

A. Natural Areas

A region is a part of the earth's land that is the same in some ways. It usually has something about it that makes it different from other nearby areas. A region may be flat or hilly or mountainous. It may be a forest or a desert. There are several regions of dense population and regions of sparse, or low, population. There are many different ways to divide land into regions.

Indiana has three distinct regions. These are shown on the map on this page. In the north is the Great Lakes Plains. Across the middle of the state is the Till Plains, and in the south is the region called the Southern Hills and Lowlands.

We have seen where these regions are. But *how* and *why* do they differ from one another? To find these answers, we must understand that much of Indiana was once covered by ice.

B. When the Ice Came

Masses of Ice Find the large island of Greenland on the map of the world on pages 352–353. It lies

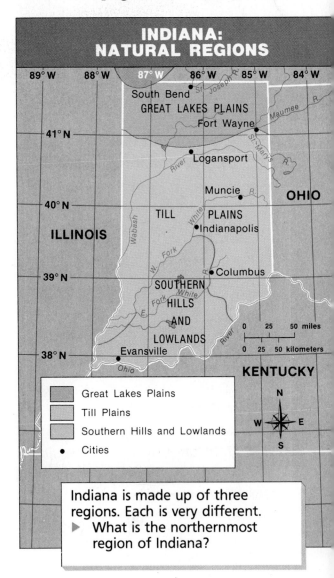

INDIANA: NATURAL REGIONS

Indiana is made up of three regions. Each is very different.
▶ What is the northernmost region of Indiana?

close to the North Pole. Greenland is covered with ice that is many hundreds of feet thick. How does the ice get there? It comes from the snow that falls on Greenland. The snow does not melt. Instead, it hardens into ice and spreads out over the land and the sea. Masses of ice break away and float southward until they melt. These huge masses of floating ice are called icebergs.

The Ice Age   More than a million years ago, the climate on the continent of North America began to grow colder. It no longer rained; it snowed. Have you ever spent time building a snowman during a snowstorm, only to find it melted in a few

Much of Indiana was once covered with ice.
▶ What was the climate like at that time?

days? You may have been disappointed to see the snow disappear. A million years ago, however, the snow did not melt. It piled up. It became thicker and thicker and stretched all the way from the North Pole to Indiana.

As more snow fell, the ice spread outward. This spread is called a **glaciation** (glay shee AY-shun). Much of Indiana was covered with ice. No people were here, and animals moved south to places that were still warm.

Moving Southward   As the ice spread down from the north, it scraped rocks and soil from the land. As the rocks were carried south by the ice, they were crushed into small pieces. When at last the climate became warmer, the ice melted and left behind a **deposit** of the crushed rocks. A deposit is a material that has been laid down by ice, wind, or water. This deposit covered hills and valleys and made the land smooth.

Look at the map on page 47. The ice once covered the Great Lakes Plains and the Till Plains. That is why these regions are almost flat. But the ice never reached southern Indiana. Here the land remains hilly.

The ice melted, but then it came again. This time the ice covered only the northern tip of Indiana, where it

Beautiful sand dunes formed along Indiana's Lake Michigan shore.
▶ What can you see growing on the dunes?

laid a new deposit on top of the old one. This newer deposit contained sand and **gravel.** Gravel is made up of small stones. This gravel formed heaps and ridges in the land. Heaps and ridges left by glaciers are called **moraines** (muh RAYNZ). At last the ice disappeared for good. Water filled many of the hollows where the ice had been. Today, there are hundreds of small lakes in northern Indiana. Look up *lake* in the Geographical Dictionary, on pages 372–375.

C. The Great Lakes Plains

On Lake Michigan The Great Lakes are to the north and northeast of Indiana. There are five Great Lakes. Read off their names from the map on pages 354–355. One of them borders Indiana. Which one is it?

Lake Michigan borders on the region of Indiana called the Great Lakes Plains. It is covered with moraines left by the second glaciation, and it is dotted with many lakes. The soil is sandy and not good for most crops. Thousands of people visit the Lake Michigan shoreline each year to see the beautiful shapes of the dunes. Dunes are hills of sand that have been formed by the wind.

Easy Transport The Great Lakes Plains region is an excellent area for manufacturing. Why is this so? Ships move easily through the Great Lakes. The Great Lakes then connect to the ocean through the St. Lawrence River. The ships bring materials such as iron into Indiana and carry goods to other places. This causes manufacturing to grow. There are factories and mills close to the lake. Look at the map on page 39. How many large cities are in this region?

From: *Moving Hills of Sand*

By: Julian May

Setting: The Great Lakes Plains

Julian May is a writer who lives in Chicago, Illinois. She has written many books and articles for children. Most have been about science and the outdoors. In the following passage from *Moving Hills of Sand*, Julian May describes the movement of the sand in the Great Lakes Plains. She tells how wind and water have created the enormous dunes that people visit today.

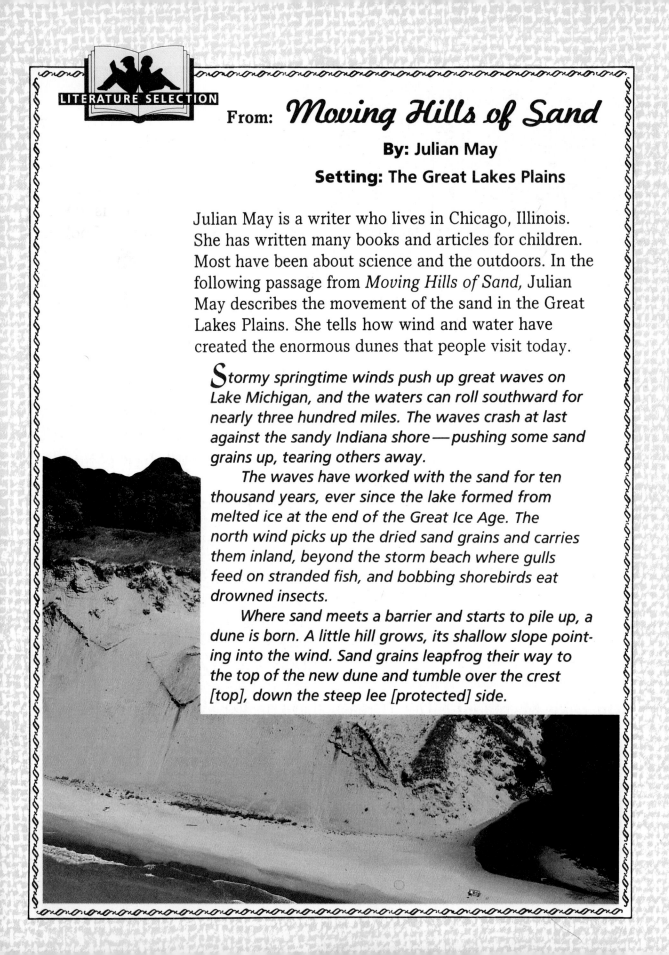

Stormy springtime winds push up great waves on Lake Michigan, and the waters can roll southward for nearly three hundred miles. The waves crash at last against the sandy Indiana shore—pushing some sand grains up, tearing others away.

The waves have worked with the sand for ten thousand years, ever since the lake formed from melted ice at the end of the Great Ice Age. The north wind picks up the dried sand grains and carries them inland, beyond the storm beach where gulls feed on stranded fish, and bobbing shorebirds eat drowned insects.

Where sand meets a barrier and starts to pile up, a dune is born. A little hill grows, its shallow slope pointing into the wind. Sand grains leapfrog their way to the top of the new dune and tumble over the crest [top], down the steep lee [protected] side.

Highways, railroads, and a river have made the city of Indianapolis a route center.
▶ What river goes through it?

D. The Till Plains

The Till Plains region covers the center of Indiana. **Till** is the name of the soft deposit left by the ice after it had melted the first time. Another name for till is boulder clay. It forms a level surface. Rivers wind their way across it. The soil is rich, and much of the land is used for farming.

Indianapolis lies in the middle of this region. Roads and railroads spread out from it. Indianapolis is a **route center,** or a place where roads and railroads have come together. Today it is one of the biggest cities in our country.

The Wabash River flows across the Till Plains. It is joined by many tributaries (TRIHB yoo tair eez), or small rivers. One of these is the White River. Indianapolis lies on the White River.

E. Southern Hills and Lowlands of Indiana

Hilly Surface   This region was never covered by the ice long ago, so the surface of the land has not been smoothed down. It is hilly. In the western part of this region is the valley of the Wabash River. Look up *valley* in the Geographical Dictionary, on pages 372–375. This valley is called the Wabash lowland. Have you ever looked at a river in southern Indiana after the snows have melted or after very heavy rain? The water flows swiftly, and it is brown. Its brown color is due to **silt.** Silt is fine mud from the Till Plains that is being carried toward the sea.

The valley of the Wabash River has soil that is good for farming.
▶ What is another name that this valley is called?

Do you remember how the ice deposited till when it melted? Well, the river does the same with its silt. Sometimes the river floods. When the flood waters draw back again, they leave behind silt. This silt then makes the soil rich and makes the Wabash lowland an excellent place for farming.

Forest Region Brown County is part of the hilly region of southern Indiana. Perhaps you have driven there in the fall to see the rich coloring of the leaves. The soil there is poor. Few people have wanted to settle there and farm the land. That is why much of the region is still covered with forest. It is rich in maple, sumac, redbud, and dogwood trees. In the spring it is alive with flowers, and in the fall it is brilliant with turning leaves. No wonder its parks are filled with so many visitors.

F. On the Banks of the Wabash

Oh, the moonlight's fair tonight
  along the Wabash,
From the fields there comes a breath
  of new-mown hay.
Through the sycamores the candle-
  lights are gleaming.
On the banks of the Wabash far away.

Have you ever sung this song? It was written by Paul Dresser, a native of Indiana, and it is the state song of Indiana. Find the Wabash River on the map on page 47. Trace it with your finger as it wanders across the Till Plains. Farther to the south, it forms part of the boundary with the state of Illinois before it joins the Ohio River.

The Ohio River forms the boundary between Indiana and Kentucky. It is a very great river. It rises in the Allegheny Mountains far to the east in Pennsylvania. The Ohio River joins the Mississippi River at Cairo (KAY roh), a city in Illinois. The Mississippi River flows past Memphis, Tennessee, and New

Much of Brown County in southern Indiana is covered with forests.
▶ How can you tell that this picture was taken in autumn?

The Ohio River forms the border between Indiana and Kentucky.
▶ What major Indiana river flows into the Ohio River?

Orleans, Louisiana, and then enters the Gulf of Mexico.

The water that you see flowing past Logansport or Muncie or Columbus will one day reach the Wabash River, and then the Ohio River, and then the Mississippi River. And after a very long journey, it will enter the sea. At the mouth of the Mississippi River in Louisiana, there is a maze of muddy islands called a **delta**. They have been built up from silt carried by the river. Look up *delta* in the Geographical Dictionary, on pages 372–375. Just think—the delta that is slowly being built on our country's faraway southern shore depends on soil from Indiana!

LESSON 3 REVIEW

THINK AND WRITE

A. What is a region?

B. When does glaciation occur?

C. Why are the Great Lakes important to Indiana?

D. Why is Indianapolis called a route center?

E. Why is Brown County still covered with so many forests?

F. How is a delta formed?

SKILLS CHECK

WRITING SKILL

Make a table showing the following information about each of the three regions of Indiana: the name of the region, its location within Indiana, and a description of the land.

53

FARM EQUIPMENT THROUGH THE TIMES

 1 Cast iron plow, 1797

McCormick's Reaper, 1831 **2**

3 Steam thresher, 1903

Kerosene-powered tractor, 1928 **4**

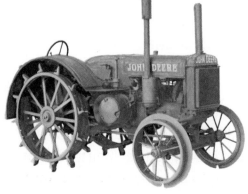

5 Modern combine, 1990

Farming has always been an important industry in Indiana. Farm equipment helps farmers with their work. Over the years, different types of farm equipment have been invented. Modern farm machinery has made farming much easier.

▶ In what ways has modern equipment helped farmers?

The Seasons in Indiana

THINK ABOUT WHAT YOU KNOW

Think back over the last season. Was it wet or dry? Was it hot, warm, cool, or cold?

STUDY THE VOCABULARY

weather	temperature
climate	thermometer
diagram	precipitation

FOCUS YOUR READING

What is Indiana's climate like?

A. Weather for a Picnic

Cloudy or Clear Have you ever planned a summer picnic? If you have, you will remember how you worried about the **weather**. You knew it would be hot because summers are always hot in Indiana. But you did not know whether it would be a bright, clear day or cloudy and humid. You may have even worried that a violent storm with thunder and lightning would send you scurrying for shelter. All these different things can happen on a summer day. They are part of the weather. Weather is the changes that occur from day to day, and hour to hour.

Rainy or Dry The kind of weather that a place has over a long period of time is called its **climate**. In Indiana,

summers are hot and rainy. The fall is warm and dry. Winter is cold and sometimes snowy. Spring is a short, in-between season. This is our climate. It is different from the climate in other places. Why are there different climates on the earth?

B. The Earth and the Sun

Look at the **diagram** on page 56. A diagram is a special kind of drawing. It is not meant to show exactly what something looks like. Its purpose is to explain how something works or why something happens. This diagram shows how the earth travels around the sun. You will notice that the earth is tilted. Not all places on the earth get the same

Indianans enjoy the beaches that surround many of Indiana's lakes.
► In what season of the year was this picture taken?

amount of the sun's light and heat. Places near the Poles often get no sun for long periods of time. Their climate is always cold. At the Equator, the sun is nearly straight overhead. There, the climate is always warm or hot. In the areas in between, such as Indiana, some seasons are warm, and others are cold. The continent of North America is tilted toward the sun in spring and summer, so these are the warmest parts of the year. It is tilted away in the fall and winter.

The earth's rotation around the sun determines the different seasons of each country.
▶ When a country is farthest from the sun, what season is it?

The way the sun reaches the earth affects many things. It affects what kinds of crops grow well in Indiana. It affects what animals live here. It also affects what people do and how they live in Indiana.

C. Learning About Temperature and Precipitation

The two most important things about climate are how hot it is and how wet it is. **Temperature** tells whether it is hot, cool, or cold. Temperature is measured in degrees with an instrument called a **thermometer.** At a temperature of 32°F (0°C), water freezes, and snow and ice form. A temperature of 70°F (21°C)

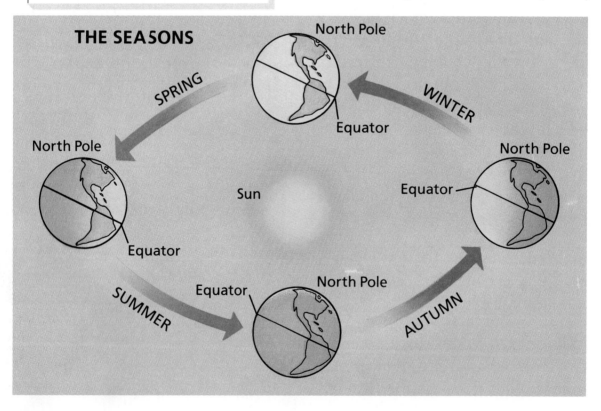

THE SEASONS

North Pole
SPRING
North Pole
Equator
WINTER
North Pole
Sun
Equator
Equator
SUMMER
Equator
North Pole
AUTUMN

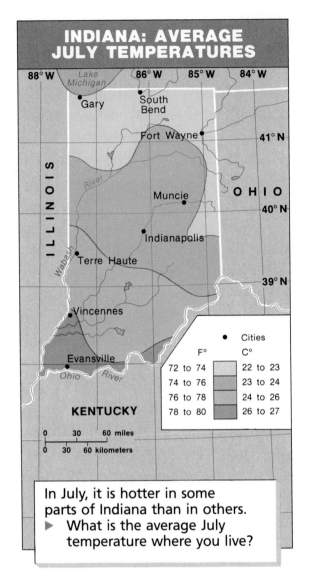

INDIANA: AVERAGE JULY TEMPERATURES

	F°	C°
	72 to 74	22 to 23
	74 to 76	23 to 24
	76 to 78	24 to 26
	78 to 80	26 to 27
•	Cities	

0   30   60 miles
0   30   60 kilometers

In July, it is hotter in some parts of Indiana than in others.
▶ What is the average July temperature where you live?

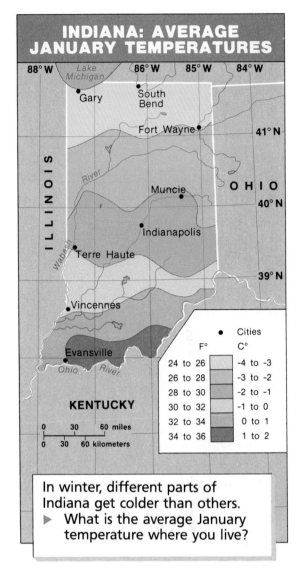

INDIANA: AVERAGE JANUARY TEMPERATURES

	F°	C°
	24 to 26	-4 to -3
	26 to 28	-3 to -2
	28 to 30	-2 to -1
	30 to 32	-1 to 0
	32 to 34	0 to 1
	34 to 36	1 to 2
•	Cities	

0   30   60 miles
0   30   60 kilometers

In winter, different parts of Indiana get colder than others.
▶ What is the average January temperature where you live?

is warm; 90°F (32°C) is so hot that we become very uncomfortable.

The maps on this page show average temperatures in Indiana in July and January. Study the maps and the map keys. You will notice that not every part of Indiana has the same average temperature. In both July and January, temperatures are lower in the northern part than in the southern part.

The other important part of climate has to do with how wet it is. Rain, hail, and snow are all forms of **precipitation** (pree sihp uh TAY shun). Precipitation is measured by means of a rain gauge. This instrument catches the precipitation that falls. A scale on the rain gauge tells how deep the precipitation is in inches or millimeters. A storm might bring 1/4 inch (6 mm) or 1/2 inch

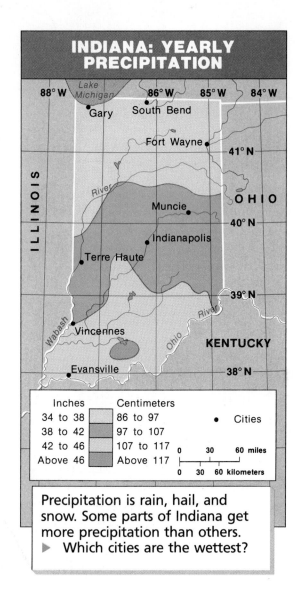

INDIANA: YEARLY PRECIPITATION

Inches	Centimeters
34 to 38	86 to 97
38 to 42	97 to 107
42 to 46	107 to 117
Above 46	Above 117

• Cities

0   30   60 miles

0   30   60 kilometers

Precipitation is rain, hail, and snow. Some parts of Indiana get more precipitation than others.
▶ Which cities are the wettest?

(13 mm). A severe storm might bring 2 inches (51 mm) or more.

When the amount of precipitation each day for a month is added up, it gives the total monthly rainfall. Adding up the monthly totals gives the total for the year. The amount of precipitation varies from month to month.

Look at the bar graphs on page 378. These show the amount of precipitation in each month for four Indiana cities. Compare the four graphs. Notice that March is the wettest month in Evansville. February is the driest month in Indianapolis. In Fort Wayne, which season has the least precipitation?

The amount of precipitation also varies from place to place. Turn to the map on this page. Which part of Indiana is the wettest? Which part is the driest?

LESSON 4 REVIEW

THINK AND WRITE

A. What is the difference between the weather and the climate of a particular area?

B. Why do all the areas on earth not get the same amount of sunlight?

C. How do you measure the monthly rainfall of an area?

SKILLS CHECK

THINKING SKILL

Look at the line graphs on page 379 that show average monthly temperatures in four cities. Which of the four cities has the hottest temperature in July and which city has the coldest temperature in January?

CHAPTER 1

PUTTING IT ALL TOGETHER

USING THE VOCABULARY

urban	glaciation
rural	till
pictograph	silt
elevation	climate
contour line	temperature

On a separate sheet of paper, write the word that best matches each definition below. Choose your answers from the vocabulary words above.

1. name for an area that is made up of farms and small communities
2. fine mud gathered by a river and deposited downstream
3. name for an area that is made up of a large city
4. the weather that a place has over a long period of time
5. a line that is drawn on a map through all the places having the same height
6. measured in degrees and tells whether it is hot, cool, or cold
7. the height of a place above the level of the sea
8. the outward spread of ice over North America
9. a graph in which symbols are used to represent numbers
10. the soft deposit left by the ice after it had melted the first time

REMEMBERING WHAT YOU READ

Write your answers in complete sentences on a separate sheet of paper.

1. Describe Indiana's location.
2. What kind of graph uses drawings to show amounts?
3. Which kind of graph best shows the parts of a whole?
4. What do relief maps show?
5. From what point is the height of land measured?
6. Name Indiana's three regions.
7. Why is the southern region of Indiana hilly and the northern and middle regions are flat?
8. What river forms the boundary between Indiana and Kentucky?
9. Are temperatures usually lower in the northern or the southern part of the state?
10. Name three forms of precipitation.

TYING LANGUAGE ARTS TO SOCIAL STUDIES: WRITING TO LEARN

Think about the three regions of Indiana. Choose one region. Imagine that you are going on a trip to that region. Write a paragraph in which you tell what you would like to see.

THINKING CRITICALLY

Write your answers in complete sentences on a separate sheet of paper.

1. What is one kind of graph that you think you might use later in this book to study Indiana?

2. How are relief maps different from other maps you have studied so far?
3. How did the glaciers help to create small lakes that are found in northern Indiana?
4. Why is the Till Plains region so good for farming?
5. What are some ways that climate affects the way people live?

SUMMARIZING THE CHAPTER

On a separate sheet of paper, draw a graphic organizer that is like the one shown here. Copy the information from the graphic organizer to the one you have drawn. Under the main idea for each lesson, write three statements that support it. The first one has been done for you.

CHAPTER THEME
Indiana has cities and farmland, a rich variety of land surfaces, and changing seasons.

LESSON 1

Indiana's location and size can be described in several ways.

1. Between the Ohio River and Lake Michigan; between Ohio and Illinois
2. 38th in land area among states
3. Urban areas with high population density and rural areas with low population density

LESSON 2

Relief maps and contour lines help us describe the surface of the land.

1.
2.
3.

LESSON 3

Indiana can be divided into three distinct regions.

1.
2.
3.

LESSON 4

Indiana's climate differs from season to season.

1.
2.
3.

1 *REVIEW*

COOPERATIVE LEARNING

In this unit you learned about the three regions of Indiana. Now you are going to work with some of your classmates to create a montage on one of Indiana's three regions.

PROJECT

• Working in groups of five, decide which region you will represent.

• One member of the group should draw an outline map of Indiana and color in your region on the map.

• The second member of the group should show the region's major cities and its main rivers and lakes, on the outline map.

• The third member of the group should cut out pictures showing land features of your region. He or she should then write a paragraph describing how the land features of your region are different from those of other regions.

• The fourth member of the group should make a montage by putting together the outline map, the pictures, and the paragraph.

PRESENTATION AND REVIEW

• Once the montage is completed, the fifth member will present the group's work to the rest of the class. He or she will read the paragraph aloud and explain the pictures and outline map to the class.

• Ask your classmates what they liked most about your montage. Did they learn anything from it? Was it neat and attractive? Did the pictures show all of the major land features?

• Talk about the montage with your own group. How might you have improved it?

REMEMBER TO:
• Give your ideas.
• Listen to others' ideas.
• Plan your work with the group.
• Present your project.
• Discuss how your group worked.

Reading SKILLBUILDER to Learn

A. WHY DO I NEED THIS SKILL?

Some books we read for fun. Other books we read to learn. Textbooks such as this one contain many ideas to learn and remember. You will do better if you have a plan of action when you study. SQR is a study-reading plan that will help you understand and remember the ideas in this book and in other textbooks, too. The letters SQR stand for **Survey, Question, Read**.

B. LEARNING THE SKILL

There are three easy steps in the SQR plan. These steps are described below.

The first step is to survey the lesson. To do this, look at the headings, questions, and vocabulary words. Also look at any photographs, maps, and other visuals in the lesson. This will give you a general idea of what the lesson is about. Then think about what you already know about the topic. Make some guesses about the ideas you think will be in this lesson.

The second step is to think of questions you may have about this topic. If questions do not come to mind, use the words *where, when, how,* and *why* to get you started. Look at the questions at the beginning and at the end of the lesson. Then look at the question that goes with each picture. Make a list of questions about the lesson and plan to find answers for them.

The third step is to read the lesson. As you read, find the answers to the questions on your list. If you think of other questions as you read, answer them as well.

C. Practicing the Skill

Turn to page 88. Practice the SQR study-reading plan on Lesson 2 of Chapter 3. The lesson is called "The Special Gifts of Native Indianans."

Start by surveying the lesson. Follow the directions given on page 62. Think about what you already know about Indiana's first people. Are there any Indian words you know, such as *tipi* or *wigwam*? What guesses can you make about the ideas in this lesson? Look at the questions in this lesson. Prepare your own list of questions. Read the lesson carefully. Find the answers to your questions. If you cannot answer all of your questions, try reading the lesson once again.

D. Applying the Skill

The SQR strategy is important to use whenever you are reading to learn. Try this strategy when you read your next science lesson.

The USING SQR chart on this page will help you remember the steps.

Make a copy of the chart and use it when you are studying.

Using SQR

Survey	Look at the questions, vocabulary words, and visuals in the lesson. Think about some things that you already know about the topic. Make predictions about the lesson content.
Question	Note questions already in the lesson. Use vocabulary words and headings to prepare other questions. Write your questions or at least make a mental note of them.
Read	Read the text to answer your questions. Write out answers or say them to yourself. Ask and answer other questions that come to mind as you read.

A. Why Do I Need This Skill?

Maps use symbols to stand for real places and things. Map symbols are explained in the map key. Learning what the symbols stand for will help you get the most information from the map.

B. Learning the Skill

Every map has symbols. The symbols may be letters, numbers, lines, colors, or a small drawing of an object. For example, a small circle can stand for a town or city. A small drawing of a picnic table can stand for a picnic area. The symbols are placed on the map to show where the places or things are located.

Map symbols can stand for many things. They can stand for roads, cities, or rivers. And they can stand for airports, railroads, or parks. Map symbols are listed and explained in the map key.

Look at the map on the facing page. This is a map of an imaginary place called Buck's Island. The map shows places and things on the island and the surrounding area.

Look at the symbols on the map. You can probably guess what some of the symbols mean by just looking at them. Find the small airplane on the

map. You may have figured out that it stands for the airport.

Other symbols are not as easy to figure out. Look at the small triangles on the map. A triangle can stand for many different things. To find out what it means on this map, you must look at the map key.

Find the triangle symbol in the map key. Read the word across from the triangle. Now you know that this symbol stands for a beach. When you look back at the map, you can tell how many beaches there are on the island and where they are located.

Look at all the map symbols shown in the key. Find each one of them on the map. The symbols help you read the map. And they help you learn about Buck's Island.

C. Practicing the Skill

Use the map of Buck's Island to answer the following questions.

1. How many towns are there on Buck's Island?
2. What does a small square on the map stand for?
3. What does a large square on the map stand for?

4. Where can people do their shopping on Buck's Island?
5. What is the highway that runs between two mountains?
6. Where is the airport located?
7. What towns on Buck's Island have ferry service?
8. What towns does the railroad link?
9. Where is the school located?
10. Where can people go fishing on Buck's Island?

D. APPLYING THE SKILL

Prepare a map of your school and the surrounding area. Begin by listing all the things you want to show on your map, such as the school building, the parking lot, and the playground. Then draw a symbol to stand for each item on your list. Draw the map, using your symbols for the real places and things. Be sure to include a map key to explain your symbols.

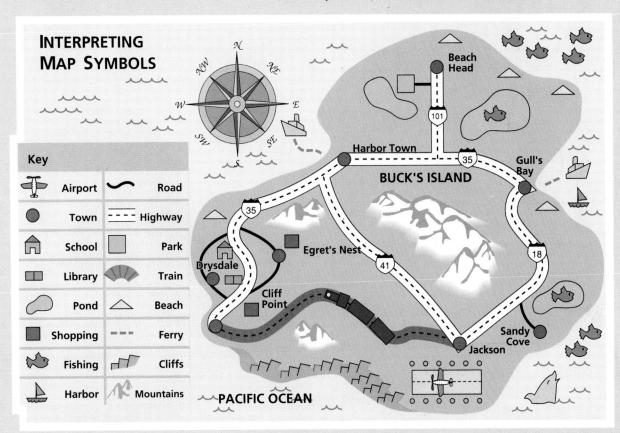

INTERPRETING MAP SYMBOLS

Key

Airport	~	Road	
Town	---	Highway	
School	☐	Park	
Library		Train	
Pond	△	Beach	
Shopping	---	Ferry	
Fishing		Cliffs	
Harbor		Mountains	

Beach Head
Harbor Town
BUCK'S ISLAND
Gull's Bay
Egret's Nest
Drysdale
Cliff Point
Jackson
Sandy Cove
PACIFIC OCEAN

▲ Long before people came to Indiana, buffalo roamed throughout the land.

◄ Native Americans were the first people to live in Indiana. Many Native Americans still live in Indiana today.

Robert de la Salle traveled through Indiana during his exploration of the New World. ▶

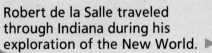

When Indiana became a state, Corydon was its capital. ▶

◀ In the late 1700s, more and more people began to move into the Northwest Territory.

UNIT 2 INDIANA: IN THE BEGINNING

Native Americans have lived in Indiana for thousands of years. European explorers came to North America and claimed the land. As the western frontier became settled, many people moved to Indiana. In 1816 Indiana became the nineteenth state.

CHAPTER 2

INDIANA'S FIRST PEOPLE

People have been living in what is now the state of Indiana for thousands of years. Indians, or Native Americans, lived in Indiana long before travelers came here from another part of the world.

Proud Indianans

THINK ABOUT WHAT YOU KNOW

Write the word *Indian* on a piece of paper. Under it write the ideas that come to mind when you hear this word.

STUDY THE VOCABULARY

explorer	heritage
tribe	prehistoric
Native	artifact
American	archaeologist

FOCUS YOUR READING

What are some ways we learn about the first Indianans?

A. The Indians and Indiana

Round the Campfire Imagine that you are sitting around a crackling campfire. You are in a deep woods. Quietly you wait for the storyteller to begin. With thoughtful eyes, he stares beyond the fire and into the woods. In the shadows, he seems to see pictures of the past. He tells a story about a time long, long before he was born:

"Have you ever been called by someone else's name? How did you feel when it happened? Long ago, a whole group of people was named by mistake. In 1492 Christopher Columbus came upon a new land. He thought he had landed in the Indies, a group of islands near Japan. He called the people he found in this land Indians.

"Columbus was an **explorer**. This means he traveled in search of new lands. After a time, Columbus returned to his home. There, he told stories of these Indians and their strange and beautiful land."

Exploring New Lands "Others were interested in exploring the new land too. About 200 years later, they found their way to our state. Of course, it was not a state then. There was not even a United States then. These explorers met people whom they also called Indians. These Indians hunted among trees like those around you now. They fished in the rivers and lakes. They roamed the flat grasslands. So the place was named Indiana. The word *Indiana* means 'Land of the Indians.'"

Native Americans have lived in Indiana for thousands of years.
▶ What method of transportation is shown in this picture?

B. Native Indianans

First People The storyteller stops for a moment. He looks slowly around the circle and asks:

"Indies, Indians, Indiana . . . do you understand how the name grew? Even after Christopher Columbus's mistake was discovered, the name still stuck.

"Indiana is no longer just the land of the early Indians. You are also an Indianan because you live in the state. You are a native of the state of Indiana if you were born in Indiana. But the Indians were the first native Indianans. They lived here thousands of years before the explorers came. They lived in **tribes,** or groups of families who shared the same way of life. Over 350 tribes of Indians have lived in America. Each tribe was different in some way. Today, more than a million Indians still live in the United States."

Long History The storyteller continues. "I am an Indian, but I like to be called a **Native American** because my people lived in America first. I am also a proud native Indianan. I was born near Indianapolis. Over 7,000 of us live here in Indiana. During the day I work in a bank. But the thing I like the best is telling young Indianans like you about my proud Indiana **heritage,** or past."

C. Learning About the Prehistoric Indians

Before Written Records As the storyteller was talking, he was telling his listeners about the past in Indiana. But today most of what we know about the past comes from written records. That was not always so, however. Indians lived in Indiana long before anyone wrote about them. Very early Indians did not even write about themselves. They are called **prehistoric** (pree-hihs TOR ihk) Indians. *Pre-* means "coming before." Prehistoric Indians came before the time when history was being written.

Over 7,000 Native Americans live in Indiana today. They work at many different types of jobs.
▶ What is this man's job?

Leaving Clues If they did not write anything down, how can you be reading about them now? Prehistoric people left their stories in other ways. They threw away broken tools and weapons. They ate meat and left bones. They ate the insides of certain fish and left shells. They left bits of food and pots in their campfires. Like you, they lost pieces of games they played. All these objects are Indian **artifacts** (AHRT uh fakts). Artifacts are things made and left behind by people. They are clues to the past.

Archaeologists (ahr kee AHL-uh jhists) are people who study the past. They learn by examining artifacts. It is a hard job but often a very exciting job.

Each artifact an archaeologist discovers shows something new about ancient people. Artifacts tell about the work people did and the way they played. Burial places can even hint at what people believed about life after death.

These archaeologists are digging for Indian artifacts.
▶ What are some of the things they might find?

LESSON **1** *REVIEW*

THINK AND WRITE

A. What is the actual meaning of the word *Indiana*?
B. Why do we use the term Native Americans for Indians?
C. In what way is an archaeologist like a detective?

SKILLS CHECK

THINKING SKILL
Discuss what you think might be some advantages of actually examining items that were used by an ancient people rather than reading about these prehistoric people.

USING SOURCE MATERIAL

PREHISTORIC INDIAN ARTIFACTS

Indiana's prehistoric people will always be somewhat of a mystery to us. Part of the mystery has been uncovered, though, by studying the objects that these people left behind. The objects shown here tell us about how the prehistoric Indians lived and what they ate. For example, we can tell that the Indians used the trowel shown here for digging in the earth. This means that they probably planted food crops. The Indians attached this arrowhead to a long stick and used it to kill animals for food. These and other artifacts help us solve the mystery of Indiana's prehistoric people.

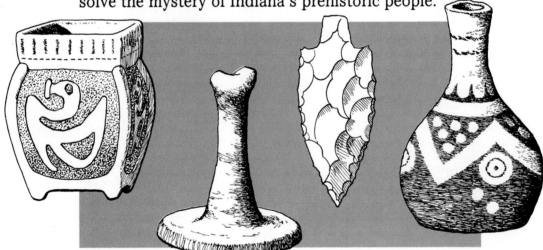

Understanding Source Material

On a separate sheet of paper, answer the questions in complete sentences.

1. What might the bottle and the jar have been used for?
2. What materials do you think were used to make the objects shown here?
3. Why is it important to study artifacts?
4. What do these artifacts tell us about the people who used them?

The Life of the Earliest Indians in Indiana

THINK ABOUT WHAT YOU KNOW

How would you feed and clothe yourself if you could not buy food and clothes in a store?

STUDY THE VOCABULARY

time line   flute
mammoth

FOCUS YOUR READING

How did the earliest Native Americans in Indiana live?

A. The First Arrivals

Different Groups The first people to live in Indiana arrived thousands of years ago. Each new group of Indians that came was very different. Each group made discoveries that helped them survive. Look at the time line on page 74 as you read this lesson. A time line is a tool. It shows you when certain things happened. It also shows you the order in which they happened.

Stone Tools Long, long ago a group of people roamed the land where you are now. Their hair was straight and black. Their eyes were deep brown. Their skin was the color of copper or bronze. They were the earliest Indians of the Stone Age.

Stone Age people were those who used stone tools. These people came soon after the glaciers drew back from Indiana. The earliest Indians hunted large animals such as buffalo and mammoths, animals that looked like hairy elephants.

The earliest Stone Age Indians invented a hunting tool. It was a stone point with a flute. A flute is a groove cut into the stone. When the fluted point struck an animal, the animal bled until it was weak. Then the hunters could easily kill it.

Wandering People These Indians also gathered berries, roots, and nuts to eat. But they did not stay in one place for long. They had to move as the animals moved. Then they would always have a source of food.

The Stone Age people hunted large animals such as mammoths.
▶ What modern animal does the mammoth look like?

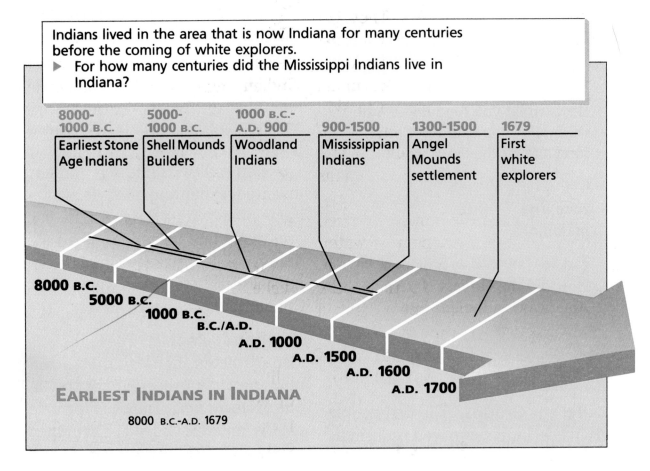

Indians lived in the area that is now Indiana for many centuries before the coming of white explorers.
▶ For how many centuries did the Mississippi Indians live in Indiana?

8000-1000 B.C.	5000-1000 B.C.	1000 B.C.-A.D. 900	900-1500	1300-1500	1679
Earliest Stone Age Indians	Shell Mounds Builders	Woodland Indians	Mississippian Indians	Angel Mounds settlement	First white explorers

8000 B.C.
5000 B.C.
1000 B.C.
B.C./A.D.
A.D. 1000
A.D. 1500
A.D. 1600
A.D. 1700

EARLIEST INDIANS IN INDIANA
8000 B.C.-A.D. 1679

B. The Shell Mounds Indians

Gathering Shellfish After the earliest Indians came the Shell Mounds Builders. From their name, what could you guess about them?

The Shell Mounds Indians gathered mussels, a type of shellfish, along the rivers of Indiana. A shellfish is a water animal with a shell. The Shell Mounds Indians did not have to follow big animals for their food. They could stay in one place longer. These Indians did hunt smaller animals, such as deer, with stone spears. But because they ate shellfish as well as animal meat, the Shell Mounds Indians had more food than earlier Indians did.

Mounds of Shells After these people ate the meat of the shellfish and animals, they threw away the shells and bones. They ate so many shellfish that their trash heaps grew into great mounds. Some of the mounds were as high as 15 feet (5 m) and covered much more land than a large house covers today!

Special Cooking Method The Shell Mounds Indians were also called the Stone Boilers. They got this name because of their special way of cooking. They did not know how to make clay pots or metal pans. Instead, they cooked in skin bags or bark pots. However, both of these materials burned over a fire. To avoid this problem, the Indians heated stones until they were very, very hot. Then the Indians dropped the hot stones into pots of water. The heated water boiled meat and vegetables without burning the pots. Sometimes the stones cracked and became part of the trash around the fire pits. These are just some of the clues that were left behind by the prehistoric Indians. By studying these clues, we learn about how these Indians lived long ago.

C. The Woodland Indians and the Mississippian People

Bow and Arrow Another group of Indians came later. They depended more on the forests for their needs. They were called the Woodland Indians. Using stone and bone, they created better weapons than earlier Indians. One weapon that appeared at this time is still used today—the bow and arrow. The Woodland Indians made bowls, bottles, and dishes and decorated them. They made jewelry and sharp tools such as fishhooks and pins.

The Woodland Indians also did a little farming. They made rules for different groups to live by. Certain people were in a higher group, or social class, than others. Chiefs lived

The Shell Mounds Indians had a special way of cooking. They dropped hot stones into pots of water. Food was cooked in the heated water.
▶ What is another name for the Shell Mounds Indians?

The Woodland Indians used the forest for many things. They used stone and bone to make weapons.

▶ What else did the Woodland Indians make?

on high mounds of dirt. They were even buried on mounds.

Permanent Villages After the Woodland Indians came the Mississippians. The Mississippian Indians built villages. These Indians began to depend on their crops for food. Because of this they lived in larger, more settled communities.

A Mystery But by about 1500, most or all of the Indians of Indiana disappeared! Why this happened is a mystery. Perhaps so much farming in one place caused the soil to become less fertile. Maybe the forests were becoming thin. Or perhaps warlike tribes drove the Mississippian Indians south.

Then, in the mid-1600s, new Indians drifted into the land. When the French arrived, these Indians were already there. The French were followed by the English and many others. But the Indians were the first to enjoy the land of Indiana.

LESSON **2** *REVIEW*

THINK AND WRITE

A. Why were the Stone Age people so named?
B. How were the Shell Mounds Builders different from some of the earlier Indians?
C. What do you know about the social life and customs of Woodland Indians?

SKILLS CHECK

WRITING SKILL

Write a paragraph explaining why you think most of the Native Americans disappeared from Indiana around 1500. You can use ideas mentioned in the text or think of your own ideas.

From: *Secret of the Indian Mound*

By: Wilson Gage (Mary Q. Steele)

Setting: The site of an ancient Indian village, 1958

Mary Q. Steele is a writer of children's books. She wrote many of her books, including *Secret of the Indian Mound,* under the name *Wilson Gage.* This book tells the story of two young boys, Alec and Jimmy, who are helping their Uncle Zan dig in an ancient Indian burial mound.

*H*e [Alec] worked vigorously, but carefully. Then he lifted out a shovelful of earth, and he knew something was there. Dropping to his knees, he began to dig with the old file. He could feel something smooth and cool and round, a jar or something. . . .

What was inside the pot? His curiosity getting the better of him, he couldn't wait until he'd dug the whole thing out. He shook the stone top gently, and it came loose. With a tug, it slid off the pot.

Quickly Alec reached his hand down inside. It was like digging into a Christmas stocking. He felt a fairly small object, something smooth and slippery. . . .

It was a polished steatite [soap-stone] pipe in the shape of a human head! . . .

'' What in the world?'' asked Uncle Zan. ''Say, this is a beautiful jar. Was this stone on top of it? Is there anything else in it?''

He reached in as Alec had done and pulled out a long, curved flint blade, a shell mask with two eyes cut in it, a piece of a bear's jawbone with four teeth embedded in it, a spearhead of white quartz about four inches long, a gorget [collar] with a rattlesnake drawn on it, a clay pipe, and a round piece of black slate with a hole in the middle. . . .

Visiting with the Indians of Angel Mounds

THINK ABOUT WHAT YOU KNOW

Suppose that you wanted to bury some objects that would tell a person in the future what life was like for you today. List five things you would bury. Explain your choices.

STUDY THE VOCABULARY

stockade   **daub**
wattle   **plaza**

FOCUS YOUR READING

What does the Angel Mounds site tell us about Indiana Indians?

A. Angel Mounds Mystery

Did you know that the southwest corner of Indiana holds a mystery? Nobody knows the original name of the town where 11 mounds, or earth piles, can be seen today. The mounds stand on a farm once owned by a family named Angel. The Angel family found many Indian artifacts as they worked on the farm.

Archaeologists soon became interested. They carefully dug into some of the mounds. They started calling the site Angel Mounds. Now much is known about the prehistoric people who lived there for about 200 years. People are still learning about the Angel Mounds Indians. You can learn, too, by visiting this state historic site located near Evansville.

B. A Safe Life in the Big Town

This town was larger than most Indian villages. There were about 200 houses and other buildings. Perhaps as many as 3,000 people lived there. It may have been an Indian capital. No one knows for sure.

The Indians who built the town knew how to make it safe. They chose to build it on the banks of the

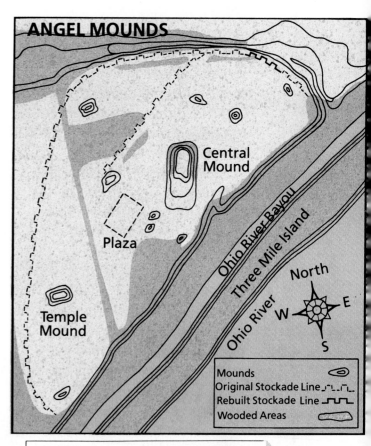

Angel Mounds holds many clues about Indian life long ago.
► What natural feature serves as a protection for the site?

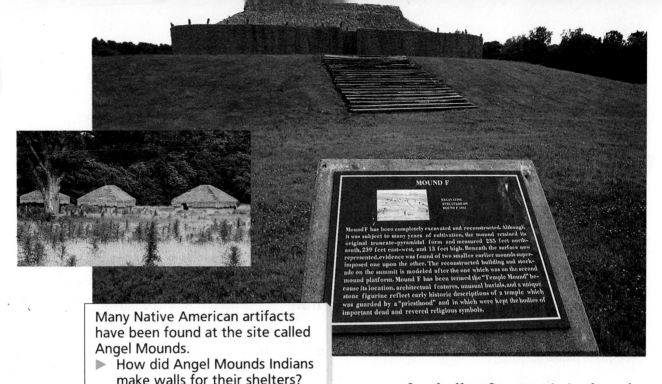

MOUND F

EXCAVATING
STRUCTURE ON
MOUND F 1941

Mound F has been completely excavated and reconstructed. Although it was subject to many years of cultivation, the mound retained its original truncate-pyramidal form and measured 235 feet north-south, 239 feet east-west, and 13 feet high. Beneath the surface now represented, evidence was found of two smaller earlier mounds superimposed one upon the other. The reconstructed building and stockade on the summit is modeled after the one which was on the second mound platform. Mound F has been termed the "Temple Mound" because its location, architectural features, unusual burials, and a unique stone figurine reflect early historic descriptions of a temple which was guarded by a "priesthood" and in which were kept the bodies of important dead and revered religious symbols.

Many Native American artifacts have been found at the site called Angel Mounds.
▶ How did Angel Mounds Indians make walls for their shelters?

Ohio River. The Indians enclosed the other sides of the town with a strong **stockade**, or fort wall. It was 20 feet (6 m) high and about 1 mile (2 km) long! To make the wall, the Indians set up thick posts side by side. They carefully wove branches between the posts. Then they pressed sticky mud around the branches and let it dry. The branches and mud, called **wattle** and **daub**, made the wall very strong. Warriors kept watch from lookout towers built along the stockade.

C. A Busy Life in the Big Town

In the center of the stockade was a **plaza**, or town square. It was about the size of a football field. The Indians played games here — but not football, of course! Archaeologists have found wheel-shaped pieces probably used for rolling games. The townspeople may also have held large meetings, colorful parades, and races in the plaza.

Near the plaza rose a very large mound. It stood over 40 feet (12 m) tall! The mound had three levels and was flat on top. This mound was probably the home of the chief. Other people may also have lived there. The chief could look across the plaza to another high mound. On this mound people worshiped in a building called a temple. What do you think the mound was called?

Other people lived in houses around the plaza. Like the stockade, these houses were built of wattle and daub. Some were square, and some were round. They had roofs made of grasses. A few had no walls so that they would be open and cool in the summer. Each family used the fire pit in the center of its house for cooking and heating. Family members sat and slept on benches made of hard mud.

D. Living with Nature

The Angel Mounds Indians knew that nature was their friend. Nature includes soil, rocks, hills, rivers, valleys, plants, and animals.

The Angel Mounds Indians chose to settle by the great Ohio River. Sometimes during spring flooding, the river left silt on the land. This made the soil good for growing crops — corn, squash, beans, and melons. The river itself provided both food and water. The townspeople caught fish to eat and carried fresh water to their houses.

In the forests, the Angel Mounds Indians hunted deer, turkeys, and other animals. They gathered fruits, nuts, and wild plants. The ancient Indianans knew how to live off the land.

E. Trading

Archaeologists have learned many other things about these Indians. They know that mound-building Indians lived at other places in Indiana. Artifacts at Angel Mounds

The forests around Angel Mounds provided food for the Indians. They hunted many types of animals, including deer.
▶ What weapon are the hunters using?

These are some artifacts from the Angel Mounds site.
▶ What do you think the face-shaped ones were used for?

show that these townspeople traded with people from far away. Pipes, jewelry, and tools in the town were made of materials not found in Indiana. But many things are still not known about the Angel Mounds Indians. What did they call their town? How did they make the huge mounds? And why did the Indians leave the town we call Angel Mounds? We will probably never know the answers.

LESSON 3 REVIEW

THINK AND WRITE

A. How did the Angel Mounds get their name?

B. How did the Indians make the town safe?

C. What is one way in which the Angel Mounds town is like a town today?

D. What effect did the river have on the crops that the Angel Mounds Indians grew?

E. How do archaeologists know that Angel Mounds Indians traded with other Indians?

SKILLS CHECK

MAP SKILL

The Angel Mounds site is found near the modern city of Evansville. Locate Evansville on the map on page 20. What is the latitude and longitude of this city?

USING THE VOCABULARY

explorer	archaeologist
tribe	mammoth
heritage	flute
prehistoric	stockade
artifact	plaza

On a separate sheet of paper, write the best ending for each sentence below. Choose your answers from the vocabulary words above.

1. A word that describes Indians who came before history was written down is _____.
2. An object made and left behind by people is called an _____.
3. The Angel Mounds Indians enclosed their town with a strong wall, or _____.
4. Another name for a person's or group's past is _____.
5. A person who travels in search of new lands is called an _____.
6. An animal that looked like a hairy elephant was a _____.
7. A group of Indian families that shared the same way of life was called a _____.
8. The Indians played games in the town square, or _____.
9. A groove that was cut into stone was called a _____.
10. A person who studies things from the past is an _____.

REMEMBERING WHAT YOU READ

Write your answers in complete sentences on a separate sheet of paper.

1. Why did Columbus give the name *Indians* to the people he found in the new land?
2. Who were the first Indianans?
3. How do we know about prehistoric people?
4. What is an archaeologist?
5. What did the earliest Indians eat?
6. How did the Shell Mounds Indians get their name?
7. Which Indians depended mostly on the forest to fill their needs?
8. How did the Angel Mounds Indians protect their town?
9. Who probably lived on the tallest mound of the Angel Mounds?
10. How do we know that the Angel Mounds Indians were traders?

TYING THE ARTS TO SOCIAL STUDIES

Will Rogers was an actor and a humorous speaker. Rogers was part Indian. One time he said: "My forefathers didn't come over on the *Mayflower*, but they met the boat." Write a paragraph that tells what you think he meant by this statement and how this ties in with what you have learned in Chapter 2.

THINKING CRITICALLY

Write your answers in complete sentences on a separate sheet of paper.

1. What are some ways we can learn about Indiana in prehistoric times?
2. Why did the Stone Age Indians need to move often?
3. Why were the Shell Mounds Indians not always on the move?
4. What allowed the Mississippian Indians to live in more settled communities than some of the earlier Indians?
5. How did the Angel Mounds Indians benefit from the Ohio River?

SUMMARIZING THE CHAPTER

On a separate sheet of paper draw a graphic organizer that is like the one shown here. Copy the information from this graphic organizer to the one you have drawn. Under the main idea for each lesson, write three statements that support it. The first one has been done for you.

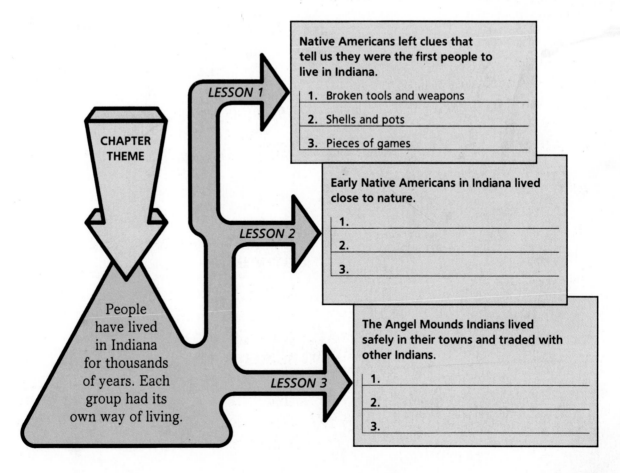

CHAPTER THEME

People have lived in Indiana for thousands of years. Each group had its own way of living.

LESSON 1

Native Americans left clues that tell us they were the first people to live in Indiana.

1. Broken tools and weapons
2. Shells and pots
3. Pieces of games

LESSON 2

Early Native Americans in Indiana lived close to nature.

1.
2.
3.

LESSON 3

The Angel Mounds Indians lived safely in their towns and traded with other Indians.

1.
2.
3.

3 LEARNING MORE ABOUT INDIANA'S FIRST PEOPLE

Native Americans all over the country had rich and varied ways of living. They shared special gifts with the early explorers and settlers. But Native Indianans have also given gifts to the people of Indiana today.

Indian Ways of Life

List all the words or phrases that you can think of that have the word *Indian* in them. What does each one mean?

stereotype   culture

How were early Indians in Indiana different from what many people think they were like?

A. Blocks to Understanding

Wrong Ideas Many people today misunderstand certain things about Native American ways of life. Studying Native Americans carefully can help people to get rid of some of these misunderstandings.

For example, some people think that all Native Americans were hunters and fighters. They picture them wearing feathers and war paint. They imagine that all Indians lived in tents that were made from animal skins. They say that Indians learned a better way to live when Europeans arrived. These ways of thinking are wrong.

No Two Alike These ways of thinking are called **stereotypes** (STER ee uh typs). One meaning of the word *stereotype* is a "copy made from a mold." All copies are exactly alike. When people believe a stereotype, they think about a whole group of people in one way. But no two people are exactly alike.

This is a parade in Kokomo. Everyone likes a parade.
▶ What is the purpose of a parade?

B. Differences Between Native American Cultures

Native American Day One reason people today use the term *Native American* is to get away from the Indian stereotype. Another way to get a true picture of the Indian people is to celebrate Native American Day on September 28. On this day, you could study about the cultures of Native American tribes. Culture is the traditions, beliefs, and way of living of a group of people.

Differences Among Tribes You will probably be surprised as you study the culture of different tribes. You will find out that the Indians in Indiana were very different from those who lived in other parts of the country, such as the Southwest. All early Indians depended on their surroundings for food, clothing, and shelter. So the climate, type of land, animals, and plants where they lived affected how they dressed, what they ate, and what types of houses they lived in.

C. Links Among Tribes

Two Main Groups The two main family groups of Indians in Indiana were called the Algonquian (al GAHNG kee un) and the Iroquois (IHR uh kwoi). In each family there were different tribes. These tribes

Native Americans had many different customs and traditions. This picture shows Indian women harvesting corn on an autumn day.
▶ What tasks are these women performing?

had both similarities and differences. Basically, though, those tribes living near each other built the same types of houses and ate the same kinds of foods. Some even spoke the same language.

Learning from Others   As one group learned a better way of hunting or farming, other tribes would use that way too. Tribes often moved, though. As some tribes moved south and west, they set up separate family groups. Then their differences became greater. But they still kept some of the customs of their original family. The map on this page shows where the tribes were living about the time the French arrived in Indiana.

The Algonquian family was much larger than the Iroquois. Within the Algonquian family, the Miami tribe was the largest tribe and was widely spread throughout the state of Indiana.

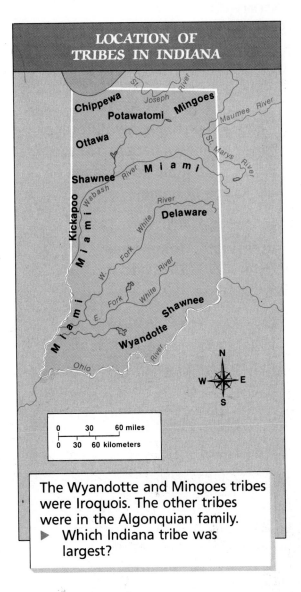

LOCATION OF TRIBES IN INDIANA

The Wyandotte and Mingoes tribes were Iroquois. The other tribes were in the Algonquian family.
▶ Which Indiana tribe was largest?

LESSON **1** *REVIEW*

THINK AND WRITE

A. What is a stereotype?
B. Why were Indians in different places different from each other in some ways?
C. What were the names of the two main Indian families in Indiana?

SKILLS CHECK

MAP SKILL

Look at the map above. Locate the area around where you live. Which Indian tribe or tribes lived nearest to the place where you live today?

The Special Gifts of Native Indianans

THINK ABOUT WHAT YOU KNOW

Think about the many different types of homes people live in today. List some advantages of each type of home.

STUDY THE VOCABULARY

architect   longhouse
tipi   lifestyle
wigwam

FOCUS YOUR READING

What have we learned from Indiana's Indians?

A. A Look at Indiana's First Mobile Homes

Movable Shelters If you had to move very often, what kind of house would you choose? You might live in a mobile home, which you could take with you when you moved.

The Indians, of course, did not have mobile homes as we know them. But many did move often. Those who hunted had to follow the animals that were their source of food. These tribes needed homes that could be moved with them. So the shelter had to be light and made of materials that were close by.

Some Indian **architects** found a clever solution. An architect plans and helps build places to live, work, and play. Indians learned how to be good architects. They cut down tall, slender trees. They placed the trees in a circle on the ground, leaning them together at the top. This made a shape like an upside-down ice cream cone. Then they wrapped deer and buffalo skins around the trees. These skins had been sewn together to make one piece. Such homes were called **tipis** (TEE peez).

Many Native Americans lived in tipis made of animal skins.
▶ What was the hole in the front of the tipi used for?

Ti means "home," and *pi* means "used for." (You may also see this word spelled *tepee* or *teepee*.)

Morning Sun Indians needed open space to set up their tipis. They usually chose flat plains, where there were few trees. Indians could pitch, or set up, and strike, or take down, their tipi in less than 30 minutes!

Tipis were built to fit the way the Indians lived. The door opening faced east, to let in the morning sun and keep out the cold west winds. At the top were flaps. When a family used its cooking fire inside, the flaps were opened to let the smoke out.

Over the years the Indians improved their tipis. They treated the hides with smoke so that they would keep out rain and snow. They learned to use different skins in different seasons. Animals' summer skins were lighter than their winter ones. Summer skins also let more light into the tipi.

B. Other Kinds of Homes

Like Bread Loaves Indians in Indiana who did not move much lived in different kinds of homes. Algonquian tribes built **wigwams,** which looked something like loaves of bread. Some were like round loaves. Others were like long loaves. To build a wigwam, the Indians would first cut slender, young trees and place them in the ground in a circle or oval. Then they bent the tops together and tied them firmly. Over this frame they threw bark, hides, or

The Indians had great respect for the land and learned to use it well.
► What is the name of the food crop planted here?

Some Indians built longhouses in which many families lived together.
▶ What was the main difference between an Indian wigwam and a longhouse?

mats of woven grass. Iroquois tribes built very large wigwams. They were called **longhouses**. In a longhouse, many families lived together. The families were usually related by birth or marriage.

More Permanent Wigwams took longer to build than tipis. What does this tell you about the **lifestyle**, or way of living, of the Indians who built them? It tells you that the Indians who lived in wigwams did not move very often. People who do not move all the time can take longer to build their homes.

In Chapter 2 you learned that the Angel Mounds Indians built houses with wattle and daub. They lived in them in winter. During the summer they used pole houses with no walls. Each type of home the Indians built was adapted to the lifestyle of the people who used it.

C. Indian Languages

Words and Signs Early Indians depended on spoken language. They did not write with an alphabet and words the way you do.

The Indian people made up words to tell about their daily lives. Each tribe had its own spoken language. But some of the different tribes could talk to one another too. The language of the Miami Indians was spoken and understood by many tribes. Study some words of the Miami Indian language on the next page. From the words they used, what can you tell about how the Miami Indians lived?

When an Indian did not know another Indian's language, he or she found other ways to share meaning. Indians invented picture and sign languages. Each picture or hand sign stood for a thought.

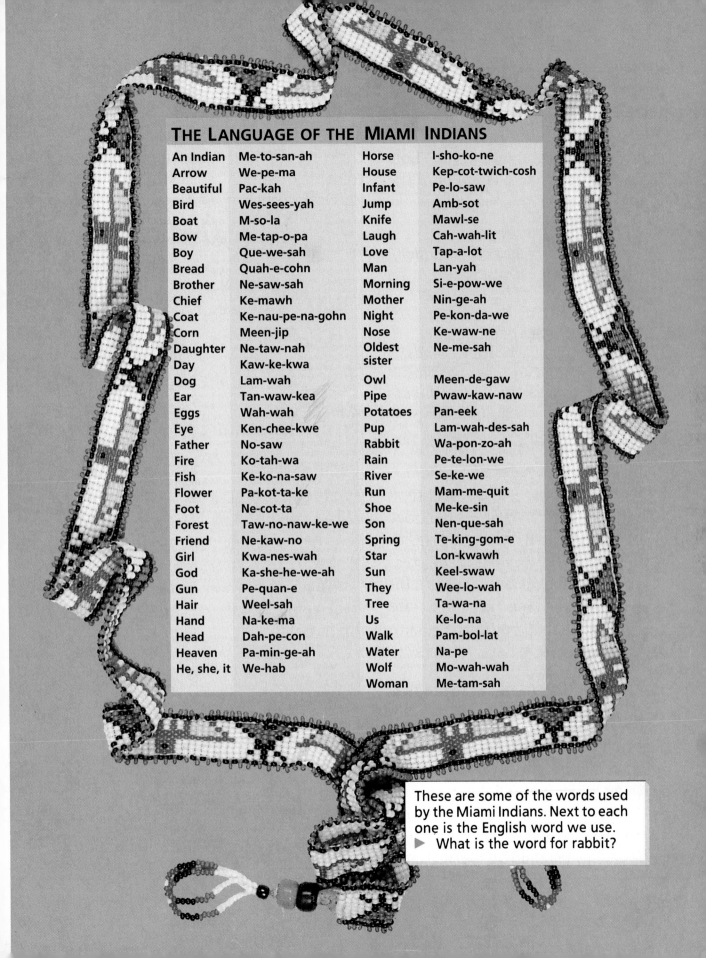

THE LANGUAGE OF THE MIAMI INDIANS

English	Miami	English	Miami
An Indian	Me-to-san-ah	Horse	I-sho-ko-ne
Arrow	We-pe-ma	House	Kep-cot-twich-cosh
Beautiful	Pac-kah	Infant	Pe-lo-saw
Bird	Wes-sees-yah	Jump	Amb-sot
Boat	M-so-la	Knife	Mawl-se
Bow	Me-tap-o-pa	Laugh	Cah-wah-lit
Boy	Que-we-sah	Love	Tap-a-lot
Bread	Quah-e-cohn	Man	Lan-yah
Brother	Ne-saw-sah	Morning	Si-e-pow-we
Chief	Ke-mawh	Mother	Nin-ge-ah
Coat	Ke-nau-pe-na-gohn	Night	Pe-kon-da-we
Corn	Meen-jip	Nose	Ke-waw-ne
Daughter	Ne-taw-nah	Oldest sister	Ne-me-sah
Day	Kaw-ke-kwa		
Dog	Lam-wah	Owl	Meen-de-gaw
Ear	Tan-waw-kea	Pipe	Pwaw-kaw-naw
Eggs	Wah-wah	Potatoes	Pan-eek
Eye	Ken-chee-kwe	Pup	Lam-wah-des-sah
Father	No-saw	Rabbit	Wa-pon-zo-ah
Fire	Ko-tah-wa	Rain	Pe-te-lon-we
Fish	Ke-ko-na-saw	River	Se-ke-we
Flower	Pa-kot-ta-ke	Run	Mam-me-quit
Foot	Ne-cot-ta	Shoe	Me-ke-sin
Forest	Taw-no-naw-ke-we	Son	Nen-que-sah
Friend	Ne-kaw-no	Spring	Te-king-gom-e
Girl	Kwa-nes-wah	Star	Lon-kwawh
God	Ka-she-he-we-ah	Sun	Keel-swaw
Gun	Pe-quan-e	They	Wee-lo-wah
Hair	Weel-sah	Tree	Ta-wa-na
Hand	Na-ke-ma	Us	Ke-lo-na
Head	Dah-pe-con	Walk	Pam-bol-lat
Heaven	Pa-min-ge-ah	Water	Na-pe
He, she, it	We-hab	Wolf	Mo-wah-wah
		Woman	Me-tam-sah

These are some of the words used by the Miami Indians. Next to each one is the English word we use.
▶ What is the word for rabbit?

Indian Legends   Older Indians passed on legends and stories by telling them to younger Indians. These Indians told the tales to their children and grandchildren. Lois Maloy's story "Swift Thunder of the Prairie" pictures this way of life.

> *Little Star-Brother was only eight. . . . He was called Little Star-Brother because, when it was dark and there were many stars in the sky, he would ask his grandfather question after question about the star legends. He looked up into the sparkling heavens where the Happy Hunting Grounds were. In the milky path across the sky, a star shone for each brave who had gone to hunt there. His grandfather said it was good for him to ask questions—for thus he could learn the lore of earth and sky and the wise ways of living.*

Places all over Indiana have Indian names. Some of them are shown on the map on this page. Are any of them near where you live?

D. Indian Scientists, Doctors, Artists, and Farmers

Science and Medicine You have learned that Indians were architects. Did you know that Indians were scientists and doctors? Indians knew that sound travels best through solids. They listened by placing their ears against the ground. They knew that warm air rises. Holes in their roofs let smoke escape. Medicine men and medicine women used bark, leaves, and roots of plants to treat sick people.

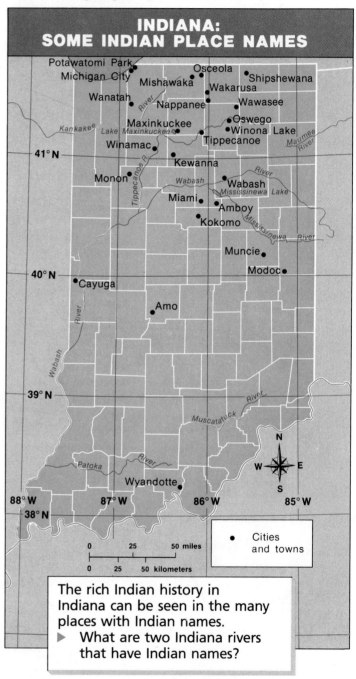

INDIANA: SOME INDIAN PLACE NAMES

The rich Indian history in Indiana can be seen in the many places with Indian names.

▶ What are two Indiana rivers that have Indian names?

This pair of moccasins, purse, and doll were made by Native Americans. They enjoyed making everyday objects very beautiful.
▶ How did they accomplish this?

Agriculture Indians were also farmers. They grew corn, tomatoes, cotton, and tobacco. Indians taught the settlers how to farm. Indians also passed on how to make snowshoes, toboggans, and moccasins.

Learning by Living As Native American tribes came to Indiana, they learned through everyday living. They discovered how to survive and live better lives. They passed what they learned to their children and to all people of today.

Indian Art Indians were artists too. Indians created poems, music, and dances. They made special designs and colors for their own tribe's baskets, clothing, and decorations.

LESSON *2* REVIEW

THINK AND WRITE

A. Why did the homes of some Indians need to be easy to carry from place to place?

B. How do tipis and wigwams show different lifestyles?

C. What are two kinds of language that Indians used?

D. What were some types of art that Indians created?

SKILLS CHECK

THINKING SKILL

You have learned that Indians used picture and sign language. How do we use these types of language today?

Claiming the Land

THINK ABOUT WHAT YOU KNOW

Most people like to explore. Describe a time when you explored an exciting place.

STUDY THE VOCABULARY

compete   trading post
wilderness   journal

FOCUS YOUR READING

Why were so many countries interested in claiming the land the Native Americans lived on?

A. The Race for the New World

French Claims Christopher Columbus claimed the New World for Spain. Yet 100 years later, it was mostly France and England that competed for the land and riches. *Compete* means "to try to win."

France sent explorers to search for new lands. They were supposed to build New France in the New World. They first settled in what is now Canada. The explorers then traveled on the Great Lakes south into what is now the United States. French explorers followed the Mississippi River south to the Gulf of Mexico. The land along the river was named Louisiana for France's King Louis XIV. It covered most of what is the west central United States. It was much larger than the present-day state of Louisiana.

British Claims While France was exploring the land from Canada south into Louisiana, England was racing from the East toward the West. You can see from the map on this page that Indiana was part of the land claimed by France. But England wanted to claim it too.

This race was not a fast one. The land was a **wilderness**, or wild

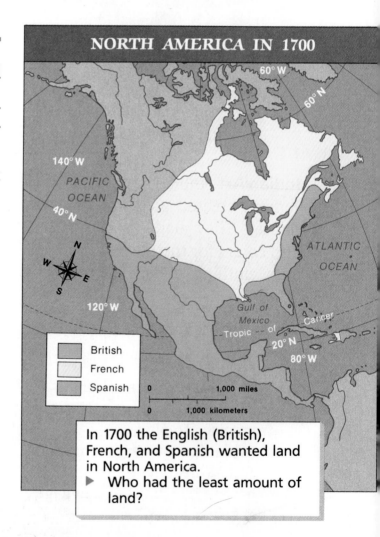

NORTH AMERICA IN 1700

British
French
Spanish

0   1,000 miles

0   1,000 kilometers

In 1700 the English (British), French, and Spanish wanted land in North America.
▶ Who had the least amount of land?

land. Travel was very difficult, slow, and dangerous.

Other Claims And have you forgotten about the Indians? They were the very first to live on the land. The Spanish and Dutch were in the race too. The Spanish were looking for gold in Florida. The Dutch were trading with Indians around what is now New York. So the Indians, Dutch, Spanish, English, and French were all in the race. And they could not all be winners.

As Indians and settlers moved west, camps like this one were set up along the way.
▶ Why did the Indians have to move west?

B. The Riches in the New World

What were the prizes for the winners? As you know, the Spanish wanted gold. The Dutch wanted to trade goods with the Indians. What did England and France want? Both countries wanted to trade for furs with the Indians. Both wanted to find a short way to reach the Indies. In addition, the French wanted to bring their religion to the Indians. The English were looking for land where their people could start new homes, farms, and towns. Again, do not forget the Indians. They wanted to keep the lands open to hunt and raise food for their own families and tribes.

La Salle may have been the first white man to explore the Mississippi River.
► Who traveled with La Salle?

C. An Explorer's Dream

One young Frenchman set out for the New World with high hopes. He was Robert de La Salle. La Salle wanted to explore the wilderness of New France from north to south. He was the first explorer to go all the way down the Mississippi River to the Gulf of Mexico.

The best wilderness highways were rivers and lakes. La Salle knew this. He planned to explore waterways and to build trading posts along them. A trading post is a store where things can be bought and sold. La Salle hoped to become rich by trading with the Indians. And he felt the posts would give France a strong claim to the land.

In 1679 La Salle began a journey that would take him through Indiana. With La Salle were an Indian guide and a French priest. The guide knew about the trails and waterways. He could speak the languages of the Indians. The priest wrote a journal. A journal is also called a diary. This was a daily record about the trip and what the explorers saw. For the first time there was a written history of the Indian natives.

LESSON **3** REVIEW

THINK AND WRITE

A. Along what major river did France claim land?

B. Why did the French want to claim the land in the New World?

C. How did La Salle travel through the wilderness?

SKILLS CHECK

WRITING SKILL

Use the Gazetteer on pages 357–364 to find out about the Mississippi River. Write two interesting facts about the Mississippi River.

Exploring with La Salle

THINK ABOUT WHAT YOU KNOW

Have you ever kept a diary or known anyone who did? Tell why you think people keep diaries.

STUDY THE VOCABULARY

portage   proclamation
council

FOCUS YOUR READING

What are three important events in the early history of Indiana?

A. The First History of Indiana

Many histories have been written about Indiana. Father Louis Hennepin, who traveled with Robert de La Salle, wrote the first. The following passage is based on Father Hennepin's actual journal. The language has been made easier to understand. As you read the journal, use the map on this page to follow La Salle's voyage.

December 3 [1679] *On this day we set out in eight canoes up the St. Joseph River. Our party of 30 is led by La Salle and a Miami Indian guide. Our guide tells of a* **portage,** *or overland route. We can carry our canoes and supplies over this land to the Kankakee River. We are very cold and hungry after our journey today.*

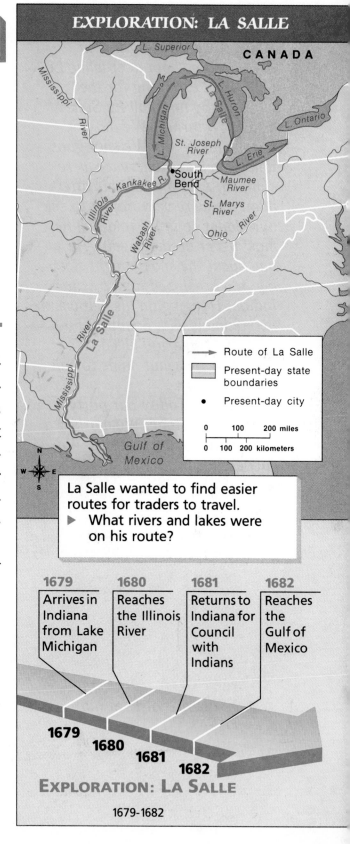

EXPLORATION: LA SALLE

La Salle wanted to find easier routes for traders to travel.
▶ What rivers and lakes were on his route?

1679	1680	1681	1682
Arrives in Indiana from Lake Michigan	Reaches the Illinois River	Returns to Indiana for Council with Indians	Reaches the Gulf of Mexico

EXPLORATION: LA SALLE

1679–1682

December 4 *We spent a very long and wakeful night. Our guide left to shoot deer while La Salle went exploring for the portage. By nightfall La Salle had not returned. We did not know what to do. We shot guns to let him know where we were camped. At 4 o'clock this afternoon we were very happy to see our leader return. I told him he must never do that again. He had spent the snowy night sleeping in a brush bed built by an Indian. Hanging on his belt were two animals with beautiful fur, which La Salle had killed. We did not know what name to call these animals.*

December 5 *Today our party found the portage. We marked a path with crosses on trees. We carried our canoes and supplies across the portage. Scattered about were many buffalo horns. There were also Indian canoes made of buffalo skins.*

December 6 *Today we reached the Kankakee River. The river begins in a great open plain. On the other side of the plain is an Indian village. There are Miami Indians there as well as some other tribes.*

December 15 *We are very short of food. Our hunters have killed a few deer, geese, and swans. The Indians have burned the tall grass nearby. This helps them hunt the buffalo. We have not seen any large animals for days.*

Eventually, the travelers got as far as the Illinois River. From this river they were then able to reach the Mississippi River.

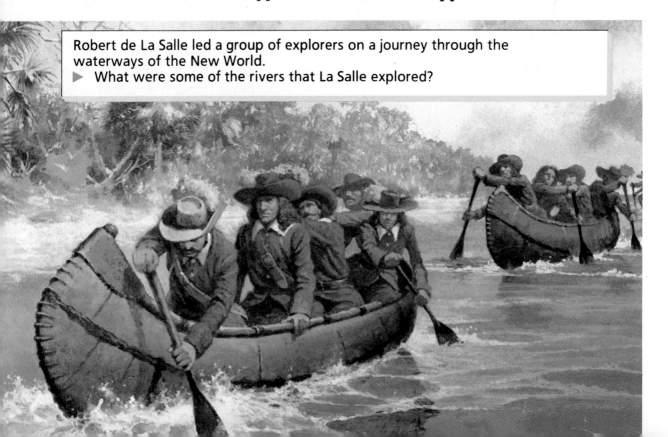

Robert de La Salle led a group of explorers on a journey through the waterways of the New World.

▶ What were some of the rivers that La Salle explored?

B. La Salle and the Indians

At South Bend La Salle made several trips to Indiana. In 1681 La Salle returned to a Miami Indian village south of Lake Michigan and at the bend of the St. Joseph River. The city of South Bend is located there today. La Salle called together Indians from many tribes. This **council** planned for trade and protection against unfriendly Indians. A council is a group that meets to discuss important subjects.

The Great Oak Tree La Salle and the Indian chiefs sat under a great oak tree. In the city of South Bend today, this tree still stands. It is called the Council Oak. La Salle and the council decided that many forts should be built in New France. Soldiers located in these forts could protect the fur trade as well as the friendly Indian tribes.

C. Building Trading Posts and Forts

Taking La Salle's Advice The French listened to the ideas that La Salle brought back from the council. They built a line of trading posts and forts. At these posts, French traders lived and kept their goods and supplies. They traded with the Indians. The Indians brought the French the

Indians met under this tree, the Council Oak, many years ago.
▶ How can people visiting this tree learn about its history?

skins of beavers, raccoons, bears, foxes, deer, and other animals. The French sent the skins to Europe.

The Indians liked many things that the French brought with them to the New World. Indians exchanged furs for metal pots and pans, iron tools, and animal traps. Guns made hunting and protecting themselves easier. They also traded for the brightly colored blankets and ruffled shirts that the French brought with them.

Building Forts The French were smart. They built their forts along rivers. That way, traders could reach

France and England were often at war because both countries wanted the same land. The Indians helped the French fight the English.
▶ Why did the Indians side with the French?

them easily by canoe. There were three main forts in Indiana. Fort Miami was built on the Maumee River. The city of Fort Wayne stands there today. Fort Ouiatanon (wee-AT uh nahn) and Fort Vincennes (vihn SENZ) were located on the Wabash River.

D. Fighting a Losing Battle

Equals and Friends The French traders and their families were fun-loving people. They loved to dance and play games much as the Indians did. The French treated the Indians as equals and friends. French men and Indian women would often marry each other.

The Indians did not get along as well with the English. The Indians were afraid that the English would settle or move onto their lands. The English settlers often cleared the forests for farms and towns. By doing this, they destroyed the things of nature that the Indians needed.

Frequent Wars Since France and England both wanted the same land, they were often at war. The Indians sided with the French. The last years

of the fighting became known as the French and Indian War. In 1763 the English won the war. The French lost both Canada and the land from the Great Lakes to the Gulf of Mexico. This included land that is now the state of Indiana.

E. Pontiac Against the English

Most of the Indian tribes did not like the outcome of the French and Indian War. They were worried

Although Pontiac did not defeat the British, he did win important gains for his people.
▶ What gains did Pontiac win for his people?

that the English settlers would come in even greater numbers to set up more farms and towns. One strong Indian chief tried to do something about it. Pontiac, chief of the Ottawa tribe, called several tribes together. He planned attacks on forts the English had taken from the French. Pontiac's war party got off to a good start. It captured Fort Miami, Fort Ouiatanon, and six other forts from the English soldiers. But because Pontiac had fewer men, the English were able to recapture the forts.

Yet, in a way, Pontiac won too. England was tired of fighting. The English passed a law. This law was called a **proclamation** (prahk luh MAY shun). In the Proclamation of 1763, England closed the Indian lands to settlers. The Indians were pleased with this law. However, the settlers who wanted to come into these lands were *not* pleased.

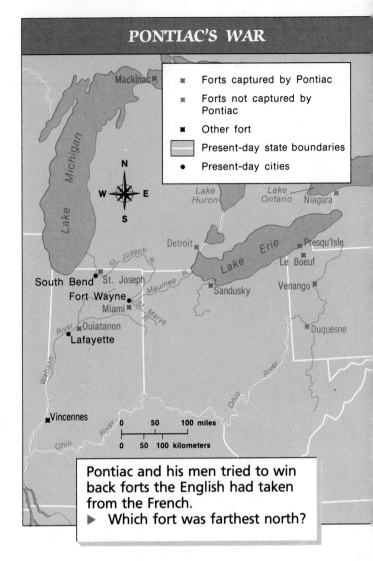

PONTIAC'S WAR

- ▪ Forts captured by Pontiac
- ▪ Forts not captured by Pontiac
- ▪ Other fort
- Present-day state boundaries
- • Present-day cities

Pontiac and his men tried to win back forts the English had taken from the French.
▶ Which fort was farthest north?

LESSON 4 REVIEW

THINK AND WRITE
A. What is a portage?
B. What does the Council Oak remind people of?
C. What were the three main French forts in Indiana?
D. Why did the French traders get along well with the Indians?

E. Why did the Indians like the Proclamation of 1763?

SKILLS CHECK

MAP SKILL
Look at the map on this page. Which three forts were Pontiac's tribes not able to capture?

THE PROCLAMATION OF 1763

On October 7, 1763, the British government signed the Proclamation of 1763. This law made rules for the settlers about land development.

And whereas it is just and reasonable, and essential to our interest and the security of our colonies, that the . . . tribes of Indians with whom we are connected, and who live under our protection, should not be . . . disturbed in the possession of such parts of our dominions and territories as, not having been . . . purchased by us, are reserved to them, . . . as their hunting-grounds; we do therefore . . . declare . . . that no Governor or commander in chief, in any of our colonies, . . . presume, . . . to grant warrants of survey, or pass any patents for lands beyond the bounds of their respective governments, . . . or for any lands beyond the heads or sources of any of the rivers which fall into the Atlantic Ocean from the west or northwest; . . .

Understanding Source Material

1. For what two reasons does the British government want to protect the Indians' lands?
2. What geographic limits does the proclamation set on western settlement?

USING THE VOCABULARY

stereotype	trading post
culture	journal
tipi	portage
longhouse	council
compete	proclamation

On a separate sheet of paper, write the best ending for each sentence below. Choose your answers from the vocabulary words above.

1. The French and the Indians could buy and sell goods at a _____.
2. In order to help the French traders, La Salle called the Indian tribes to a _____.
3. An Indian home that could be taken down and moved easily is called a _____.
4. Some people who keep a diary call it their _____.
5. People who think one way about a whole group of people show that they believe a _____.
6. To make an effort to win something is to _____.
7. A very large Indian wigwam was called a _____.
8. The traditions, beliefs, and way of living of a particular group of people is called _____.
9. Another name for a law is a _____.
10. An overland route is a _____.

REMEMBERING WHAT YOU READ

Write your answers in complete sentences on a separate sheet of paper.

1. What is culture?
2. Which Algonquian Indian tribe was spread throughout Indiana?
3. Why did some Indians build tipis?
4. What is a wigwam?
5. In what ways did the Indians help the settlers?
6. What two European countries competed for the land of Indiana?
7. What did the English want in the New World?
8. What is a portage?
9. Why did La Salle call a council of Indian tribes?
10. Who was Chief Pontiac?

TYING LANGUAGE ARTS TO SOCIAL STUDIES: WRITING TO LEARN

Pretend that you are either a Native American or a French or English explorer in the New World. If you are a Native American, write a paragraph describing your reaction to the explorers. If you are an explorer, write a paragraph describing your reaction to the people you found in the New World.

THINKING CRITICALLY

Write your answers in complete sentences on a separate sheet of paper.
1. How did the surroundings of Indian tribes affect their ways of life?
2. How did tipis reflect the lifestyle of some Native Americans?
3. Why is it so important for people to be able to communicate?
4. Why was there conflict over the land in Indiana?
5. Why were forts important to those competing for land in the West?

SUMMARIZING THE CHAPTER

On a separate sheet of paper draw a graphic organizer that is like the one shown here. Copy the information from this graphic organizer to the one you have drawn. Under the main idea for each lesson, write three statements that support it. The first one has been done for you.

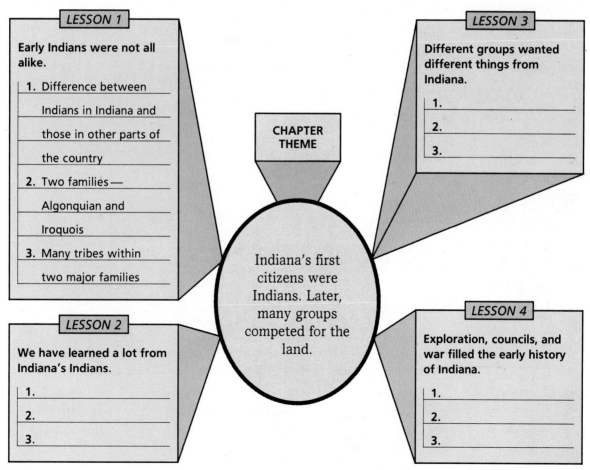

LESSON 1

Early Indians were not all alike.

1. Difference between Indians in Indiana and those in other parts of the country

2. Two families — Algonquian and Iroquois

3. Many tribes within two major families

LESSON 2

We have learned a lot from Indiana's Indians.

1. _____
2. _____
3. _____

CHAPTER THEME

Indiana's first citizens were Indians. Later, many groups competed for the land.

LESSON 3

Different groups wanted different things from Indiana.

1. _____
2. _____
3. _____

LESSON 4

Exploration, councils, and war filled the early history of Indiana.

1. _____
2. _____
3. _____

4 INDIANA: THE WESTERN FRONTIER

This country grew and changed before it became the United States of America. The Indians, the British, and the Americans all claimed the land. Some great leaders helped settle the question of land ownership.

Moving into the New Frontier

THINK ABOUT WHAT YOU KNOW

How would you feel about obeying a rule that you thought was unfair? What, if anything, would you do about it?

STUDY THE VOCABULARY

frontier   preserve
independent

FOCUS YOUR READING

What were the reasons for the conflict among the Native Americans, the settlers, and the British government?

A. The Settlers and the Indians

The Moving Frontier Sometimes you hear people refer to Indiana and other states around it as the Midwest. They call states such as Colorado and California the West. But in the 1700s and 1800s, Indiana was part of the West! It was part of the western **frontier.** A frontier is the outer edge of a settled area.

Not everyone agreed about the frontier. Settlers said, "We will move west over this frontier and tame it. We will build our houses and begin our farms on the frontier."

The Indians said something else. "We live here already. We have built our villages and hunted in the forests and on the plains for many, many years now. We do not want the American settlers taking over our hunting grounds."

Some Indians were becoming angrier. They had already been driven from their homes in the East by the English settlers.

Claiming the Frontier Who had the better claim to the West—the Indians or the settlers? You have already learned that the Native Americans were the first to live on the

Seeking land of their own, settlers moved west in wagon trains.
► What animals are pulling the first wagon in this picture?

land. But Indians did not believe in owning land. They believed in sharing it with other members of their tribe and with other tribes.

The settlers had different ideas, however. Each wanted to own a piece of land. The settlers pushed farther into the West. Did they have a right to the land? The Indians said, "No!" Remember that in the Proclamation of 1763 the British government had also said, "No!"

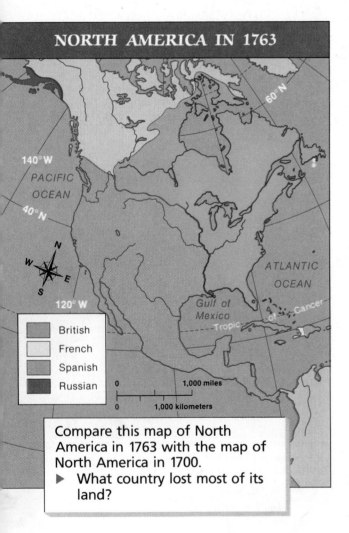

NORTH AMERICA IN 1763

British
French
Spanish
Russian

0   1,000 miles
0   1,000 kilometers

Compare this map of North America in 1763 with the map of North America in 1700.
▶ What country lost most of its land?

B. The Settlers and the British

The Proclamation of 1763 was made by a government far away in Britain. It closed the West to settlers. Do you think that stopped them? It did not. The settlers had to be brave to go to a new land. They were **independent** people. That means they thought for themselves. Many had already begun to think of themselves as Americans. They did not like being told what to do by the British government.

The settlers saw no reason to stay out of the frontier. "We helped force the French out," they said. "The East Coast is getting crowded. Cities, towns, and farms are growing here. We want more land." The land they wanted was in the West. So they went west!

The British wanted to stop the westward movement. To them, the Indian fur trade was important. If settlers cleared the land, the fur-bearing animals would disappear. To keep control over western land, the British sent their soldiers to forts in the West.

C. Conflict in the East

There were problems in the East too. The French and Indian War had cost the British money. For this reason, the government taxed the settlers. It also passed some

Outnumbered by the colonists, the British retreated from Concord to Boston.
▶ What were the colonists fighting for?

strict new laws. Most colonists did not like that at all!

The settlers thought that their freedom was being taken away. Many began thinking about fighting to **preserve** it, or keep it from being lost. The result was the War for Independence. *Independence* means "to be free of something." This war started in 1775. The Americans fought this war in order to be free from the British.

LESSON *1* REVIEW

THINK AND WRITE

A. Why were the Indians angry with the settlers?
B. Why were the settlers unhappy about the Proclamation of 1763?
C. Why did the settlers believe their freedom was being taken away?

SKILLS CHECK

MAP SKILL

Compare the map on page 94 with the map on page 108. Describe the similarities and differences between the two maps.

INDIANS AND SETTLERS WORKING TOGETHER

Sometimes when we think of the Indians during the early history of the United States, we think of bad feelings and wars. In fact, the Indians were protecting their land and defending their way of life. Some settlers ignored the needs of the Indians and broke promises made to them. Yet the relationships between the Indians and the settlers were usually friendly at first. Without help from the Indians, the early settlements would surely not have survived.

There are many examples of cooperation and goodwill between Indians and settlers. One such example occurred in Indiana. The first permanent European settlement in Indiana was the fort at Vincennes. It was built in 1731 by the French. The French treated the Indians as equals. They traded such items as beads, blankets, knives, and paint for animal furs from the Indians. The French and the Indians lived in peace for many years.

When the British moved into the area, they also traded peacefully with the Indians. In fact, they tried to gain the Indians' favor by paying them higher prices for the furs than the French. Soon the French and the British began to compete for the fur trade. Unfortunately, the Indians were drawn into the conflicts and the wars that followed.

A careful look at history will show that where there was cooperation between the Indians and the settlers, there was friendship. And where there was friendship, there was peace.

Thinking for Yourself

On a separate sheet of paper, answer the questions in complete sentences.

1. Why do you think cooperation between different groups of people is important?
2. In your opinion, could more of the conflicts between the settlers and the Indians have been settled peacefully? Explain your answer.
3. How do you think cooperation and friendship help keep peace?

Planning the War in the West

THINK ABOUT WHAT YOU KNOW
What kinds of skills help a person survive in the wilderness? Make a list of at least three skills.

STUDY THE VOCABULARY
survey   **rapids**

FOCUS YOUR READING
Why was George Rogers Clark an important leader?

A. Clark in the Wilderness

Becoming a Surveyor   George Rogers Clark was born in Virginia in 1752. He grew up on a farm. At school he learned reading and math. But his favorite place to learn was from nature. George's grandfather taught him to survey, or to measure and map land. This was a good skill to have, because surveyors were needed in the West. Before settlers could claim land, it had to be surveyed so that the boundaries could be marked correctly.

Clark grew into a tall, broad-shouldered young man. He had blue eyes and reddish hair. At 19, Clark went west to survey. He kept a journal on his travels. At one time he wrote, "A richer and more beautiful country . . . has never been seen in America yet." Clark decided he wanted to live in the West. When the War for Independence started, George Rogers Clark was living in a settlement in Kentucky.

Attacking Settlers   Henry Hamilton was the British leader in the West. Hamilton's headquarters were at Fort Detroit. The British also had three other important forts. Fort

George Rogers Clark learned a lot about nature from the Indians.
► How does his clothing show some of the things he learned from the Indians?

Vincennes was in Indiana. Fort Kaskaskia (ka SKAS kee uh) and Fort Cahokia (kuh HOH kee uh) were in Illinois. Find each of the forts on the map on this page.

After the War for Independence started, the British encouraged the Indians to attack the settlers in the West. The British gave the Indians supplies from the British forts.

B. Clark's Secret Plan

Protecting Settlers In 1777 George Rogers Clark came up with a plan. He wanted to protect the western settlers from the British and also from the Indians who had sided with the British.

If you had been Clark, which fort would you attack first? Fort Detroit was the largest and the strongest. The other forts were small. Few British soldiers guarded the small forts. Clark chose to take the small forts first — by surprise!

Asking for Help To carry out his plan, Clark needed soldiers and supplies. He went back to Virginia. There, he asked friends for help. These friends were leaders in Virginia. One of them was Virginia's governor, Patrick Henry. George Rogers Clark's friends believed that his plan might work. But the plan had to be kept secret.

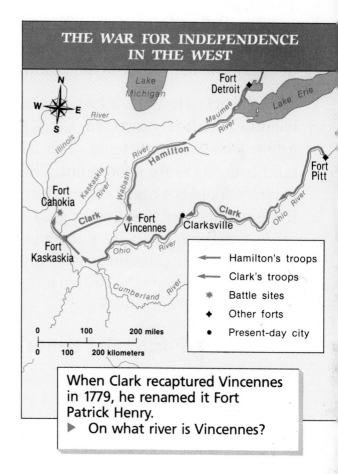

THE WAR FOR INDEPENDENCE IN THE WEST

Legend:
← Hamilton's troops
← Clark's troops
✳ Battle sites
◆ Other forts
● Present-day city

0   100   200 miles
0   100   200 kilometers

When Clark recaptured Vincennes in 1779, he renamed it Fort Patrick Henry.
▶ On what river is Vincennes?

C. A Fort on Corn Island

Fake Orders Clark returned to the West. With him were 175 soldiers, 20 settler families — and two sets of orders! His soldiers thought they were going only as far as Kentucky to fight. Only Clark knew what their real mission was.

Clark and the others traveled by flatboat along the Ohio River. At one point the flat, boxlike boats reached **rapids.** Rapids are places where water flows quickly over rocks. At that place, Clark spotted Corn Island. It is near the present-day city of Clarksville. You can see Clarksville on the map on page 113. Clark decided to set up camp on the island.

Island Fort He built a fort on the island. The fort protected Clark's group from Indian attacks. The island had one more good point. The soldiers could not easily escape from it. Clark imagined that they might be quite unhappy when he told them what their real mission was. They were going to attack the British forts 300 miles (483 km) away!

D. Winning Forts and Friends

Many Miles to Go Clark and his soldiers set out from Corn Island in June 1778. They spent four days and four nights covering 200 miles (322 km) on the Ohio River. Then they had to march more than 100 miles (161 km) overland. By the end of the summer, they had captured the three forts. Few shots had been fired! Clark's plan was working.

French Friends French traders still lived near the forts. They wondered: *Who is this tall, red-haired leader with his ragged army?* At first they were afraid of the rough-looking soldiers. But Clark wanted to make the French traders his friends, so he was very kind to them. The French then decided to be loyal to the Americans.

At a gathering of Indian tribes, Clark stood before the braves. He held a red belt in one hand, and a white belt in the other.
▶ What did the two belts mean?

Big Knives Clark also wanted the Indians as friends. Again, he had a plan. He knew that the Indians would be curious about him. So he waited. Soon he received a message that there would be a gathering of tribes. The Indians invited the Big Knives, as they called the Americans, to come. (The Americans got

this name because of the long hunting knives the soldiers carried on their belts.)

At the Meeting For three days Clark listened in silence to the Indians' speeches. Then he called a meeting. He stood up proudly in front of the tribes. In his right hand he held a blood-red belt. In his left he held a white belt. He said in a clear, strong voice: "Men and warriors! Pay attention! . . . the Great Spirit . . . brought us together, . . . and what ever may be agreed to by us, . . . I expect that each party will strictly adhere to [support]. . . . I carry in my right hand war and peace in my left. . . . Take which you please."

The Indians liked this brave soldier. They decided to take the white belt of peace from the leader of the Big Knives.

LESSON *2* REVIEW

THINK AND WRITE

A. What were the names of the four British forts in the West?

B. Which forts did Clark decide to attack first?

C. Why did Clark decide to stop at Corn Island?

D. What did Clark offer the Indians?

SKILLS CHECK

THINKING SKILL

What were some of the reasons that the Indians might have had for choosing the white belt offered by George Rogers Clark? Write your answer using complete sentences.

The End of the War

THINK ABOUT WHAT YOU KNOW

You have probably played games in which you were part of a team. How does it feel to know that you have had a part in helping your team win?

STUDY THE VOCABULARY

gunport   **Declaration of**
cannon   **Independence**
surrender   **memorial**

FOCUS YOUR READING

What did George Rogers Clark do for the Americans?

A. Fighting with the British

Renamed Sackville At Fort Detroit, the British general Henry Hamilton was hearing some bad news. Clark had captured the three small forts! Hamilton could hardly believe what the small band of Americans had done! In the fall of 1778, Hamilton gathered an army of British troops and friendly Indians. They marched to Vincennes and recaptured that fort. They renamed it Fort Sackville.

Help from Vigo When the British captured the fort, they also captured a rich fur trader named Francis Vigo. Hamilton put him in prison at first but then released him. This turned out to be a mistake! One night in January 1779, Clark received a visitor at Fort Kaskaskia. It was Vigo. He told Clark that Hamilton had recaptured Fort Vincennes (now Fort Sackville). Vigo told Clark that Hamilton had only about 80 soldiers there. In the spring, though, Hamilton's army would be large. Then he was going to try to gain back the other two forts.

Flooded Land Clark had another important decision to make. If he waited until spring to attack Hamilton, the general's army would probably defeat Clark's small band. About half of Clark's soldiers had

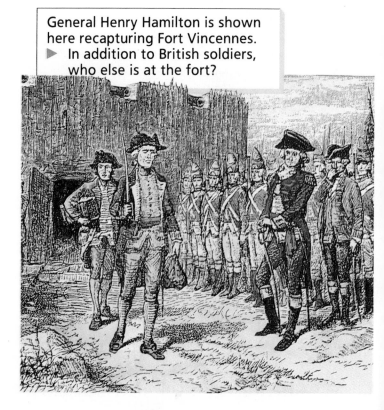

General Henry Hamilton is shown here recapturing Fort Vincennes.
▶ In addition to British soldiers, who else is at the fort?

Clark's soldiers were cold and tired. They regained their strength and courage when the little drummer boy bravely floated past on his drum.
▶ Which fort were the soldiers on their way to recapture?

gone back home. What if he attacked now? No one would expect an attack in the winter. One big problem was that the land between Kaskaskia and Vincennes was flooded. If only Clark could move his army through the marshy land so that he could surprise the British.

Clark decided that he had to take the chance. Again, Francis Vigo helped. He lent money to Clark for guns, gunpowder, and bullets. Clark sent these supplies by boat down the Mississippi and up the Ohio and Wabash rivers. The supply boat was going to meet Clark at Vincennes.

B. A Heroic Return

The small army carried no tents. They had very little food and gunpowder. The army marched for 16 days. The soldiers were wet, cold, and hungry.

At one point a small drummer boy floated on his drum and made the men laugh. They covered more than 150 miles (241 km).

When they reached the fort, they hid outside the walls. The boat with the supplies had not arrived. The soldiers had only one thing going for them. The British did not know they were there.

C. The Battle of Sackville

Carrying Flags Clark spread his soldiers out behind a hill. With him he had 20 American flags that the women in Kaskaskia had sewn. Clark spread these flags among the men. Carrying them, the men marched in a zigzag line. People in the town and fort could not see the men. They could see only the flags. They thought a large army was ready to attack. Hamilton and his soldiers thought there were about 1,000 men in Clark's army!

Opening Fire The British opened the gunports. These were small doors in front of the cannons, or large guns. Clark's men had crept forward and were close to the fort. When Clark gave the order to fire, his men shot through the gunports.

They had to make every shot count. "Boom!" the cannons roared. Clark's men were so close to the fort that the cannonballs just sailed harmlessly over their heads.

Offering Help Do you remember how Clark made friends with the French who lived around the forts he captured? Now the Americans received help from these friendly people. The French townspeople brought out food and gunpowder. Some Indians arrived too, and offered to help.

A White Flag Clark demanded that General Hamilton surrender, or give up. At first, the British leader refused angrily. Clark again demanded surrender. Finally, at ten o'clock on February 25, 1779, Hamilton and his soldiers marched out with the white flag of surrender. Clark's ragged, surprisingly small army marched in.

The British surrendered to Clark's army at the battle of Sackville.
▶ How can you tell that the British have surrendered?

Delegates from all 13 colonies met in Philadelphia, Pennsylvania, to sign the Declaration of Independence.

▶ What did the Declaration of Independence say?

D. Victory in the West and the East

The British turned Fort Sackville over to the Americans. Instead of going back to the French name of Fort Vincennes, Clark gave it another name. He wanted to repay a friend who had stood by him. The American flag rose over Fort Patrick Henry! Governor Henry of Virginia must have been proud of the young Clark and his secret plans.

Throughout his life, Clark was disappointed that he had not taken Fort Detroit. But he *had* captured the British leader in the West. Other Americans won battles in the East.

The **Declaration of Independence** had been signed by the Americans on July 4, 1776. This paper said that Americans wanted to be free of the British. As the War for Independence drew to a close in 1783, Americans were finally free! A new and glorious nation was born —the United States of America.

E. Clark the Hero

Paid with Land To win the West, Clark had used all his own money and had borrowed more from others. He had fed soldiers and bought supplies. The young country could not afford to pay him in money. Instead,

119

he and his soldiers were given 150,000 acres (60,750 ha) of land north of Corn Island. This land was called Clark's Grant. It was the beginning of the town of Clarksville. His soldiers became the first settlers in the area. They started the first American settlement in what is now Indiana. Today, some families of those soldiers still live on this land in Clark, Floyd, and Scott counties.

Reminders of the Past A street along the west line of the grant is called Grant Line Road. It reminds travelers of Clark and his brave soldiers. Today, a town, a county, a school, a bridge, and a street are named for the man some people call the George Washington of the West. Many people visit the George Rogers Clark Memorial in Vincennes each year. A **memorial** is a way of honoring an important person or group of people.

The George Rogers Clark Memorial is one of many historical places in Vincennes.
▶ What is a memorial?

George Rogers Clark understood people and knew how to make decisions. This, along with his bravery, made him a great leader.

LESSON 3 REVIEW

THINK AND WRITE

A. How did Francis Vigo help his friend Clark?

B. What kinds of problems did Clark's soldiers face?

C. How did Clark pretend he had a large army?

D. For whom did George Rogers Clark rename Fort Sackville?

E. What are two things that help us remember George Rogers Clark?

SKILLS CHECK

WRITING SKILL

Use the Gazetteer on pages 357–364 to find out about Clarksville. Then write one fact about Clarksville that is not mentioned in this lesson.

Indians After the War

THINK ABOUT WHAT YOU KNOW

Do you think keeping your promises is important? Tell why or why not.

STUDY THE VOCABULARY

treaty   territory

FOCUS YOUR READING

Why was the Treaty of Greenville important to Indiana?

A. The Treaty of Paris

At the end of the War for Independence in 1783, an important treaty was signed. A treaty is an agreement between two or more persons or groups. This agreement is called the Treaty of Paris, because it was signed in the city of Paris, France. The treaty said that the United States of America was an independent country.

The treaty set the boundaries of the new country. The northern boundary was the Great Lakes. The Mississippi River was the western boundary. Florida was the southern boundary. The British and new Americans signed the treaty. What group was left out?

If you said Native Americans, you are right. Do you think that was fair? The Indians had no part in the treaty. They were angry. Although one war was over, peace did not yet come to the West.

B. Indians' Conflicts with the Settlers

After the war, the United States set up a new government. The government passed laws. One law allowed for land to be settled. This area of land, called a territory, was north of the Ohio River and stretched to the Mississippi River. The Northwest Territory, as it was called, later included six states: Ohio, Indiana, Illinois, Michigan, Wisconsin, and part of Minnesota. (See the map on page 131 of Chapter 5.) For years after the war, settlers moved into this territory. The Indians, though, wanted to use the land to farm, hunt, and fish.

A powerful Miami Indian chief named Little Turtle called a council

Chief Little Turtle planned raids against the settlers to chase them away. His people believed the land belonged to them.
▶ How did the Indians want to use the land?

The reckless General "Mad Anthony" Wayne attacked the British at Stony Point.
▶ How does this painting show his recklessness?

of Indians. The Indians planned raids against the settlers. The settlers were very frightened. They built small forts where they could go for protection. Both men and women carried guns as they worked.

C. Mad Anthony Wayne

Who could protect the settlers from the angry Indians? Their raids grew worse in the years after the

for wilderness fighting. General Wayne spent two years training soldiers to fight the Indians. Little Turtle had great respect for Wayne. He called General Wayne "the man who never sleeps."

D. Heading for Battle

Wayne prepared his army, but he did not want war with the Indians. He asked the tribes for peace. Little Turtle told his people that Wayne's army was very strong. He thought they should vote for peace. But the Indians thought that Little Turtle had lost his nerve. They named a new chief who wanted war.

An important battle occurred in a place called Fallen Timbers. It got its name because huge trees had been blown down by a windstorm.

Wayne tricked the Indians. He let it be known that he planned to attack on August 17, 1794. Wayne knew that the Indians did not eat right before a battle. Wayne waited until August 20 to attack. By then the braves were weak with hunger. Some had gone in search of food. The soldiers attacked, and in one hour the battle was over. The Indians had been defeated. They realized that Little Turtle had been right. The Indians decided to make him their chief again.

war. General Anthony Wayne had proved in the War for Independence that he was a good fighter. His recklessness had gained him the name Mad Anthony Wayne.

He also knew the ways of Indians. He knew how to train soldiers

General Wayne's soldiers attacked the Miami Indians at a place called Fallen Timbers.
▶ Which side seems to be winning the battle at Fallen Timbers?

E. The Treaty of Greenville

Wayne met with Little Turtle and many other Indian chiefs to make peace. They traveled to a place called Greenville, in Ohio. Every chief who wanted to speak was allowed to do so. Together they wrote a treaty. The Indians promised to give up certain lands located in the Northwest Territory to the settlers and not to attack them.

In the Treaty of Greenville, signed in 1795, the Indians gave up most of Ohio. They also gave up part of southeastern Indiana. For all this land, the Indians received $20,000 in goods and an additional $9,500 in goods each year.

The Treaty of Greenville was signed by General Wayne and Chief Little Turtle in 1795.
► What did the Indians lose by signing the treaty?

Little Turtle placed his mark on the treaty as the Indian leader. He promised: "I have been the last to sign this treaty; I will be the last to break it."

Little Turtle kept his promise. For 15 years the Native Americans and the new Americans lived in peace. The treaty helped bring new settlers into Ohio and Indiana. The treaty also helped Ohio and Indiana to become states.

LESSON 4 REVIEW

THINK AND WRITE

A. What was the Treaty of Paris?

B. Why did the Indians plan raids against settlers?

C. What were two good points about General Anthony Wayne?

D. In what three ways were General Anthony Wayne and George Rogers Clark alike?

E. What was the purpose of the Treaty of Greenville?

SKILLS CHECK

WRITING SKILL

Write a sentence telling how the Treaty of Paris and the Treaty of Greenville were alike. Write a sentence telling how they were different.

USING THE VOCABULARY

frontier	cannon
preserve	surrender
survey	memorial
rapids	treaty
gunport	territory

On a separate sheet of paper, write the word that best matches each definition below. Choose your answers from the vocabulary words above.

1. to measure and map land
2. an area of land
3. the outer edge of a settled area
4. an agreement between two or more persons or groups
5. to give up
6. a large gun
7. to keep something from being lost
8. small doors in front of cannons
9. a way of honoring an important person or people
10. a place where water flows quickly over rocks

REMEMBERING WHAT YOU READ

Write your answers in complete sentences on a separate sheet of paper.

1. Why didn't the settlers obey the Proclamation of 1763?
2. Why did the British government tax the English settlers?
3. What was Clark's purpose in going west in 1777?
4. What two groups did Clark manage to gain as friends?
5. Who gave news that helped Clark decide when he should attack Fort Sackville?
6. Who led the march from Fort Kaskaskia to Fort Sackville?
7. Who offered help to Clark at the battle of Sackville?
8. For Clark's work in the West, what did the government give Clark and his men?
9. What were the boundaries of the United States, according to the Treaty of Paris?
10. At what battle did Anthony Wayne defeat the Indians?

TYING LANGUAGE ARTS TO SOCIAL STUDIES: WRITING TO LEARN

Imagine that you are George Rogers Clark. You have just landed on Corn Island. Now you must tell the soldiers about your secret plan. Write what you will say to them so that you can convince them that they should go with you to capture the forts.

THINKING CRITICALLY

Write your answers in complete sentences on a separate sheet of paper.

1. How did the Proclamation of 1763 affect settlers moving west?
2. Why did George Rogers Clark take soldiers into the West?
3. How do you feel about the way George Rogers Clark kept his real plans hidden from the settlers and soldiers who traveled with him?
4. What were good and bad reasons to attack Fort Sackville in winter?
5. Why was the Treaty of Greenville important in Indiana history?

SUMMARIZING THE CHAPTER

On a separate sheet of paper draw a graphic organizer that is like the one shown here. Copy the information from this graphic organizer to the one you have drawn. Under the main idea for each lesson, write three statements that support it. The first one has been done for you.

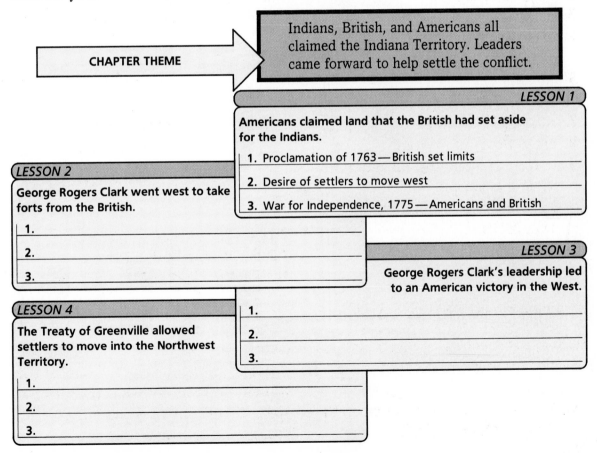

CHAPTER THEME

Indians, British, and Americans all claimed the Indiana Territory. Leaders came forward to help settle the conflict.

LESSON 1

Americans claimed land that the British had set aside for the Indians.

1. Proclamation of 1763—British set limits
2. Desire of settlers to move west
3. War for Independence, 1775—Americans and British

LESSON 2

George Rogers Clark went west to take forts from the British.

1.
2.
3.

LESSON 3

George Rogers Clark's leadership led to an American victory in the West.

1.
2.
3.

LESSON 4

The Treaty of Greenville allowed settlers to move into the Northwest Territory.

1.
2.
3.

CHAPTER 5

FROM TERRITORY TO STATEHOOD

*W*orking together with a group helps everyone grow. Cooperation helped Indiana grow. Indiana became a model state. Many other territories went on to become states by following Indiana's plan.

INDIANA CAPITOL

The capital of Indiana Territory was moved to Corydon from Vincennes, 1813. This building became first State Capitol, 1816. Offices were moved to Indianapolis in 1825.

Forming a New Territory

What do you think would happen in our country if there were no laws to follow?

Congress   **township**
ordinance   **capital**
squatter

How did the Indiana Territory come into being?

A. A Growing Country

Each year you grow a little taller and heavier. The United States also grew, step by step. In 1783 the War for Independence ended. The United States became a new country. The country was small. It was made up of 13 states. They were the 13 original colonies.

The United States also claimed land that reached to the Mississippi River. As you read in Chapter 4, part of the land was the Northwest Territory. The rest of that land was claimed by individual states. You can look at the areas claimed on the map on page 131.

The states and territories were governed by the United States **Congress**. Congress is a group of men and women who are chosen by the people of the country. They speak for the people and make laws. Congress passed laws that helped Indiana grow into a state.

B. Settling Quarrels over Land

Dividing the Land As more people moved into the Northwest Territory, they needed laws that would help them divide the land. In 1785 Congress passed a new **ordinance** (ORD un uns). An ordinance is a law. This law helped people keep order. It was called the Land Ordinance of 1785.

The Northwest Territory was divided into equal squares. Today, you can still see these sections.
▶ What law helped people divide the land?

A TOWNSHIP IN THE INDIANA TERRITORY

← 6 miles →

1	2	3	4	5	6
7	8	9	10	11	12
13	14	15	16	17	18
19	20	21	22	23	24
25	26	27	28	29	30
31	32	33	34	35	36

6 miles

16 = Income used to support public schools

Surveyors divided each township of the Indiana Territory into 36 equal sections.
▶ How large was each section?

Many families had already cleared land and built cabins. Some marked the boundaries of their land. To them, the land was theirs. These settlers were called squatters. Squatters are people who claim land without paying for it. Congress changed all that. In the Land Ordinance of 1785, Congress said that settlers must pay for the land. This was one way for Congress to get money for its debts. The War for Independence had cost the new country a great deal of money.

Forming Townships Surveyors began to measure off the land into 6-mile (10-km) squares. Each square was called a township. Each township was then cut into 36 equal sections, each 1 mile (2 km) square. In each township, the income from one section was set aside to support public schools. The other sections were sold for $640 each.

For most settlers this was a very great amount of money. They had a hard time raising it. Also, not everyone wanted that much land. But the Land Ordinance of 1785 did create an orderly way to settle land.

Today, Indiana is still divided into townships. What is the name of your township?

C. Providing Freedoms Through Laws

Needing Government Once people began settling in the new territory, they needed a government. Congress passed another law. It was called the Ordinance of 1787. This law gave certain freedoms to people in the Territory of the United States Northwest of the River Ohio, as the area was officially called.

Same Rights First, the law gave them freedom of speech, press, and religion. This means that they could speak, write, and worship as they pleased, as long as they did not hurt

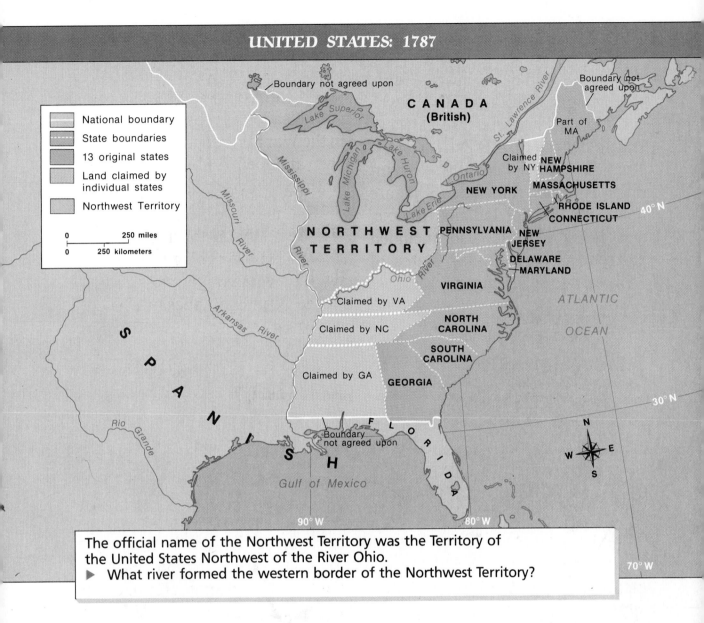

Boundary not agreed upon

CANADA
(British)

Boundary not
agreed upon

Lake Superior

St. Lawrence River

Part of
MA

Mississippi River

Lake Michigan

Lake Huron

Claimed NEW
by NY HAMPSHIRE

Missouri River

Ontario

NEW YORK

MASSACHUSETTS

Lake Erie

RHODE ISLAND
CONNECTICUT

40° N

N O R T H W E S T
T E R R I T O R Y

PENNSYLVANIA NEW
JERSEY

Ohio River

DELAWARE
MARYLAND

VIRGINIA

ATLANTIC

Arkansas River

Claimed by VA

Claimed by NC

NORTH
CAROLINA

OCEAN

S
P
A
N
I
S
H

Claimed by GA

SOUTH
CAROLINA

GEORGIA

30° N

Rio Grande

Boundary
not agreed upon

F
L
O
R
I
D
A

N

W E

S

Gulf of Mexico

90° W

80° W

70° W

Legend:
- National boundary
- State boundaries
- 13 original states
- Land claimed by individual states
- Northwest Territory

0   250 miles
0   250 kilometers

The official name of the Northwest Territory was the Territory of
the United States Northwest of the River Ohio.
▶ What river formed the western border of the Northwest Territory?

others. The ordinance also said that people could not own slaves. It said that settlers were to treat the Native Americans fairly. The settlers were encouraged to build schools.

The ordinance stated that three to five states would be created out of the Northwest Territory. Any part of the territory could become a state when it had 60,000 people. That was a lot of people! Until the territory had enough people, a territorial governor ruled it. The governor was selected by the Congress. Once a part of the territory became a state, its citizens would have the same rights and privileges as the citizens of the original 13 states.

131

D. Getting a Governor and a Capital City

By 1800 the Northwest Territory had grown so much that it was cut into smaller parts. One part was still called the Northwest Territory. The other part was called the Indiana Territory. It included what are now the states of Indiana, Illinois, and Wisconsin. It also included parts of the present-day states of Minnesota and Michigan.

In 1800 Congress chose 27-year-old William Henry Harrison as the first governor of the Indiana Territory. Harrison was a strong, courageous leader. He had fought bravely in the War for Independence. He had been at Fallen Timbers with General Anthony Wayne. Harrison knew the Indians' ways of fighting and how to talk with them in councils.

Vincennes was the **capital** of the Indiana Territory. A capital is a city where government leaders meet

As governor, William Henry Harrison tried to remain friends with the Indians.
▶ Why did Harrison build his house in Vincennes?

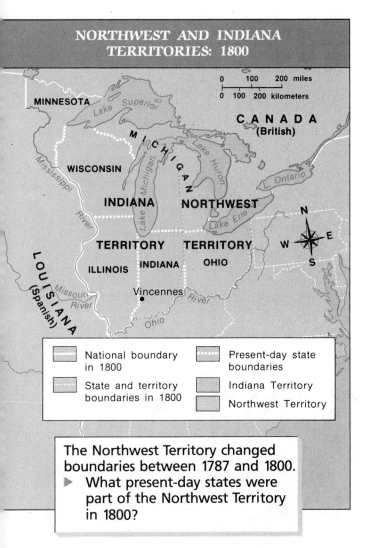

NORTHWEST AND INDIANA TERRITORIES: 1800

The Northwest Territory changed boundaries between 1787 and 1800.
▶ What present-day states were part of the Northwest Territory in 1800?

Legend:
- National boundary in 1800
- State and territory boundaries in 1800
- Present-day state boundaries
- Indiana Territory
- Northwest Territory

to make laws. In January 1801, Governor Harrison arrived in Vincennes. He was pleased by its beauty, even in winter. But spring was breathtaking. The apple and peach trees in the capital burst into bloom. The strawberry patches were filled with plump, bright fruit. In this fine season, Harrison brought the rest of his family to Vincennes. Soon, he began to build a large brick house he called Grouseland. He enjoyed hunting grouse, in his spare time. Grouse are birds caught for sport.

In Vincennes, Governor Harrison set up his government and started to work. He made many treaties with the Indians. In these treaties, the Indians agreed to move from their lands. Sometimes the United States government paid them. Sometimes the Indians just moved to lands farther west.

LESSON 1 REVIEW

THINK AND WRITE

A. What is Congress?

B. How did the Land Ordinance of 1785 divide the land in the Northwest Territory?

C. Why could you call the Ordinance of 1787 the Freedoms Ordinance?

D. How did Governor Harrison help the United States to grow?

SKILLS CHECK

WRITING SKILL

Look at the maps on page 131 and above. Compare the Northwest Territory in 1787 with the Northwest Territory in 1800. Write a paragraph describing the changes that took place during these years.

DWELLINGS THROUGH TIME

1 Log cabin, 1830

City home in
Indianapolis, 1880 2

3 Prairie-style home, 1920

Modern home that draws
heat from the sun, 1990

5

4

Ranch home, 1950

Long ago, pioneers moved to Indiana and built log cabin homes. As the area
became settled, people built larger, more permanent homes in which to live.
Over the years, people's needs have changed and the styles of their homes
have changed to meet these needs.
▶ In what ways is your home different from homes of long ago?

Another Indian War

THINK ABOUT WHAT YOU KNOW
Imagine how you would feel if someone told you that you had to leave your home and not come back. What would you do?

STUDY THE VOCABULARY
defeat   **legend**

FOCUS YOUR READING
Why did wars continue in the Indiana Territory?

A. A Frightening Visit

Indian Brothers   Some Indian tribes were not pleased with the treaties made with Governor Harrison. They believed that no tribes had the right to make treaties that gave up land to the settlers. With these treaties Indians were losing their best hunting grounds. They were being pushed from their homes.

A Shawnee chief named Tecumseh (tih KUM suh) was one of those who was not pleased. Tecumseh was a strong Indian leader. When he was born, his mother saw a light streak across the sky. So she named him Tecumseh, which means "shooting star." One of Tecumseh's younger brothers had the name that meant "the Prophet." He became a spiritual leader of the Shawnee. The Prophet taught that Indians had to separate themselves from settlers.

Talking About Treaties   After Harrison became governor, Tecumseh began to organize the tribes along the Wabash River. They planned to attack nearby settlements. First, though, they decided to try talking to Governor Harrison at the capital. Tecumseh wanted to talk to Governor Harrison about treaties. They talked under the trees at Grouseland, the governor's home. Sadly, the leaders could not agree. The Indians left.

Hoping to avoid a war, Tecumseh went to Vincennes to talk with Governor Harrison.
▶ What did the men talk about?

From: *TECUMSEH: Destiny's Warrior*

By: David C. Cooke

Setting: Vincennes, Indiana, 1810

David C. Cooke has written many books for children. *Tecumseh: Destiny's Warrior* tells the story of Tecumseh, the great Shawnee leader. In 1810, Tecumseh visited Governor William Henry Harrison at Vincennes. Tecumseh hoped to come to some agreement about the rights of Indians to the land.

On the morning of the eleventh of August [1810], a small army of warriors moved down the sun-swept Wabash a few miles above Vincennes.
Proud and splendid in simple but elegant deerskin, a single eagle's feather thrust into his shining ebony [black] hair, Tecumseh sat erect [straight] in the leading canoe. Though his face was composed [calm], his eyes constantly darted to either shore. A long rifle rested against his moccasined foot in the bottom of the canoe, and the pair of braves manning the paddles were fully armed.
Directly behind, in another canoe, rode the Prophet . . . And following the Prophet's craft came eighty more canoes . . . , each jammed with men. Harrison had sent directions that Tecumseh should limit his party . . . , but he had ignored the message.

Although this meeting ended peacefully, it did not end in an agreement between Governor Harrison and Tecumseh.

B. Losing a Battle

Both Tecumseh and Harrison started getting ready for war. Tecumseh traveled throughout the Northwest and Indiana territories. He talked with many tribes, asking them to join him in his fight against the settlers. In the fall of 1811, Governor Harrison marched a small army north along the Wabash. The army camped close to an Indian village on the Tippecanoe River. The village was close to what is now the city of Lafayette.

Tecumseh was not in the village, but the Prophet was. Before Tecumseh had left, he had warned his brother not to attack Harrison's army. The Prophet did not listen. He planned an attack for the early hours of November 7. He told his warriors that their enemies would be powerless and that the soldiers' bullets would be as soft as rain. Believing him, the braves attacked.

The soldiers were ready. They were sleeping with their guns beside them. Harrison's army scattered the Indians and destroyed their village. It was a terrible **defeat**, or loss, for the Indians.

The Battle of Tippecanoe was the last great battle that the Indians of Indiana fought. After that, William Henry Harrison was nicknamed Old Tippecanoe.

The Battle of Tippecanoe was the last big battle fought by the Indians of Indiana. The Indians were defeated.
▶ What flag are Harrison's men carrying?

C. Continuing War

By 1812 the Indian villages south of the Wabash were gone. But still there was no peace. The British were still using their forts in the Northwest to encourage Indians to attack settlers. And the British and the French were at war. To fight this war, the British navy needed more sailors. It boarded American ships and took sailors who could not prove that they were Americans. This made the people in the United States very angry! America and England went to war again. The War of 1812 lasted more than two years. On Christmas Eve in 1814, the British and the Americans finally signed a peace treaty to end the war.

The British seized American sailors, forcing them to serve on British ships.
▶ How did the Americans react?

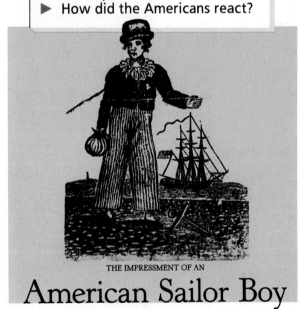

THE IMPRESSMENT OF AN

American Sailor Boy

D. A Last Meeting

Harrison and Tecumseh did meet again after Tecumseh's visit to Vincennes. During the War of 1812, Harrison led American armies. Tecumseh fought in the British army. In October 1813, Harrison won an important battle against Tecumseh. It was the Battle of the Thames in Canada. During this battle, Tecumseh was killed. The Indians had lost their land. Now they had lost their last great and beloved leader.

Many legends surround this great Shawnee warrior. A legend is a story that may or may not be true. Tecumseh was admired by both the British and the Americans, as well as by his own people. You read earlier that Tecumseh traveled in the Northwest and Indian territories to band the Native Americans together. But after his death, people reported having seen him as far east as New York and as far west as Oklahoma. He was also spotted in the South, supposedly. Perhaps these people who said they saw him wanted their friends to think they had met the great Indian leader.

Even if the legends about Tecumseh are not true, history shows that Tecumseh was a great Indian leader. He was a brave fighter, but never a cruel one. He was a fine speaker, who was admired even

VAN BUREN AND RUIN.

HARRISON AND PROSPERITY.

These pictures were part of Harrison's campaign.
▶ What did he want voters to believe about the election?

by his enemies. Tecumseh always fought for his beliefs.

William Henry Harrison was a brave leader too. Because of his success in the wars against the Indians and the British, people wanted him to become President. He was elected the ninth President of the United States. No one knows if Harrison would have been a strong President because he died only a month after he took office.

LESSON 2 REVIEW

THINK AND WRITE

A. Why did Tecumseh visit with Governor Harrison?

B. Why was the Battle of Tippecanoe important?

C. What was one reason that the War of 1812 was fought?

D. Why was Tecumseh a great Indian leader?

SKILLS CHECK

THINKING SKILL

Describe at least two ways in which William Henry Harrison and Tecumseh were similar to one another. Then describe at least two ways in which the two men were different from each other.

The New State of Indiana

You have changed and grown a lot in the last five years. What changes in your life and your home have occurred because of your growth?

census   **delegate**
constitution

What steps did Indiana follow to become a state?

A. Moving to Corydon

Growth of the Territory The Ordinance of 1787, the Indian treaties, and the War of 1812 made the Indiana Territory a safer place to live. As a result, many new settlers came into the Indiana Territory.

The territory grew in the number of people, but it grew smaller in size. One part broke away to become the state of Ohio. Other parts were almost ready to become states. By 1809 the Indiana Territory was just about the size and shape that Indiana is today.

A New Need With changes in size and number of people, the Indiana Territory had to change in other ways. Vincennes was no longer the best place for the capital. It was no longer close to most of the people in the territory. A new capital was needed. Several towns wanted to become the next capital. Finally, a small town in the hills of southern Indiana was chosen. The small town was called Corydon. The territorial capital was moved there in 1813.

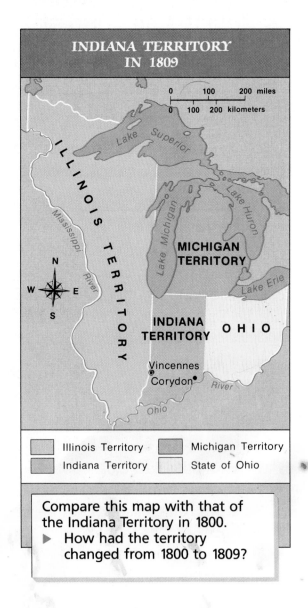

INDIANA TERRITORY IN 1809

Compare this map with that of the Indiana Territory in 1800.
▶ How had the territory changed from 1800 to 1809?

B. On the Way to Statehood

Toward Statehood The government worked hard to improve life. New laws were made. Some roads and schools were built. As more and more settlers came in, people began asking, "Is Indiana ready to become a state?" The Ordinance of 1787 had said that 60,000 people were needed for statehood. A **census** was taken in 1815. A census is a government count of the number of people in a place. There were 63,897 people in the territory. That was more than enough people to form a state!

Writing Laws Another leader of Indiana stepped forward. Jonathan Jennings was a member of the United States Congress. He spoke for the people of the Indiana Territory. Jennings asked Congress to make the territory a state. Congress, too, thought that Indiana was ready. But another step was needed.

In 1816 the United States Congress said that a state **constitution** (kahn stuh TOO shun) should be written. A constitution is a set of laws by which a state or country is governed. The writers of the constitution were elected by the people of the territory. These writers were called **delegates** (DEL uh guts). A delegate is a person who has the right to act or speak for others.

C. Writing Indiana's First State Constitution

June 10, 1816, was scorchingly hot. The air in the Corydon courthouse was very stuffy. The delegates needed relief from the heat. They walked to the banks of Indian Creek and sat in the welcome shade of a huge elm tree. There, they talked and wrote about Indiana's state constitution. Working for 18 days, they produced a fine constitution.

The tree they worked under became famous as the Constitutional Elm. The elm died many years later, but the trunk was saved. Today, the old elm trunk reminds visitors to Corydon of this important step in Indiana's journey toward statehood.

This is a meeting room in the first state capital at Corydon.
► What kind of lighting was used in this room?

D. Celebrating a Birthday

Many important thoughts were written into Indiana's first constitution. The constitution gave people the same freedoms found in the Ordinance of 1787. In addition, free schools were promised for all children, both black and white. Also, libraries would be built.

Jonathan Jennings was the first to sign the new constitution. Jennings was elected Indiana's first state governor. Governor Jennings's job was to make the new government work. This was not an easy job. There was very little tax money. Tax money was needed to build schools and roads. At that time, the roads were only Indian and buffalo trails that had been made wider. Tax money was also needed to pay people to enforce the laws. Money was even needed to pay the people who collected the taxes!

Jonathan Jennings worked hard to help Indiana become a state.
▶ With Indiana's statehood in 1816, how many states were in the nation?

Indiana's birth date was December 11, 1816. On this day it became the nineteenth state of the United States. This was a great event for Indiana!

LESSON **3** *REVIEW*

THINK AND WRITE

A. Why was the territorial capital moved from Vincennes?

B. How did Jonathan Jennings help Indiana become a state?

C. What is the importance of the Constitutional Elm?

D. Why was Jonathan Jennings's job as state governor so difficult?

SKILLS CHECK

MAP SKILL

Look at the map on page 131. Then look at the map of the United States on pages 354–355. Which of the three territories were very similar in size to states that have the same names? Which territory included parts of more than one present-day state?

Growth Through Cooperation

THINK ABOUT WHAT YOU KNOW
Have you ever worked together with others in a group? What kinds of things can make working with others hard?

STUDY THE VOCABULARY
amend   amendment

FOCUS YOUR READING
How did people in Indiana cooperate to build a strong state?

A. Pushing the Frontier Farther North

Today Indiana has 92 counties. In 1816, as a new state, it had only 15 counties. Some had very few people, but some were very large in land size. As people settled in the new state, boundary lines were drawn to make more counties. This made it easier to govern and collect taxes. Look at the county table on pages 381–382. The last column in the table shows the date when each Indiana county was formed. In what year was your county formed?

The first Indiana settlers came from the East. The large rivers were like highways that brought people west. People settled along the Wabash and Ohio rivers first. That is the reason why the oldest Indiana counties are located along these two rivers. As Indian treaties made the northern part of Indiana safe, the frontier moved northward.

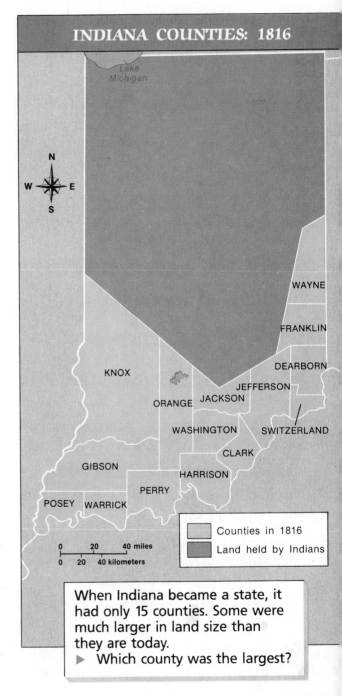

INDIANA COUNTIES: 1816

Counties in 1816
Land held by Indians

When Indiana became a state, it had only 15 counties. Some were much larger in land size than they are today.
► Which county was the largest?

This is how Indianapolis looked in 1825, the year it became the new state capital.
▶ What street is shown here?

B. Moving the Capital Again

Another Move You guessed it! As more people came to Indiana, more changes were needed. By 1820 Corydon was no longer the center of population. Besides, it was a small town. It was not located on a big river. In winter, the capital was almost impossible to reach because it was in the hills.

So, just four years after Indiana became a state, planning for the new capital began. The state's leaders thought about the future of Indiana. They knew that people were settling in the northern part of the state. They believed that Indiana would someday have large cities and farms in the north. They wanted a capital in the center of the state. That way, it could be easily reached from all different directions.

The state's leaders chose Fall Creek Settlement because it was located in the center of the state. Of course, in 1820 this place was very rural. The capital was not moved from Corydon until 1825. This was because Indiana's leaders needed time to plan the new capital.

A New Name In the meantime, Indiana's leaders chose a new name for the capital. Some people wanted to name the capital Tecumseh.

Other people suggested the name Indianapolis. This name would honor both the Indians and the state. *Polis* is the Greek word meaning "city." The word *Indianapolis* means "city of Indiana."

C. Outgrowing the Indiana State Constitution

New Laws Needed By 1850 Indiana had grown up. The new capital was then 25 years old. The government workers worked in a beautiful State House. The state had 91 counties and almost 1 million people. Although most people lived on farms, cities were beginning to grow. Indiana had grown so much that it had outgrown its constitution. With so many people, a new constitution was needed—one that would make a stronger state government.

Unequal Citizenship Delegates met in Indianapolis. They came from all counties. By 1851 the people of Indiana voted to accept Indiana's new constitution. It started with the people's rights. Again, all people were promised freedom of speech, press, and worship. But not all people shared all rights. The right to vote was not given to all. White men of Indiana could vote. Blacks, Native Americans, and women could not vote. Do you think this was fair?

D. Providing for Change

Increased Services The new constitution said that leaders were to be elected by the voters. The state could not borrow money to run the government. Schools would be open to all. The state would provide education and health care for handicapped people. In many ways this was a good constitution.

Making Changes But the writers of the constitution knew that the state would continue to grow and change. They put in a part that told how the constitution could be **amended,** or changed. The changes are called **amendments.** An

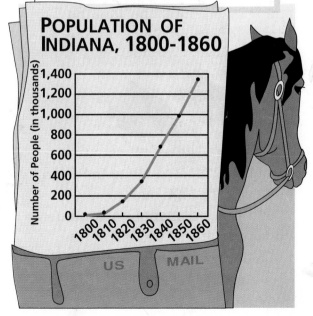

By 1815, Indiana's population had grown to more than 60,000.
▶ Why was the 1815 census important to people in the Indiana Territory?

POPULATION OF INDIANA, 1800-1860

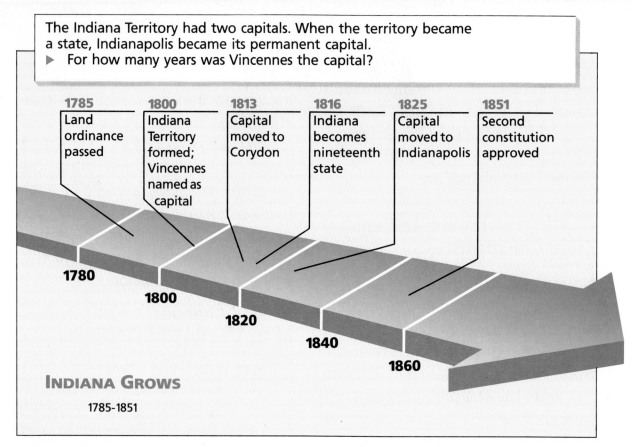

The Indiana Territory had two capitals. When the territory became a state, Indianapolis became its permanent capital.

▶ For how many years was Vincennes the capital?

1785 Land ordinance passed

1800 Indiana Territory formed; Vincennes named as capital

1813 Capital moved to Corydon

1816 Indiana becomes nineteenth state

1825 Capital moved to Indianapolis

1851 Second constitution approved

1780

1800

1820

1840

1860

INDIANA GROWS
1785-1851

amendment is an addition that changes a set of laws.

So much had changed in Indiana already! The time line on this page helps you see some of these changes. In 1800 the Indiana Territory was formed. Sixteen years later, in 1816, Indiana became a state. The territory and the state had had three capitals. Many Indians moved to the West. People from the East and the South poured into Indiana. People from other countries came too. The settlers spread throughout the state. They made homes and put down roots in Indiana.

LESSON *4* REVIEW

THINK AND WRITE

A. Why are the oldest counties in Indiana located along the Ohio and Wabash rivers?

B. Why is Indianapolis a good name for Indiana's capital?

C. What groups could not vote, according to Indiana's 1851 state constitution?

D. How did the writers of the new state constitution prepare for future change?

SKILLS CHECK

WRITING SKILL

Write a sentence explaining why Indiana leaders wanted a capital in the center of the state.

USING THE VOCABULARY

Congress	legend
ordinance	census
squatter	constitution
township	delegate
capital	amendment

On a separate sheet of paper, write the best ending for each sentence below. Choose your answers from the vocabulary words above.

1. A law is sometimes referred to as an _____ .
2. When the government counts the people in a place, it takes a _____ .
3. The set of laws by which a state or country is governed is its _____ .
4. A person who has been given the right to speak or act for others is called a _____ .
5. A story that may or may not be true is a _____ .
6. A settler who claimed land without paying for it was a _____ .
7. An addition that changes a set of laws is an _____ .
8. The group of men and women who speak for the people and make laws is called _____ .
9. A 6-mile square of measured land was called a _____ .
10. The city where government leaders meet in order to make laws is the _____ .

REMEMBERING WHAT YOU READ

Write your answers in complete sentences on a separate sheet of paper.

1. What did the Land Ordinance of 1785 say?
2. Where was the capital of the Indiana Territory located?
3. Why was Tecumseh unhappy with Governor Harrison's treaties?
4. Why was Governor Harrison nicknamed Old Tippecanoe?
5. How did Americans show their appreciation for Harrison's success in the Indian wars?
6. Who spoke in Congress to help Indiana become a state?
7. When did Indiana become a state?
8. To what city was the state capital moved in 1825?
9. When did Indiana vote to accept the new state constitution?
10. How did the writers of Indiana's constitution provide for future change and growth?

TYING MATH TO SOCIAL STUDIES

The delegates that met in Indianapolis in the 1850s came from 91 counties. Look at the map of Indiana on page 37. Use a ruler and a map scale to figure out the distance between the following county seats and Indianapolis: Evansville, Fort Wayne, Lafayette, New Albany, Richmond, and Terre Haute.

THINKING CRITICALLY

Write your answers in complete sentences on a separate sheet of paper.

1. Why would squatters not have liked the Land Ordinance of 1785?
2. In what ways were Tecumseh and his brother, the Prophet, different?
3. What did the moving of the capital to Corydon and then to Indianapolis show about settlement in Indiana?
4. What was one important reason Indiana's leaders chose Fall Creek for the new capital?
5. Why are amendments important to a constitution?

SUMMARIZING THE CHAPTER

On a separate sheet of paper draw a graphic organizer that is like the one shown here. Copy the information from this graphic organizer to the one you have drawn. Under the main idea for each lesson, write three statements that support it. The first one has been done for you.

CHAPTER THEME
Indiana grew and changed as its leaders learned to cooperate to get things done.

LESSON 1

New laws and freedoms, along with new settlers, helped Indiana become a territory.

1. Land Ordinance of 1785—orderly land settlement
2. Ordinance of 1787—freedoms given and rules for statehood
3. 1800—Harrison became governor, Vincennes the capital

LESSON 2

Governor Harrison and Tecumseh led their people in battles over land.

1.
2.
3.

LESSON 3

The people worked hard to prepare Indiana for statehood.

1.
2.
3.

LESSON 4

Indiana's leaders adjusted to changes in the state.

1.
2.
3.

2 REVIEW

COOPERATIVE LEARNING

You have just learned about the early people who lived in Indiana. Now you are going to put together a 15-minute television talk show called "Life in Early Indiana."

PROJECT

- Working in a group of five students, decide who will be the four guests on the show and who will be the host of the show.

- One member of the group will be an Indian architect. The second group member will be an Indian doctor. The third will be an Indian artist. The fourth will be an Indian farmer.

- Talk together about the questions that the host will ask each guest. Here are some sample questions: What do you do in your job? Do you work alone or with other people? How were you trained for your job? Do you like what you do?

- Each guest will do research in the library to find answers to these questions.

- The host will draw up a plan for introducing the show and the order of the guests and questions.

- After all the members of the group have completed their research or plan, they should talk together and prepare for the show.

PRESENTATION AND REVIEW

- Present the show to your class.

- Ask your classmates what they liked most about the show. Did it seem like a real talk show? What did they learn? Did it seem like everyone had researched his or her role?

- Talk about the show with your own group. How might you have improved your show?

REMEMBER TO:
- Give your ideas.
- Listen to others' ideas.
- Plan your work with the group.
- Present your project.
- Discuss how your group worked.

A. WHY DO I NEED THIS SKILL?

This book has many special parts to help you learn about Indiana. To get the most from your textbook, you need to know how to use its special parts. You also need to know what kind of information is contained in each part.

B. LEARNING THE SKILL

The first special part of the book is the Table of Contents, or Contents. Look at the Contents at the front of this book. Notice that the book is divided into units and chapters. The Contents also lists the page number on which these units and chapters begin.

Other special parts are found at the end of the book. The Atlas is a special collection of maps. In the Contents you will find a list of the maps included in the Atlas. These maps show the location of physical features, boundaries, cities, and roads.

The Gazetteer gives information about the places and geographical features discussed in the book. The entries are listed in alphabetical order. For many of these places, the Gazetteer also gives latitude and longitude.

The Glossary is another important part of the book. It defines the vocabulary terms and special social studies words. These are the words that are listed at the beginning of each lesson. Like words in a dictionary, glossary words are listed in alphabetical order.

The Index is an alphabetical listing of the important topics in the book. The Index lists the page numbers on which these topics are discussed. Turn to the Index, starting on page 387. On what pages can you find information about the Declaration of Independence?

4. What is the meaning of *artifact*?
5. On which pages does the Map Skills Handbook appear?
6. What is the longitude and latitude of Fall Creek?
7. What is Spring Mill?
8. What is the title of Unit 2?
9. What makes the town of French Lick famous?
10. Who was John Chapman?

C. Practicing the Skill

Use the special parts of this book to answer the following questions. After each answer, write the part that helped you find each answer.

1. What states border Indiana?
2. What is the total number of chapters in this book?
3. On what page or pages are Hoosiers discussed?

D. Applying the Skill

Select another textbook that you use in class. Examine the book carefully and make a list of its special parts. Does the book include a table of contents, a glossary, and an index? Does the book have any special parts that are not found in your social studies textbook? What are they? What information is contained in these other special parts? Write your answers on a separate sheet of paper.

A. WHY DO I NEED THIS SKILL?

One thing sometimes causes something else to happen. For example, an earthquake in California in 1989 caused a bridge to collapse. We call this cause and effect. The cause of what happened was the earthquake. The effect was the collapse of the bridge. Identifying cause-and-effect relationships is part of thinking critically. It is especially important in social studies to learn how one event causes another to happen.

B. LEARNING THE SKILL

Read the following sentences.

The Indians were angry because they had been left out of the Treaty of Paris. They decided to attack the settlers.

To see if a cause-and-effect relationship exists, ask yourself these questions: What happened? Why did it happen? In this example, the Indians decided to attack the settlers. This is the effect. The Indians had been left out of the Treaty of Paris. This is the cause.

Identify the cause and effect in the following example:

The British government passed strict new laws and taxed the settlers. The settlers became angry and went to war against England.

What happened? The settlers became angry and went to war against England. This is the effect. Why did it happen? The British government passed strict new laws and taxed the settlers. This is the cause.

C. PRACTICING THE SKILL

In social studies you will read about many events that have cause-and-effect relationships. The War for Independence occurred because the British taxed the colonists unfairly.

Fold a sheet of paper in half lengthwise. Label one column *Cause* and the other *Effect*. Write the numbers 1 to 5 at the left. Then read the following pairs of sentences. Identify the cause and effect in each pair and write them in the correct column.

1. The French and Indian War had cost the British government much money. They taxed the colonists to pay for the war.

2. The British were angry at the colonists for starting a war. They encouraged the Indians to attack the settlers in the West.
3. The Prophet did not listen to Tecumseh's warning. The Prophet's braves were defeated and their village was destroyed.
4. Surface mining harmed the land and caused erosion. Today mining companies replace the soil after removing the coal.
5. George Hammond's meat-packing business was a great success. A town grew up around his factory.

D. APPLYING THE SKILL

Think about something that happened to you recently that has a cause-and-effect relationship. Write two paragraphs about the event. In the first paragraph describe the event and explain what caused it. In the second paragraph state what effects it had.

UNIT 3 THE YOUNG STATE GROWS UP

In Indiana's early days, people from many different places decided to settle in our state. All these different people have become known as Hoosiers. They helped Indiana to grow and change.

▲ Many of Indiana's early pioneers cleared the land and built log cabins in which to live.

Although Amish children have many chores, they have some time to
▼ have fun and play games.

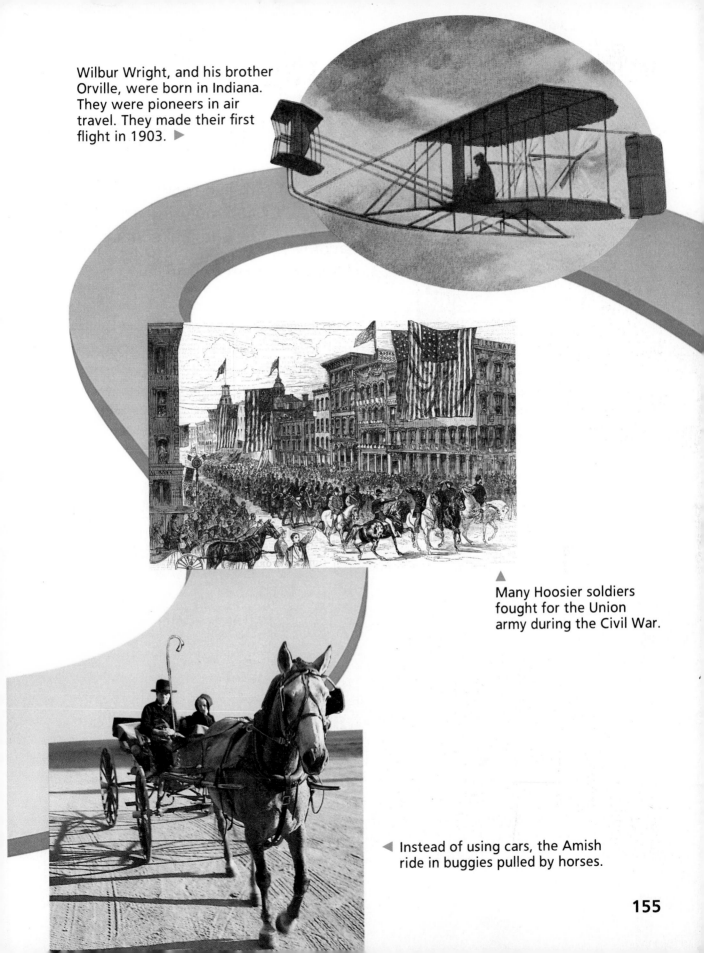

Wilbur Wright, and his brother Orville, were born in Indiana. They were pioneers in air travel. They made their first flight in 1903. ▶

Many Hoosier soldiers fought for the Union army during the Civil War.

◀ Instead of using cars, the Amish ride in buggies pulled by horses.

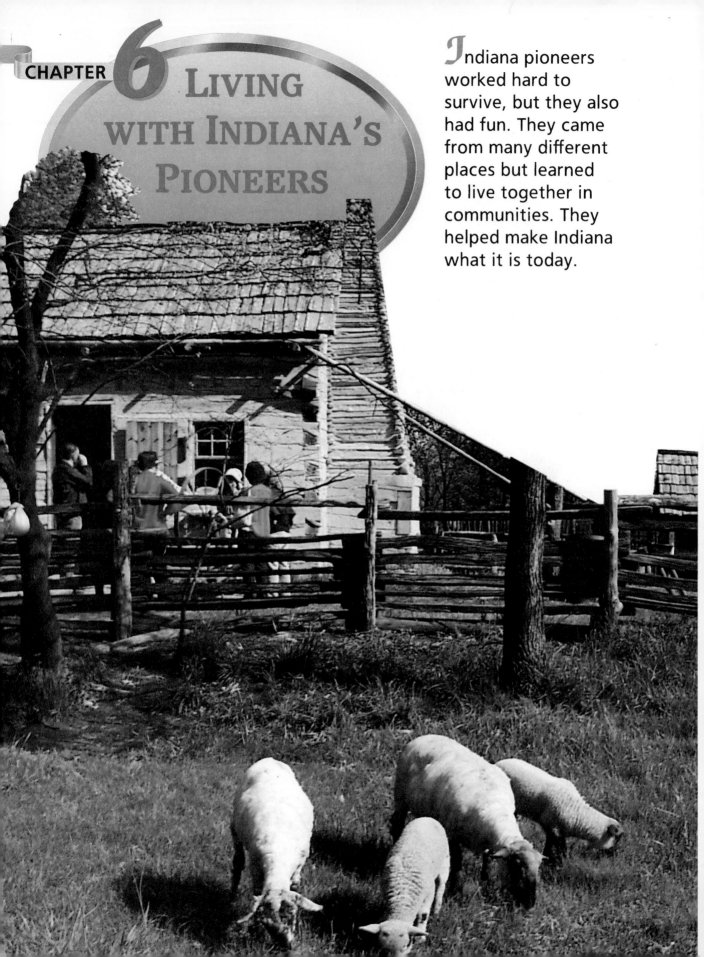

CHAPTER 6

LIVING WITH INDIANA'S PIONEERS

*I*ndiana pioneers worked hard to survive, but they also had fun. They came from many different places but learned to live together in communities. They helped make Indiana what it is today.

Clearing the Land for the Wilderness Farm

THINK ABOUT WHAT YOU KNOW

What kinds of activities does your neighborhood or community get together to do? Do you ever take part in these activities?

STUDY THE VOCABULARY

fell   **house-raising**
girdle   **logrolling**

FOCUS YOUR READING

What was life like for the early pioneers when they first arrived in Indiana?

A. Time to Move

Leaving Kentucky The Lincoln family looked back at the log cabin in Kentucky they had called home. It seemed to be saying a sad goodbye to Thomas and Nancy Lincoln and to their children, nine-year-old Sarah and seven-year-old Abe. It was December 1816. They were starting on a long, 100-mile (161-km) journey. They were on their way north to the Indiana wilderness.

Nancy Lincoln pulled Sarah close to her underneath the animal skin covers. They had brought cornmeal, corn seed, some cooking pots and a spinning wheel to make cloth. They also carried Thomas Lincoln's tools. Mr. Lincoln was a skilled carpenter. He made things out of wood. Mr. Lincoln also carried his ax, hunting knife, and gun. Abe darted in front of and behind the family to explore the rough trail.

Coming to Indiana It took the Lincoln family three days to make the trip through the wilderness. As they went, they had to clear away the trees and brush. It was a tiring journey. More than 40 years later, President Abraham Lincoln remembered the trip to Pigeon Creek—his boyhood home in Indiana.

> The Lincolns made a long journey through the wilderness on their way to their new home in Indiana.
> ▶ What are some of the items being carried by the horse?

157

From: ABRAHAM LINCOLN

By: Genevieve Foster

Setting: Southern Indiana, 1816

Genevieve Foster wrote books about great Americans such as George Washington and Theodore Roosevelt. The following quotation is from her book called *Abraham Lincoln*. As you know, Lincoln was born in Kentucky. But when he was seven, his family left Kentucky for Indiana. As the passage begins, the family has just crossed the Ohio River into Indiana.

From the river, there were sixteen miles more to go, back into the deep woods. Deeper and thicker woods than any in Kentucky. In places there wasn't even a trail. Abe's father had borrowed a wagon to carry in supplies for the winter, and he often had to chop down trees in order to get through. And when they got there, there was nothing to be seen.

Just a pile of brush and some notched trees to mark the spot.

First thing to do, his father said, was to make a pole shed to live in, till they could get a cabin built. Abe helped. They cut down saplings [young trees] and stood them up into a three-sided shed, open in the front.

There, in that open shed, they spent the long winter. The cold rain and snow blew in upon them, and sometimes smoke from the log fire outside. They cooked their meals of game and wild turkey over the fire, and kept it burning all night to scare away the wolves, howling in the darkness.

B. Work for the Whole Family

The Lincolns wanted to build a log cabin. First they had to clear the land so that they could grow food. Their cornmeal was running out, and food was more important than a cabin. Mr. Lincoln cleared a little patch, or small space of land. Abe and Sarah helped plant corn seeds. This was called the "hurry-up-and-get-in-a-crop." Pioneer families depended on corn. Mrs. Lincoln cooked it in some form for each meal every day.

Water was very important too. The Lincolns needed it for drinking, cooking, and washing. They chose a place near a spring. Abe carried water to their home.

Abe and his father **felled**, or cut down, the small trees to make room for the corn patch. Then they piled the small trees around the larger, standing trees and set the cut trees on fire. The fire killed the standing trees. Then the sunshine could reach the crop through the burned, leafless trees.

Some pioneers cleared the forests by **girdling** the trees. They cut a deep ring around the tree trunk. This cut off the sap from the leaves. Sap to a tree is as your blood is to you. Without the sap being able to reach the leaves, the leaves died. Then the sunlight could come in.

The pioneer family's first task was to clear the land.
▶ How did this family get its drinking water?

C. Working and Playing as a Community

Helping Neighbors At last the Lincolns were ready to build a log cabin. In pioneer times, the whole community gathered together to help build a new house. They called this a **house-raising**. Abe was sent through Pigeon Creek, calling: "The Lincolns are having a house-raising!" People were glad to help, and the Lincolns were grateful for it.

Erecting the Walls First came the **logrolling**. Men formed teams to cut trees. Then they rolled the logs to where the Lincolns wanted their cabin. The team that cut the most logs won the contest. When the men finished, the four walls of the cabin were standing.

Celebrating Together Everyone shared the food that the women cooked. After the people ate, they watched or took part in games, races, singing, and dancing.

Abraham Lincoln and his family lived in this log cabin.
▶ What was used to make a lining for the chimney?

D. A Poor But Proud Home

Thomas Lincoln had to split boards for the cabin roof. He cut openings for the door, window, and fireplace. Mrs. Lincoln and the children mixed grass with mud to fill cracks between the logs. Abe crawled inside the fireplace chimney to spread mud mixed with cattails over each log. The lining kept the chimney from catching fire. It did not always work. To be safe, people kept a long pole outside the cabin. With this pole they could push away a burning chimney. Then the fire would not spread to the wood cabin.

The family hung animal skins over the door and window openings. The cabin had only a dirt floor. Still, the Lincolns were glad to move into their new home.

LESSON *1* REVIEW

THINK AND WRITE

A. What were some things that the Lincolns took with them to their new home in Indiana?

B. Why did the pioneers want to clear the forests?

C. How did the Lincolns' neighbors help them?

D. How did pioneers protect their cabins from fire?

SKILLS CHECK

THINKING SKILL

What are the first tasks to be done by a pioneer family arriving at their new home?

Pioneer Life in the Southern Part of Indiana

THINK ABOUT WHAT YOU KNOW

Where do you go when you want to go shopping? Tell how you think this is different from what pioneer families did.

STUDY THE VOCABULARY

blab school   **water power**
horsepower   **general store**
buhr

FOCUS YOUR READING

What brought changes to the pioneer way of life?

A. The Young Lincolns in Their New School

Abe and Sarah walked 3 miles (5 km) to school. In school the teacher listened for mistakes as pupils studied out loud. The school was called a **blab school.**

The teacher was paid in animal skins, food, and a place to stay. A teacher would live for some time with each family in the community.

At school Abe and Sarah learned reading, writing, math, and manners. But the children did not get to school much. They were often needed to work on the farm. Even so, Abe was able to learn to read, write, and speak well.

B. Changes Occurring in the Lincoln Family

No Medical Care There were no doctors and very little medicine in pioneer villages. The closest doctor might be several days away by horseback. Disease spread quickly. Sometimes whole villages were wiped out by sickness.

Milk sickness started in the fall of 1818. The weather was very dry. The cows were very hungry. They even ate the snakeroot plant, which was poisonous. Their milk became poisoned. People who drank the milk became sick. Many died. Abe's mother was one. Abe was only nine, but he never forgot this sad time.

Pioneer children often walked long distances to attend school.
▶ How far from home is your school and how do you get there?

161

Many people enjoy visiting Lincoln's boyhood home in Indiana.
► In what special way is the guide dressed?

The Second Mrs. Lincoln Abe's sister Sarah tried to cook, sew, and clean for the family. But a pioneer family needed a mother. Mr. Lincoln returned to Kentucky and married Sarah Bush Johnston. She arrived at the Lincoln cabin with her three children and a wagonload of furniture. Abe grew to love Sarah Bush Johnston. She understood this tall boy who had a love for learning.

When Abe was 21 years old, the Lincolns left Pigeon Creek. They joined other settlers heading west. Mr. Lincoln wanted to try farming in Illinois. Also, Mrs. Lincoln would be near her married daughters there. Even as he moved away, Abraham Lincoln remembered fondly his years growing up in Indiana.

C. New Indiana Villages

The Lincolns left Indiana, but many other pioneer families came. They built towns and cities. These were often centered around small village mills. The pioneers needed mills to grind their corn into meal. The Native Americans had taught the first settlers to grind corn. They rubbed the grains between stones. The pioneers built mills that used the same idea to grind the corn. Rather than grinding by hand, some mills used **horsepower.** A horse pulled a pole that was attached to a round stone. This stone was called a **buhr** (BUR). As the horse walked in circles, the buhr turned against another stone. The corn was ground between the two stones.

D. Busy Spring Mill

Going to the Mill Back in 1859, George Hamersley walked into the village of Spring Mill. He had a bag of corn over his shoulder. It was only six o'clock in the morning, but the village was already busy. Other men and boys were arriving with the family corn. They made this trip to the mill every two weeks. They came to have the corn ground.

George Hamersley heard the huge mill wheel turning. This mill did not use horsepower. It used **water power.** Water from a spring poured into buckets on the wheel. As the buckets filled, the wheel turned. This wheel turned the stones inside the mill. As the corn passed between the stones, it was ground.

Up the street, people were saying goodbye as they climbed into a stagecoach. Their corn had been ground the day before. Most of them had spent the night in the village inn. With a crack of the whip, the stagecoach was off.

George Hamersley hurried into the big stone mill. He had a busy day ahead. He was going to work in the mill for a whole day. For 12 hours of work, he would be paid only $1.

The General Store Later in the day, the village really came alive! Big red wagons full of goods from far away arrived at the **general store.** A

This diagram shows how a waterwheel works. The waterwheel was used to grind the corn in the mill.
▶ What is this type of power called?

WHEEL

WATER

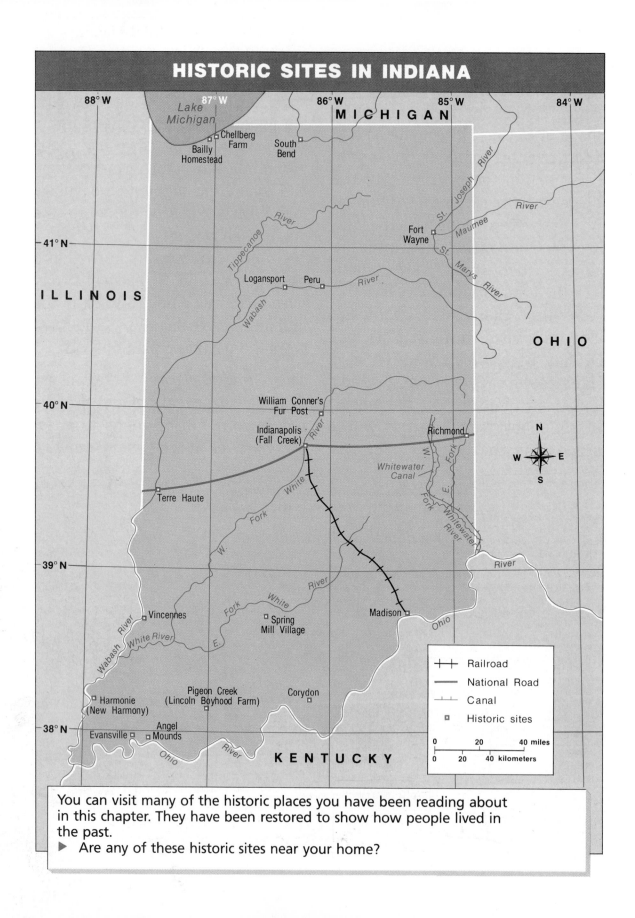

HISTORIC SITES IN INDIANA

Lake Michigan

MICHIGAN

Chellberg Farm
Bailly Homestead
South Bend

ILLINOIS

Tippecanoe River

41° N

Logansport   Peru   River

Wabash

OHIO

St. Joseph River
St. Maumee River
River
Fort Wayne
St. Marys River

40° N

William Conner's Fur Post
Indianapolis (Fall Creek)
River
Richmond

Whitewater Canal

W. Fork

Terre Haute

White River

E. Fork

Whitewater River

39° N

W. Fork

White River

Vincennes
Spring Mill Village

E. Fork

Madison

Ohio River

River

38° N

Wabash River
White River

Harmonie (New Harmony)
Pigeon Creek (Lincoln Boyhood Farm)
Corydon

Angel Mounds
Evansville

Ohio River

KENTUCKY

N
W   E
S

┼┼┼ Railroad
━━━ National Road
┼┼┼ Canal
▫ Historic sites

0   20   40 miles
0   20   40 kilometers

You can visit many of the historic places you have been reading about in this chapter. They have been restored to show how people lived in the past.

▶ Are any of these historic sites near your home?

general store is a store that carries many kinds of things. The large red wagons were owned by Hugh and Thomas Hamer. They also owned the general store and the mill. They were very successful!

Everyone rushed to watch the unloading of the wagons. There were fancy laces, beautiful new hats, and fine shoes. There were also axes, hoes, knives, and many other goods.

Work for Goods When the milling day ended, Mr. Hamer did not pay George Hamersley the dollar. Instead, George exchanged his work for goods at the general store. George, like other pioneers, did not have much use for money. They

The Hamers recorded the hours George Hamersley worked and the goods he received in trade.
▶ When was this record dated?

Mills need water power to run them. That is why they were built near running water.
▶ What were mills used for?

usually traded one thing for another. Farmers paid to have their corn ground by giving the miller part of the corn. They paid for store goods with furs, farm crops, or work.

E. Sleeping Spring Mill

People and goods once came to Spring Mill by stagecoach and wagon. Then railroads were built. But the railroads did not come to Spring Mill. Since people wanted to ship their goods by train, they stopped coming to Spring Mill. The big mill wheel no longer creaked and turned. Those people who lived in the village moved away.

Many years later, though, the mill and the village around it were restored. Today, the mill grinds corn the same way it did when people lived in the village many years ago.

At the restored Spring Mill, you can see how candles were made.
▶ Why were candles important to the pioneers?

LESSON 2 REVIEW

THINK AND WRITE

A. Why were the Lincoln children not able to go to school often?

B. Why did diseases spread quickly in pioneer times?

C. Who taught the settlers how to grind corn?

D. How did the mill make Spring Mill a busy town?

E. Why did people move away from Spring Mill?

SKILLS CHECK

MAP SKILL

Look at the map on page 164. How far is Spring Mill Village from the railroad at Madison? Use the mileage scale to figure out the distance.

Settling in the Central Part of Indiana

THINK ABOUT WHAT YOU KNOW
Have you ever moved or helped a friend move? What kinds of things have to be done when people and belongings are being moved to a new place?

STUDY THE VOCABULARY
representative   **granny cure**

FOCUS YOUR READING
How did central Indiana change in pioneer days?

A. Living on the Central Plains

Forced to Leave   Central Indiana was still the land of Indians when William Conner settled there. The soil was rich and black. William Conner married the daughter of Chief Anderson, who was the leader of the Delaware tribe.

One day William Conner stood with tears in his eyes. His wife and six children were leaving him. They sadly joined a long line of Delaware Indians. Chief Anderson had made a treaty selling the tribe's land to the government. The Delaware Indians had a law that said members of the tribe must follow their chief. William Conner respected the Indians. He hated to see them, tribe by tribe, leaving the state. And he was going to miss his family very much.

Businessman   Conner owned a trading post. His business was very successful. He built a brick home in the village that grew up around the post. The village was considered as a place for the new capital. But Fall Creek, farther south, was chosen.

> William Conner was very sad to see his wife and children leave Indiana.
> ▶ Why did his family have to leave the state?

167

This is an Independence Day celebration at Conner Prairie in Noblesville, Indiana.
▶ What special pioneer headdress are some women wearing?

Lawmaker Conner became very well known. Later, he was chosen to be a state **representative**. This means that he was chosen to speak in the state capital for the people of central Indiana. Today, Conner Prairie, near Noblesville, is a museum of living history. People who work there play the roles of settlers in the 1820s and 1830s.

B. Planning a Circle City

You read in Chapter 5 that Indiana's leaders started planning the new capital city of Indianapolis in 1820. They asked Alexander Ralston, a surveyor, to help. He had been one of the planners of the city of Washington, D.C.

Ralston planned the city of Indianapolis to look very much like the nation's capital. He began with a large circle that was within a grid. A grid is made up of crossing lines. Ralston planned the city to be 1 mile (2 km) square.

Look at the plan below. You can see that in the center is a circle, the Governor's Circle. Four wide streets run out from the center to the corners of the square. These and many other streets in the capital are named for states.

C. Sickness in the New Capital

Building a City People were clearing land, building homes, and planting farms in the new capital. Then one hot, rainy summer, sickness struck! Mosquitoes caused this sickness. There were only three doctors in the city. They could not take care of all the sick. Many people died. Everyone was frightened. Some families packed up and fled so quickly that they left the doors to their homes and stores wide open!

> Indianapolis was a carefully planned city. Its design resembles that of Washington, D.C.
> ▶ What was planned for the center of the city?

Homemade Cures Other people decided to stay in the capital anyway. For help, they turned to **granny cures,** or home remedies. These were cures usually made up by older women. As mothers, they had doctored their children for years and had cures for everything. The grannies would say: "Step across a creek backwards and you will get well." Or they might tell you: "Rub an onion on your head to cure a headache." We laugh at granny cures today. But it seems that some of them really did work!

There were granny cures for many different types of sickness, including those shown here.
▶ Why were these home remedies called granny cures?

D. The Big Land Sale

When the rain stopped and the cool weather came, the mosquitoes disappeared. People went back to building the city. They decided to have a big land sale. The money from the sale of the land would help to pay for state government buildings. The sale was a big success.

After the sale, the city grew quickly. Sawmills and brickyards opened. Carpenters, chair makers, wagon makers, and sign painters opened businesses. Storekeepers sold things the settlers needed.

Settlers soon demanded services too. They wanted a post office, churches, and schools. Riders were hired to carry mail by horseback. Preachers rode in to hold Sunday

GRANNY CURES: In the early 1800s the causes and the cures of many diseases were unknown. The settlers made up their own remedies. These remedies were known as granny cures.

Warts: Use a washrag; wipe the warts; bury the rag secretly.

Sore throat: Take a sock that you have worn inside a boot for about a week. Make sure it has a bad odor. Tie it around your neck.

Chicken pox: To cure a patient, shake a chicken three times over the patient.

services. The first church services in Indianapolis were held in Governor's Circle. Logs were rolled in to be used as seats. Later, log churches were built. These churches also served as schools.

E. Moving and Changing

The State Records   It was early January 1825 and time to move the capital. Four large wagons were loaded at Corydon. The wagons carried the state's papers, books, and money. The wagons arrived in Indianapolis two weeks later. The government used the Marion County Court House to make its laws and do its business. The new state house was not finished until 1835.

The Governor's House   In 1825 Governor James B. Ray did not have a house, either. One was planned. But Governor Ray and his wife did not like the plans. One problem was that the house was going to stand in the middle of Governor's Circle. That meant it had no private back yard. Mrs. Ray refused to hang out the family's wash for the whole city to see! So the governor's house was never finished. The unfinished building was eventually torn down in 1857.

The center of Indianapolis looks very different today than it did in the 1800s.
► What do you see in this picture that would not have been there in the 1800s?

Indianapolis grew into a busy and beautiful city. Horse-drawn carriages moved people from place to place. Gas lamps lighted the streets. A firefighting company was formed. A hospital was built. Factories that made carriages and wagons opened, and so did a medicine company. More schools and more churches were also built.

Building New Roads Even a large highway went through the city. It was called the National Road. The United States Congress agreed to pay for building it. It started in the East and ran into Illinois in the West. The National Road ran along Washington Street in Indianapolis. Other roads came, too, including several railroads. A big train station called Union Station was built. All Indianans were very proud of their new capital city.

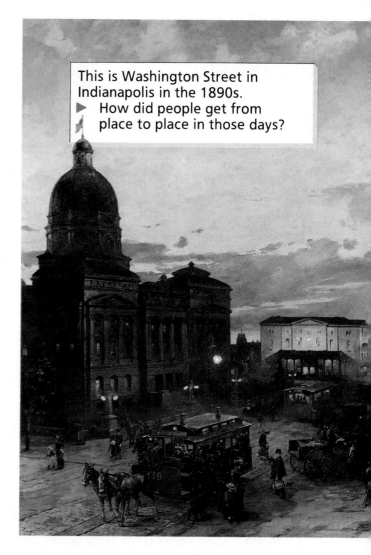

This is Washington Street in Indianapolis in the 1890s.
► How did people get from place to place in those days?

LESSON 3 REVIEW

THINK AND WRITE

A. Why did William Conner's wife and children leave him?

B. How is Indiana's capital like the national capital?

C. In what way did serious illness affect the capital?

D. How did Indianapolis change after the big land sale?

E. What were two things that made people proud of Indianapolis in the 1800s?

SKILLS CHECK

WRITING SKILL

Look at the chart of granny cures on page 170. Write a granny cure of your own.

USING SOURCE MATERIAL

PIONEER TOYS

The lives of the early pioneers in Indiana were often difficult. They did not have the modern conveniences that we have today. Although pioneer children did many chores around the house and farm, there was still some time for fun. Pioneer children played games and had toys. The pioneer toys shown here are all handmade.

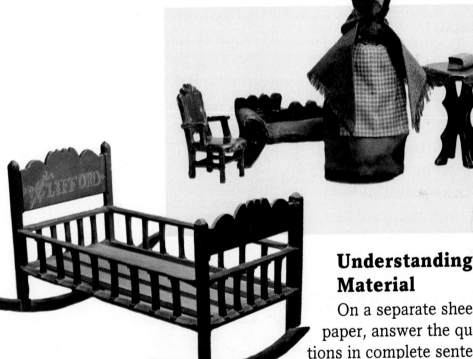

Understanding Source Material

On a separate sheet of paper, answer the questions in complete sentences.

1. What materials were used to make these toys?

2. Do you think these toys were used by pioneer boys or girls? Explain your answer.

3. How are these toys similar to or different from toys today?

4. What can you learn about pioneer children from their toys?

Settling Indiana's Northern Frontier

THINK ABOUT WHAT YOU KNOW
What kinds of changes have occurred, during the last five years, in the area you live in?

STUDY THE VOCABULARY
blockhouse   homestead barracks

FOCUS YOUR READING
What was life like in northern Indiana in the 1800s?

A. Protecting the People

Many settlers in Indiana's wilderness still lived in fear of Indian attacks. They built forts for protection. Most forts were single log houses called **blockhouses**. Whole families rushed to these forts when Indian raids were expected. Some forts were much larger. These forts had blockhouses with overhanging second floors. A blockhouse stood at each corner of the fort. Strong stockade walls connected the blockhouses. Many families and animals could be protected within the walls.

B. Life in the Frontier Forts

A Hard Life   What would it have been like to live in a fort? Today, you can visit historic Fort Wayne. There, you can meet and even talk to a person who is acting the part of Polly Baily. Polly Baily lived in General Anthony Wayne's fort.

Life was not easy for Polly Baily. She had come to live in Fort

With so many buildings, large forts were much like small towns.
▶ Which two buildings were next to the gunsmith's house?

THE OLD FORT COMPLEX

1. North Blockhouse
2. Commanding Officers' Quarters
3. Commanding Officers' Privy
4. Hospital Barracks
5. Powder Magazine
6. South Blockhouse
7. Enlisted Men's Barracks
8. Privies
9. Officers' Quarters
10. Indian Agent's House
11. Gunsmith's House
12. Woodcrafter's House
13. Bakers Oven
14. Baker's House
15. Inn
16. Meloche House
17. Blacksmith's Shop
18. Blacksmith's House
19. Peltier House
20. Indian Council House
21. Stable

ITEMS THAT PIONEERS PRESERVED

Bear

Fish

Beef

Fruit

Deer

Vegetables

Turkey

Ham

This chart shows the food items the settlers preserved for the winter. Without these things, they might not have survived the cold winters.
▶ Why was it necessary to preserve foods before storing them?

Wayne with her soldier-husband. The whole Baily family lived in the **barracks.** The barracks was a large building in which all the soldiers slept. Polly wished her husband were an officer. Officers and their wives had houses.

Women's Work While soldiers guarded the fort, the women worked at special jobs. Some served as nurses. Others, like Polly, were paid to wash the soldiers' clothes.

Polly also had to see that her family was fed. The family grew vegetables in the soldiers' garden. The children picked cranberries and other fruit near the fort. Private Baily hunted for wild game and fished. In the winter the family ate the food they had preserved. Preserving keeps food from spoiling. Meats, vegetables, and fruits were sun-dried, smoked, and pickled in vinegar and salt.

A Time for Fun With all the work at the fort, Polly had little time for fun. One day a year was set aside as a special time. It was the Fourth of July, or Independence Day.

The day started early with booming shots from the large cannon. Everyone stood proudly as the United States flag was raised. Games and contests followed. A fine dinner was served. Afterward, men and women danced. Not even Polly Baily had anything to quarrel about on this day.

C. A Pioneer Family in Northern Indiana

Moved to Indiana Joseph Bailly, who was not related to Polly Baily, was born in Canada. The Bailly family came south to Indiana in 1822. It settled in the wilderness near the Great Lakes.

The Baillys built a farm and trading post. They lived in harmony with the Indian tribes that camped close by. The Indians trapped wolves, beavers, and muskrats for their fur.

A Lively Business At their trading post, the Baillys kept a supply of blankets, guns, and cooking pots. These were goods that Indians wanted in exchange for their furs.

The Baillys were good businesspeople. They built their post near where Indian trails crossed. So it was easy for Indians to get their furs to the post. The post was also near the Great Lakes. The Baillys were able to ship their furs from there to fur companies.

When fur-bearing animals became scarce, the Baillys opened an inn along the road. They were very successful at that too.

D. Changes in the Land

Improving the Land The wilderness of northern Indiana began to change. As more people came, they pushed the Indians west. The settlers traded their farm products for goods they needed. Soon they were able to build larger homes. These people **homesteaded** their

This is a trading post. Here the Indians exchanged furs for the supplies that they needed.
▶ What are some of the supplies the Indians traded for?

land. This means that they built homes, lived in them, and worked to improve the land.

Owning the Land President Abraham Lincoln made the Homestead Act a law in 1862. The Homestead Act said that any head of a family could own land that he or she had cleared and lived on for at least five years. This act was very important because it opened up lands in the West. Thousands of people came to the United States from many other parts of the world. Many of these people homesteaded in Indiana and in the neighboring states.

After the Homestead Act was passed in 1862, many people came to Indiana to live.
► What are these men doing?

LESSON 4 REVIEW

THINK AND WRITE

A. Why were forts built in the Indiana wilderness?
B. In what ways was Polly Baily's life hard?
C. Why was the Bailly family successful in business?

D. What does *homesteading* mean?

SKILLS CHECK

MAP SKILL
Look at the map on page 164. What are three Indiana cities that the National Road passed through?

USING THE VOCABULARY

fell	water power
house-raising	representative
blab school	granny cure
horsepower	blockhouse
buhr	homestead

On a separate sheet of paper, write the best word to complete each sentence below. Choose your answers from the vocabulary words above.

1. To build a home and improve land in pioneer times was to _____ it.
2. Someone who is elected to speak for the people of a particular area is called a _____.
3. When an Indian raid was expected, a pioneer family might seek protection in a _____.
4. When pioneer families got together to help a family build a new cabin, they held a _____.
5. Mills that are powered by a flowing stream use _____.

REMEMBERING WHAT YOU READ

Write your answers in complete sentences on a separate sheet of paper.

1. Why did settlers try to build their homes near water?
2. How did the pioneers clear the land so they could plant crops?

3. What did pioneer families do at a house-raising?
4. What tragedy came to the Lincoln family two years after it moved to Indiana?
5. What was the source of power for the mill at Spring Mill?
6. Who was William Conner?
7. How was the money from the land sale in Indianapolis used?
8. What large road ran along Washington Street in Indianapolis?
9. What do people do when they preserve food?
10. What was the name of the law that said that heads of families could own land that they had cleared and lived on for five years?

TYING LITERATURE TO SOCIAL STUDIES

Find a biography of Abraham Lincoln in your school library. A biography is an account of the life of a well-known person. Write the name of the biography on a sheet of paper. Also write the name of the author. Look through the biography to find out things about Abraham Lincoln that you have not learned before. Write three interesting things about Abraham Lincoln on your paper. Be prepared to share what you learned with the class.

THINKING CRITICALLY

Write your answers in complete sentences on a separate sheet of paper.

1. A house-raising meant a lot of work, but what else did it mean?
2. In what three ways was schooling for children in the Lincolns' community different from what it is for your community?
3. Why were towns often centered around village mills?
4. How did the lives of people in Indianapolis change after the land sale?
5. Why did Joseph Bailly build his trading post where he did?

SUMMARIZING THE CHAPTER

On a separate sheet of paper draw a graphic organizer that is like the one shown here. Copy the information from this graphic organizer to the one you have drawn. Under the main idea for each lesson, write three statements that support it. The first one has been done for you.

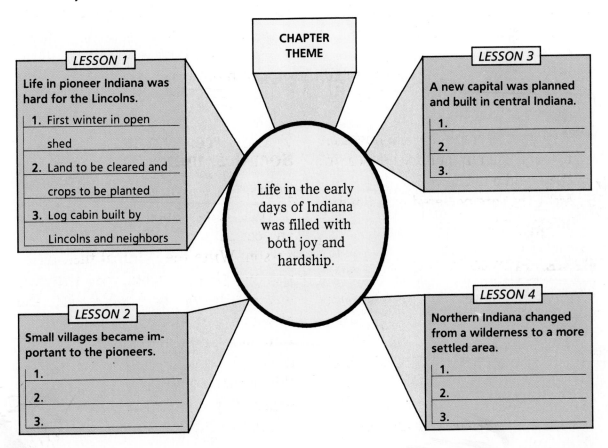

CHAPTER THEME

Life in the early days of Indiana was filled with both joy and hardship.

LESSON 1
Life in pioneer Indiana was hard for the Lincolns.
1. First winter in open shed
2. Land to be cleared and crops to be planted
3. Log cabin built by Lincolns and neighbors

LESSON 2
Small villages became important to the pioneers.
1.
2.
3.

LESSON 3
A new capital was planned and built in central Indiana.
1.
2.
3.

LESSON 4
Northern Indiana changed from a wilderness to a more settled area.
1.
2.
3.

179

OUR GROWING HOOSIER HERITAGE

*Y*ou have learned about many groups who settled in Indiana. In this chapter you will learn about some people who came to Indiana for very special reasons. They are part of Indiana's rich heritage.

THINK ABOUT WHAT YOU KNOW

Imagine what it would be like to live with people whose way of life is very different from yours. Try to describe what problems you might have.

STUDY THE VOCABULARY

ancestor   **minority**
custom   **majority**
shun

FOCUS YOUR READING

How are the Amish different from those around them?

A. A True Pioneer

Rows of Apple Trees   People sometimes asked John Chapman why he did what he did. He told them that he was kicked by a horse when he was 26 years old. After that, he had a religious vision. In his vision, heaven was filled with rows and rows of apple trees in full bloom. John Chapman spent the rest of his life—from about 1800 to 1845—trying to make that vision come true on earth. We know him today as Johnny Appleseed.

Chapman wore a shirt made from a coffee sack. He had a cooking pot for a hat and no shoes. Both Indians and settlers treated him with respect and kindness. He hated to harm anything living. One time a rattlesnake bit him, and he killed it. But he always felt sad that he did so.

Sowing Seeds   Chapman would collect apple seeds in Pennsylvania. Then he planted them throughout the Ohio River valley and also in Indiana. Today many of his orchards still blossom and bear fruit.

John Chapman is typical of many Hoosiers. He was not afraid to think in ways that were different from the ways others thought. He acted on his beliefs. In this chapter you will meet more Hoosiers of yesterday and today.

Johnny Appleseed planted appleseeds in Indiana. Many of his apple orchards still bear fruit.
► What was his real name?

B. Plain and Simple Living

Early to Rise "Jacob Yoder! Schnell!" Jacob's feet hit the cold floor at his father's first call. *Schnell* is a German word that means "quick." German is the language spoken in Jacob's home.

It is only four-thirty in the morning, but Jacob knows he must obey his father. He pulls on his heavy clothes and boots. The moon is still shining as he crunches through the snow to the big barn.

A Simple Farm Mr. Yoder has already begun milking the cows by hand. There are no milking machines in the barn. In fact, there is no electricity at all on the farm. The Yoders do not own a car or a truck. Jacob's family belongs to the "strict," or Old Order, Amish (AHM ihsh). They believe in living the same way as their **ancestors** (AN ses turz), or family members in the past. They follow the same **customs**, or ways of living.

Jacob's job is to feed the calves, pigs, and horses. He carries ears of corn and buckets of warm milk. Just last summer, Jacob picked the corn by hand from tall stalks. Now the calves nudge him playfully as they push their pink noses into the milk.

Working for the Future Jacob loves these chores. He knows that

Amish farmers do not use modern tractors or any electrical equipment.
▶ What are these farmers using to help with the farm work?

one day this farm will be his. Many times he has heard his father and grandfather say, "We borrow the land for our children." When Jacob, the youngest son, grows up and marries, a house will be built for him. It will be attached to his parents' house. When Jacob's parents get older, they will move into the small house where Jacob's grandparents now live. Jacob and his family will then live in the big house. That is why Amish homes are made up of several attached houses.

C. Living Close to Nature

Sounds of Nature Jacob finishes his chores and heads to the plain white house. He is guided by lamplight shining through curtainless windows. Jacob listens to the big windmill whirling in the wind. He thinks, *How wonderful nature is. The wind is pumping water up from the well for my family and our animals. It is doing work for me.*

Outside, Jacob picks up an armload of wood. Inside, he places the wood behind the kitchen stove. His mother and his sisters Sarah and Becky are making breakfast.

Family Closeness The family gathers around the big kitchen table. The meal begins and ends with a prayer spoken in German. Jacob thinks, *I am glad that I am Amish.* The Amish are a religious group named for their founder, Jacob Ammann (AHM ahn). They have three main beliefs. They believe in simple living and worship. They believe in close families and communities. They have a deep respect for nature.

From Europe The first Amish people came to the United States from Germany and Switzerland in the 1700s. The Amish, along with other groups, were being mistreated in parts of Europe. Now the Amish people live in 23 states. But they are found mostly in Pennsylvania, Ohio, Indiana, Illinois, and Iowa.

D. Respect for the Community

Community Life Jacob and his sisters are eating *knepp* for breakfast. This food is made by dripping flour into bubbly hot milk. They also

Amish homes are quite often made up of several small buildings that are attached to a main house.
▶ Why is this done?

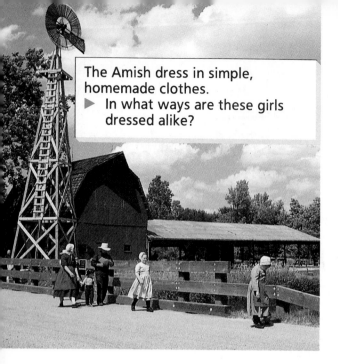

The Amish dress in simple, homemade clothes.
▶ In what ways are these girls dressed alike?

have cornmeal mush, eggs, bread, and butter. The children listen to the older Yoders talk about church this coming Sunday. It will be held here in their house. They are excited, but there is much work to do!

Every other Sunday, church is held in a home that is large enough for many families. The house must be cleaned and polished during the week. Food must be prepared. Sometime before Sunday, a wagon full of benches will arrive. Neighbors will help the Yoder men push back the furniture in the house. Then they will set up rows of benches in the kitchen, the living room — even the first-floor bedroom! Not everyone will be able to see the speaker, but all will hear.

Jacob groans inside as he thinks of the three-hour service —

long hours for children sitting on backless benches! But even the small children have learned to sit quietly and not to cry.

Punishment As they continue to eat their breakfast, the Yoder children do not even glance at their older brother, Levi. Nobody talks to him as he eats in the corner of the room. He is being shunned. That means that no one can speak to him or eat with him. No one can have anything to do with him — not even his own family!

Against the Rules Levi is being punished because he went against the rules of the Amish. He was working as a carpenter in a job away from the farm. There was not enough work on the small Yoder farm for all the men. When Levi saw other ways of living, he wanted to live in those ways too. To the Amish, a community is not a place. It is a group of people who share the same beliefs. So when Levi began to cast off Amish beliefs, he was considered to be out of the community.

Levi soon changed his mind. He missed his family and their customs. Now he has to prove that he again shares the Amish beliefs. Jacob thinks, *It will be good when the people of the church vote to take him back. I am sad to have to shun him.*

THINGS THE AMISH DO NOT USE

Musical Instruments · Televisions · Mirrors · Safety Pins · Telephones · Buttons · Electricity

The Amish follow strict rules first started by Jacob Ammann. They are religious people who avoid any luxury, including buttons on clothing.
▶ What other items do the Amish avoid using?

E. Learning at Home and Learning at School

Traditional Ways Sarah and Becky wash the breakfast dishes. They learn how to clean, cook, and sew from their mother and grandmother. The girls dress exactly alike. Their long, plain dresses and white aprons have been made at home. The clothes for the men and boys are also homemade. Before leaving for school, each girl glances at the one small mirror in the house. No more than 1 inch (3 cm) of hair can show from under their bonnets!

Jacob leads the younger children to the main road. He looks at the fields. This spring he will be old enough to help plant the crops. He will drive the horses back and forth across the fields. Jacob knows about rotating the crops, or changing them each year. Rotating crops keeps the soil from wearing out.

Going to School The Yoders wait for the "school bus." The clippety-clop of horses' hooves tells them that the bus is coming. The children climb into the unheated yellow buggy. The Amish usually ride in black or gray buggies. The Amish have been forced to follow safety laws to avoid accidents. A plain buggy must have a bright orange and red triangle on the back so that car drivers can see it at night.

Amish children go to Amish schools, but only to the eighth grade. Their parents believe this is all the formal education they need. The following passage was written by an Amish schoolgirl.

The Amish usually use horse-drawn buggies for transportation.
▶ Why are there orange and red triangles on the buggies?

Oct. 2nd, Thurs.

It's hard to believe that I've gone to this school a whole month now. . . ! I'm sure I would never want to go back to the public school. This school is much more like a big casual sort of family. . . . We all have arithmetic every day except Friday, also spelling and phonics. Monday and Tuesdays we have History and/or Geography, Wednesday afternoon we have German (someone comes in to teach it as we have a non-Amish teacher). Thursdays we have reading and Fridays we have health and special activities — art, spelling bees, or games.

For the Yoders, the Amish school is also fun. Sarah and Becky talk during recess. Jacob and his friends play marbles, roll hoops, and play a game that involves throwing a ball over the school roof. The children are never supposed to brag or fight. They are never supposed to let a child stand alone. Everyone is to be included in some activity.

F. Sharing Happy and Sad Times

Helping One Another The Amish have problems just like those of other people. They solve their problems together — by sharing. For example, if crops fail or a barn burns, the Amish community shares food or rebuilds the barn.

Communicating Amish friends and families keep in touch through letters and newspapers. The arrival

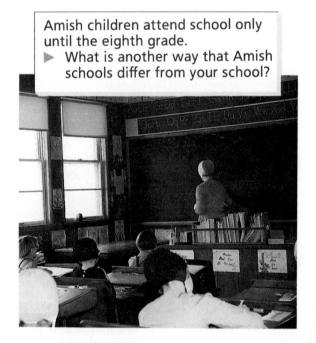

Amish children attend school only until the eighth grade.
▶ What is another way that Amish schools differ from your school?

of the mail is usually a happy occasion for everyone. The entire family gathers to share a letter. Then it adds its own news and mails the letter on to family and friends who live far away. It also welcomes the arrival of *The Budget,* a newspaper for Amish families everywhere.

Being Different The Amish are a minority (mye NOR uh tee) in the United States. A minority is a group that is smaller and also different in some way from most people around it. The majority (muh JOR uh tee), or larger group of people in the United States, are not Amish.

Is it all right to be different? After meeting Jacob, what do you think about being Amish? Of course, not all Amish are exactly like Jacob's family. That is what is so wonderful about our country and our state. The law says that people

The Amish girls are enjoying some free time between classes.
▶ Why are there no children standing alone?

can live by their beliefs unless they are harmful to others.

Still, some people do not understand the Amish and their beliefs. They tease them and even harm their property. They do not respect the right to be different. But most people are glad that the Amish have chosen to be Hoosiers.

LESSON *1* REVIEW

THINK AND WRITE

A. How was Johnny Appleseed like other Hoosiers?

B. What do Amish people mean when they say, "We borrow the land for our children"?

C. What are the three main beliefs of the Amish people?

D. When do the Amish shun a member of their community?

E. Why do the Amish rotate crops?

F. How do the Amish share their news with one another?

SKILLS CHECK

THINKING SKILL

Write a paragraph comparing and contrasting some part of an Amish child's day with that same part of your day.

SETTLERS AND RELIGIOUS FREEDOM

In some countries, most people belong to one religion and worship in the same way. Sometimes these people think that their religious beliefs are the only correct beliefs. They feel that other religions are wrong. In many of these countries, the religion of the majority is officially recognized as the religion of the state.

In the past, people who did not share the religious beliefs of the majority were mistreated. Often, they had to move from place to place to avoid abuse. Some left their homelands in order to find places where they could practice their religion freely.

In the 1600s, most European countries had a state religion. Anyone living in a country who did not practice the state religion of that country was mistreated. Eventually, some of these people left Europe.

One such group of people was the Amish. The Amish lived in Switzerland and in southern Germany. They did not like the rules of the official church. When the New World became settled, many Amish people left Europe. They came to America where they hoped to practice their religion freely. They settled in Indiana and other states such as Pennsylvania, Ohio, and Iowa.

In the late 1700s, our nation's leaders thought that freedom of religion was very important. In fact, they decided to make it part of our Constitution. The first amendment of the United States Constitution states that the nation will have no official state religion. The people of the United States may practice any religion they choose or no religion at all. As a result, the United States is a country where people from all religious backgrounds can worship openly and freely.

Thinking for Yourself

On a separate sheet of paper, answer the questions in complete sentences.

1. How does respect for the religious beliefs of others benefit everyone?
2. Imagine that you are a member of the Constitutional Convention. Develop an argument for making freedom of religion part of our country's Constitution.
3. In what ways might our country be different if we did not have freedom of religion?

Living in Harmony

THINK ABOUT WHAT YOU KNOW

List five words you think of when you hear the phrase "pioneer life in Indiana." This chapter may help you think of a few more.

STUDY THE VOCABULARY

harmony   **greenhouse**
communal living   **granary**

FOCUS YOUR READING

What are the reasons why the Rappites and Owenites are still remembered today?

A. A Town Called Harmonie

Hard Work and Sharing Another group that came to live in Indiana were called Harmonists. To live in **harmony** is to agree. The Harmonists agreed on certain beliefs. In Germany, their home, they could not practice those beliefs. Their leader, George Rapp, led a group of 125 families to America in 1803. Their first community was in Pennsylvania.

The Harmonists were also called Rappites, after their leader. They believed in hard work. They believed in sharing work and goods as a community. This is called **communal** (KAHM yoo nul) **living**. They also believed that the world would end in their lifetime. For this reason, the Rappites saw no need to marry or have children.

A Comfortable Place In 1814 the Rappites bought land along the Wabash River in Indiana. There, they began a community called Harmonie. In less than ten years, the Rappites had built a large community. In the town were four large brick buildings. These were comfortable houses where the men and women lived separately. The houses were heated with special fireplaces. The walls were made thick and warm with mud-wrapped cattails.

Harmonie had many other buildings—more than 100! There were cloth, flour, and lumber mills, along with an oil well. A church shaped like a cross stood in the center of town. Harmonie was known as the "wonder of the wilderness."

George Rapp was the leader of the Harmonists.
► What were three beliefs of the Harmonists?

B. Working in Harmonie

Fruit and Grain   The Rappites farmed over 2,000 acres (810 ha). They had many farm animals, and they raised silkworms. Plump grapes grew in their vineyards. In greenhouses, they tended lemon and orange trees. A greenhouse is a building made of glass and used for growing plants. The sun shining through the glass keeps the plants warm in winter. The hard-working Rappites also built a large granary for storing grain.

Flatboats left Harmonie regularly. They were loaded with goods for sale in New Orleans. The boats carried wagons, cloth, rope, leather goods, and hats—all made in the town of Harmonie.

Leaving Harmonie   George Rapp became well known. He was one of the writers of Indiana's first constitution. Eventually, he sold Harmonie. No one knows why. Some people feel that the Rappites wanted to start a new kind of business. Perhaps they thought it would work better in the East. The Rappites went back to Pennsylvania, where they had come from. They named their new community Economy.

The visitors' center in New Harmony is a beautiful modern building. Many of the old New Harmony buildings have been restored.
▶ What were some of the original buildings?

C. A Town for Sale

Different Ideas Robert Owen was a rich man from the country of Wales, near England. He owned many factories there. He was very different from most owners at that time. Workers in most factories worked long hours. They received little money. Some of the workers were young children. Robert Owen raised wages and lowered hours. He would not hire children. He believed that children should play, not work. He also believed that children should go to school. He thought schooling was the best way to a better life. Owen's partners in Europe did not like his ideas. They forced him to leave.

Buying a Town The town built by the Rappites in Indiana was a perfect place for Robert Owen to live out his dream. In January 1825 he, along with several other people, bought the town. They named the town New Harmony.

Like the Rappites, Robert Owen believed in communal living. Everyone was to work hard and share equally. Many people liked Owen's ideas. Famous scientists, artists, teachers, and others came to New Harmony and were called Owenites. However, too few of those who came were farmers. Many

In the 1800s, working conditions in English factories were harsh.
▶ In what ways were conditions better in Owen's factories?

of those who came were not hard workers. They began to quarrel. After a while, the Owenites could not live in agreement anymore.

Some Successes Robert Owen's plan did not work, but some of his dreams did come true. The first kindergarten in the United States was started in New Harmony. The town had the first free public schools. It had the first free public library. There was a school for teaching work skills. New Harmony had the first women's club. Robert Owen's thinking *was* ahead of his time!

D. Carrying on Good Ideas

Robert Owen left New Harmony in 1827. Some members of his family carried on his ideas. His son, Robert Dale Owen, was later elected to the United States Congress. He worked hard for the rights of women. He also believed that it was wrong for people to own slaves.

Today, some of the old buildings in New Harmony have been restored and rebuilt. A beautiful visitors' center has been added, along with a roofless church. Close by is the 3,000-acre (1,215 ha) Harmonie State Park. Every year many visitors come to New Harmony to see where the Rappites and Owenites dreamed of living in harmony.

New Harmony's church has no real roof. But it does have a wooden cover.
▶ What does this cover protect?

LESSON *2* REVIEW

THINK AND WRITE

A. Why did the Harmonists come to the United States?
B. What did the Rappites grow in greenhouses in Harmonie?
C. What ideas of Robert Owen continue today?
D. How did Robert Owen's son carry on his ideas?

SKILLS CHECK

MAP SKILL
Use the Gazetteer on pages 357–364 to find the latitude and longitude of New Harmony. Then find the town on the map on page 356. In what part of the state is the town of New Harmony found?

Searching for a New Life

THINK ABOUT WHAT YOU KNOW
What modern people do you know of who have risked their lives to help others?

STUDY THE VOCABULARY
Society of Friends   festival   immigrant

FOCUS YOUR READING
To what people has Indiana offered a chance for a new life?

A. The Underground Railroad

Against Slavery Indiana's constitution said that no one in the state could own slaves. To the north of Indiana were other states where slavery was not allowed. To the south were states that allowed slavery. Sometimes slaves escaped from the South to Indiana. Owners and slave catchers often came after them. Then the slaves were beaten and taken back to slavery. The slaves needed to go farther north—to Canada. Only then could they be sure of freedom. So, many people traveled through Indiana on their way to freedom in Canada.

Helping Runaway Slaves Many people in Indiana helped slaves run away from their owners. This was unlawful, so they worked in secret. Part of the secret plan was called the Underground Railroad. It was not really a railroad. Most of it was not even under the ground. It was called the Underground Railroad because of the quick, quiet way that slaves were helped to escape.

Routes and Stations The Underground Railroad involved three main routes through Indiana. The routes passed through more than 30 Indiana towns. The road that is now U.S. Highway 27 was one of the main routes.

Homes, barns, and churches with special hiding places were called stations, or depots (DEE-pohz). Station by station, the slaves were helped along the routes. The

Many people in Indiana worked in the Underground Railroad. They helped slaves escape to freedom.
▶ Where were the slaves going?

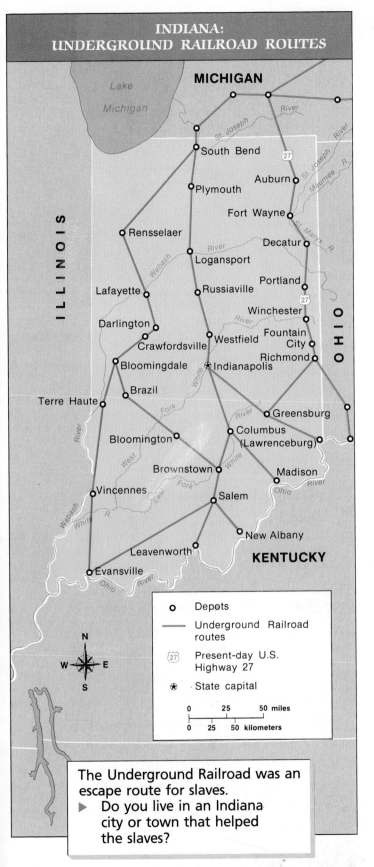

INDIANA: UNDERGROUND RAILROAD ROUTES

MICHIGAN

Lake Michigan

ILLINOIS

South Bend
Auburn
Plymouth
Fort Wayne
Rensselaer
Decatur
Logansport
Portland
Lafayette
Russiaville
Winchester
Darlington
Fountain City
Westfield
Crawfordsville
Richmond
Bloomingdale
Indianapolis
Brazil
Terre Haute
Greensburg
Bloomington
Columbus (Lawrenceburg)
Brownstown
Madison
Vincennes
Salem
New Albany
Leavenworth
KENTUCKY
Evansville

OHIO

Wabash River
St. Joseph River
Maumee R.
St. Mary's R.
White River
West Fork
East Fork
Ohio River

Legend:
- o Depots
- — Underground Railroad routes
- (27) Present-day U.S. Highway 27
- ✪ State capital

0   25   50 miles
0   25   50 kilometers

N W E S

The Underground Railroad was an escape route for slaves.
▶ Do you live in an Indiana city or town that helped the slaves?

slaves often walked to the next station by night. They hid during the day, when they rested and were fed. The slaves were always in danger, and so were the friends who helped them. Would you have been willing to take the risk of helping them?

B. The Society of Friends

Understanding Freedom A religious group called Quakers helped with the Underground Railroad. The Quakers are also known as the Society of Friends, or just Friends. This group was a real friend to many slaves who would never have escaped without their help.

The Friends could understand the problems of the slaves. Their group, founded by George Fox, had begun in England. But, they could not practice their beliefs there. They, too, had had to travel to freedom. The first Quaker colony in this country was in Pennsylvania.

Quaker Leaders Two leaders of the Underground Railroad were Friends. They were Levi and Katie Coffin. The Coffins lived in a large house in Fountain City. Between 1827 and 1847, the Coffins sheltered about 2,000 slaves in hidden rooms. Aunt Katie, as Mrs. Coffin was called, often nursed sick slaves until they were well enough to travel.

Levi and Katie Coffin were active in the Underground Railroad. They hid slaves in secret rooms in their house.
▶ How could this door be hidden from view?

Today, the Friends still work for peace and freedom. They do not believe in war, but they help those who have been hurt by war.

C. Immigrants Who Decided to Become Hoosiers

New Settlers The word *migrate* means "to move." **Immigrants** are people from one country who move to another to live. The largest group of immigrants who settled in Indiana were the Germans. The next largest were the Irish and the Swedish. They all brought their special ways of doing things to this new land.

The Kjellberg family lived on a small rocky farm in Sweden. But Anders, Johanna, and their son Cahrl wanted to come to America. In 1863 they arrived in Indiana. There was already a Swedish community near the Great Lakes.

Becoming Citizens It took the Kjellbergs 11 years of hard work to buy their own farm. Then they wanted to become American citizens. The Kjellbergs still spoke Swedish at home. They celebrated Swedish holidays, and they were proud of their Swedish heritage. But they decided to change the spelling of their names. Kjellberg became Chellberg and Cahrl became Carl. They were becoming real Hoosiers!

At first, the Chellbergs grew wheat, oats, corn, and rye. When Carl was grown, he bought a herd of

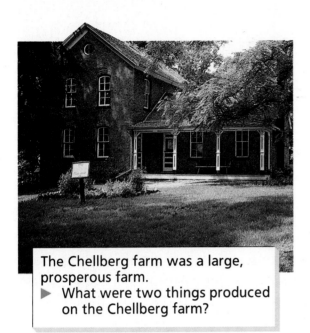

The Chellberg farm was a large, prosperous farm.
▶ What were two things produced on the Chellberg farm?

Sometimes immigrants gave their Hoosier towns the same names as ones they had left. On the map on this page you can see some of these place names. More than 300 Indiana

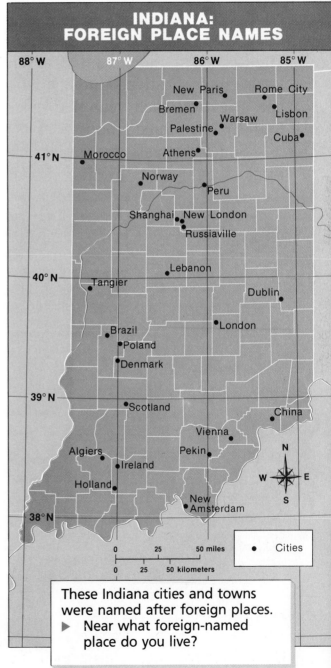

INDIANA: FOREIGN PLACE NAMES

These Indiana cities and towns were named after foreign places.
▶ Near what foreign-named place do you live?

cows and went into the milk business. He sent milk to the city by wagon. Later, the railroad provided better transportation. One after another, buildings were added to the farm. The Chellbergs built a maple sugar house and sold the maple sugar. Later, they replaced the farm's windmills with electric power.

Today, you can visit the Chellberg Farm at the Indiana Dunes National Lakeshore. You can see the house, barn, and farm as they were when the Chellbergs lived there.

D. Celebrating a Rich Heritage

Change and Tradition All over Indiana, immigrant groups settled in small communities. Most changed like the Chellbergs. Others, such as the Amish, kept their communities much the same.

place names are borrowed from other countries.

Things to Celebrate Today, Hoosiers love to celebrate their heritage. Every year groups gather for **festivals.** A festival is a special celebration. The Germans in Vevay and other towns celebrate Oktoberfests. The Italians in Clinton celebrate the Little Italy Festival. Indianapolis has a festival each year that celebrates many ethnic groups.

Some festivals are based on local scenery or events. Parke County has a Covered Bridge Festival. Fulton County celebrates a Round Barn Festival. Many people in communities around Indiana celebrate Old Settlers Days or Pioneers Days. Fort Wayne celebrates its Three Rivers Festival.

Hoosier Pride All over Indiana, Hoosiers celebrate things they are proud of. Why do Hoosiers have such celebrations as the Rose, Strawberry, Blueberry, Persimmon,

Puppet shows are popular events at many festivals.
▶ What is the man behind the curtain doing?

These colorful marchers are parading through Thorntown in the annual Festival of the Turning Leaves.

▶ At what time of year is this event held?

Sunflower, Egg, Popcorn, Mint, Pumpkin, Tomato, Maple Sugar, Turtle Days, and Apple festivals?

In your community you can find clues to people's heritage. Look at place names, headstones in old cemeteries, and architecture. Study art, festivals, languages, music, dance, dress, foods, and religions. Where did the Hoosiers in your community come from? Why did they come to Indiana? What customs and beliefs did they bring with them? Hoosiers should be proud of their heritage!

LESSON 3 REVIEW

THINK AND WRITE

A. How did the Underground Railroad work?
B. Why could the Quakers understand the problems of the slaves?
C. How did the Chellbergs change in their new homeland?
D. Why do Hoosiers celebrate so many festivals?

SKILLS CHECK

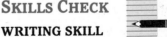

WRITING SKILL

Look carefully at the map on page 197. Use the map scale to answer the following questions. What city is found 15 miles southwest of Vienna? About how many miles lie between Bremen and Peru? Write your answers in complete sentences.

CHAPTER 7 PUTTING IT ALL TOGETHER

USING THE VOCABULARY

ancestor	greenhouse
minority	granary
majority	Society of
harmony	Friends
communal living	immigrant
	festival

On a separate sheet of paper, write the word or words that best match each definition below. Choose your answers from the vocabulary words above.

1. another name for the Quakers
2. a group that is smaller and also different in some way from most people around it
3. sharing as a community
4. a place for storing grain
5. a family member from long ago
6. the larger group of people
7. a person from one country who moves to another country to live
8. agreement
9. a building made of glass that is used for growing things
10. a celebration

REMEMBERING WHAT YOU READ

Write your answers in complete sentences on a separate sheet of paper.

1. Who are the Amish?
2. What does it mean to be shunned by the Amish community?
3. What is the main kind of transportation used by the Amish?
4. What is the difference between a majority and a minority?
5. Which two groups practiced communal living in early Indiana?
6. Who built the town of Harmonie?
7. What were two of Robert Owen's ideas?
8. What was the purpose of the Underground Railroad?
9. What religious group helped the Underground Railroad?
10. How do Hoosiers from other countries celebrate their heritage?

TYING LANGUAGE ARTS TO SOCIAL STUDIES: WRITING TO LEARN

Pretend that George Rapp has given you the job of writing an advertisement to sell the town of Harmonie. It will be placed in several local newspapers. Write an ad that will show the good things about Harmonie and make someone want to buy it. Make your ad as convincing as you can!

THINKING CRITICALLY

Write your answers in complete sentences on a separate sheet of paper.

1. How is the Old Order Amish way of life different from yours?
2. How is communal living different from how people live today?
3. What kind of person do you think Robert Owen was?
4. Why did the Underground Railroad have to be kept secret?
5. What kinds of qualities do you think the Chellbergs had that allowed them to move to America and be so successful in business?

SUMMARIZING THE CHAPTER

On a separate sheet of paper draw a graphic organizer that is like the one shown here. Copy the information from this graphic organizer to the one you have drawn. Under the main idea for each lesson, write three statements that support it. The first one has been done for you.

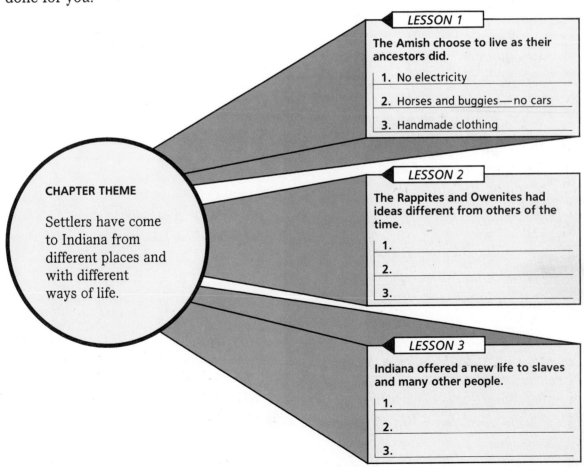

CHAPTER THEME

Settlers have come to Indiana from different places and with different ways of life.

LESSON 1

The Amish choose to live as their ancestors did.

1. No electricity
2. Horses and buggies—no cars
3. Handmade clothing

LESSON 2

The Rappites and Owenites had ideas different from others of the time.

1.
2.
3.

LESSON 3

Indiana offered a new life to slaves and many other people.

1.
2.
3.

8

INDIANA IN PEACE AND WAR

*T*hrough the years, Indiana has asked for and received the support of its citizens. Indiana has also faced its responsibilities to provide for the needs of all its citizens.

Indiana and the Civil War

THINK ABOUT WHAT YOU KNOW

How is a country like a family? Think of as many ways as you can.

STUDY THE VOCABULARY

Union   civil war
slavery   secede
plantation   Confederacy
free state

FOCUS YOUR READING

Why was the Civil War known as the "terrible war"?

A. The Free State of Indiana

Part of a Family When Indiana became a state in 1816, it was part of the Union. The Union was like a family of states. The Union was the early United States.

Slavery in the South Like members of a family, the states in the Union did not always agree. By 1861 the states were faced with a problem. The problem was slavery, the practice of owning people. In the South, some farmers owned plantations (plan TAY shunz), or very large farms. They used slaves to work on their plantations. The farms in the North were smaller, so these farmers did not use slaves. Indiana did not allow slavery. That made it a free state. In 1861, when Abraham Lincoln became President, the Union was made up of 19 free states and 15 slave states.

B. Splitting in Two

War in the Nation Between 1861 and 1865, a terrible war was fought. This war is called the Civil War. A civil war is a war between groups of people in the same country. In a civil war, members of families sometimes take different sides. They fight against each other.

People who study history have never agreed on the exact causes of the Civil War. One cause was slavery. Those who were against slavery wanted Congress to keep slavery out of any new territory. Slave owners in the South wanted to keep their slaves and allow slavery in new territories. Another cause of the Civil War was that the Southern states wanted to secede (sih SEED), or leave, the Union because of slavery.

Splitting the Nation So there were two important questions that split the Union. Was it right to own slaves? Did a state have the right to leave the Union?

President Lincoln did not believe in slavery. He also did not believe that states had the right to secede from the Union. In a famous

SLAVE STATES AND FREE STATES BEFORE THE CIVIL WAR

State	Date admitted to the Union	Status	State	Date admitted to the Union	Status
Delaware	1787	Slave	Louisiana	1812	Slave
New Jersey	1787	Free	Indiana	1816	Free
Pennsylvania	1787	Free	Mississippi	1817	Slave
Connecticut	1788	Free	Illinois	1818	Free
Georgia	1788	Slave	Alabama	1819	Slave
Maryland	1788	Slave	Maine	1820	Free
Massachusetts	1788	Free	Missouri	1821	Slave
New Hampshire	1788	Free	Arkansas	1836	Slave
New York	1788	Free	Michigan	1837	Free
South Carolina	1788	Slave	Florida	1845	Slave
Virginia	1788	Slave	Texas	1845	Slave
North Carolina	1789	Slave	Iowa	1846	Free
Rhode Island	1790	Free	Wisconsin	1848	Free
Vermont	1791	Free	California	1850	Free
Kentucky	1792	Slave	Minnesota	1858	Free
Tennessee	1796	Slave	Oregon	1859	Free
Ohio	1803	Free	Kansas	1861	Free

■ Slave ■ Free

This table shows when each state was admitted to the Union and if it was a free or slave state.
▶ When was Indiana admitted?

The Civil War lasted four years and tore the nation apart.
▶ What weapons are being used by these soldiers?

speech, he quoted from the Bible, saying: "A house divided against itself cannot stand."

Soon the time came when 11 Southern states *did* leave the Union. They became the Confederate States of America. The Civil War was fought between the Union and the **Confederacy** (kun FED ur uh see).

C. Learning the Costs of War

Hoosiers and the War   At first, Hoosiers did not want to get into the Civil War. However, Governor Oliver P. Morton was a strong supporter of President Lincoln. So the

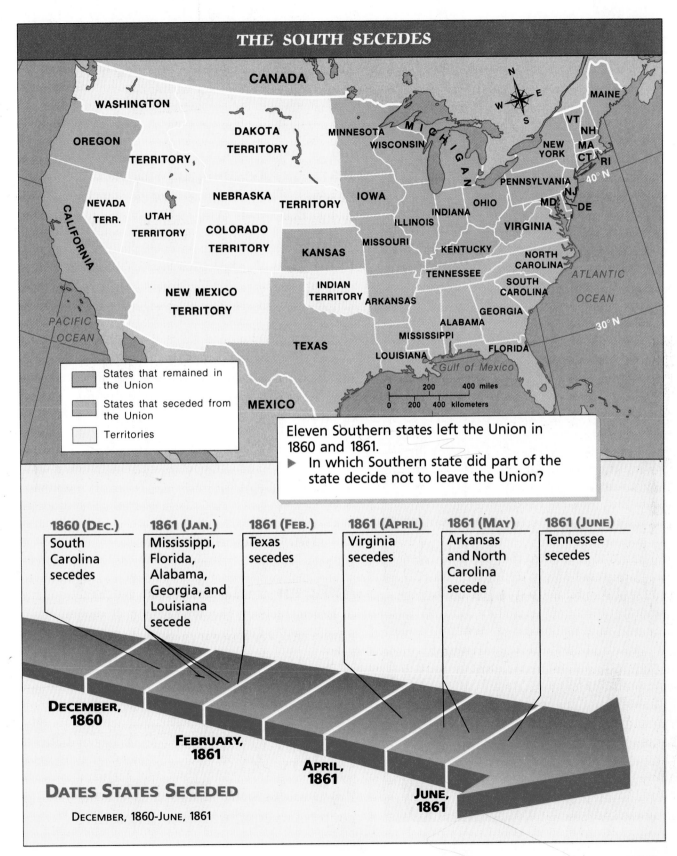

THE SOUTH SECEDES

CANADA

WASHINGTON

OREGON

TERRITORY

DAKOTA
TERRITORY

MINNESOTA

WISCONSIN

MICHIGAN

MAINE

VT
NH

NEW
YORK

MA
CT
RI

NEVADA
TERR.

UTAH
TERRITORY

NEBRASKA

TERRITORY

IOWA

PENNSYLVANIA

40° N

NJ

CALIFORNIA

COLORADO
TERRITORY

ILLINOIS

INDIANA

OHIO

MD

DE

MISSOURI

VIRGINIA

KANSAS

NEW MEXICO

TERRITORY

INDIAN
TERRITORY

ARKANSAS

KENTUCKY

TENNESSEE

NORTH
CAROLINA

SOUTH
CAROLINA

ATLANTIC

OCEAN

GEORGIA

30° N

PACIFIC
OCEAN

TEXAS

ALABAMA

MISSISSIPPI

LOUISIANA

FLORIDA

Gulf of Mexico

MEXICO

| | 0 | 200 | 400 miles |
| 0 | 200 | 400 kilometers |

States that remained in
the Union

States that seceded from
the Union

Territories

Eleven Southern states left the Union in
1860 and 1861.
▶ In which Southern state did part of the
state decide not to leave the Union?

DATES STATES SECEDED
DECEMBER, 1860–JUNE, 1861

1860 (DEC.)
South
Carolina
secedes

1861 (JAN.)
Mississippi,
Florida,
Alabama,
Georgia, and
Louisiana
secede

1861 (FEB.)
Texas
secedes

1861 (APRIL)
Virginia
secedes

1861 (MAY)
Arkansas
and North
Carolina
secede

1861 (JUNE)
Tennessee
secedes

DECEMBER,
1860

FEBRUARY,
1861

APRIL,
1861

JUNE,
1861

governor used the little money the state had to support the Union.

Governor Morton also borrowed money to help the Union. He used this money to train, clothe, and feed Hoosier soldiers and nurses.

No major battles were fought in Indiana. But even so, Indiana sent many soldiers and nurses—about 200,000—to the battlefields. Most soldiers were farmers. After they went to war, their wives and children kept the farms going. Hoosier

Many soldiers from Indiana lost their lives during the Civil War.
▶ Why were few Indiana farms and mills lost during the war?

THE MUFFLED DRUMS SAD ROLL HAS BEAT
THE SOLDIERS LAST TATTOO
NO MORE ON LIFE'S PARADE SHALL MEET
THAT BRAVE AND FALLEN FEW

farms helped to feed the Union army. Trains and boats carried large loads of corn, wheat, and pork from Indiana to the Union soldiers.

The Cost of War The war cost many lives. The trains and boats that took food returned with sadder cargo. They came back with wounded and sick soldiers who went to hospitals in the state. Also, more than 24,000 Hoosiers died— one of every eight Indiana soldiers. How many sad families there were in those days!

Few Indiana farms and mills were destroyed. However, in the South, Union armies burned mills, farm buildings, and crops. They took farm animals for food and transportation. Some of the great plantations were never rebuilt.

D. Hoosier Contributions to the War

At Home Many Hoosiers worked at home to help the war effort. If you could talk to Hoosiers who lived in Indiana during the Civil War, this is what they might say.

"I remember when Governor Morton called on the women of Indiana to help the war effort," Hannah said. "We were asked to supply the soldiers with things that would keep them comfortable and healthy.

During the Civil War, Indiana women made clothes for soldiers.
▶ What were some of the clothes made by the women?

I knitted so many woolen socks, gloves, blankets, shirts, and pairs of underwear that I thought my fingers would fall off. My friends and I spun, knitted, and wove late into the night. This was after spending a full day working in the fields. We were happy to help, though."

Far Away from Home The men who were away fighting were grateful for the hard work of those at home. They were happy to get anything that reminded them of Indiana. The following passage is from a letter written home to Indiana by James Simpson. Simpson had gone off to fight with the 14th Indiana Regiment in the spring of 1861.

You ought to have seen us pitch into [dig into] the peaches and black-berries—As I helped each of the mess [the people he ate with] to some they would remark "that puts me in mind of Indiany"—"who-ever put them up understood the business"—"bully [cheers] for old Indiany" and other like remarks were continually going around.

LESSON *1* REVIEW

THINK AND WRITE

A. Why were Southern farmers more likely than Northern farmers to use slaves?
B. What were the two important questions that split the Union?
C. What are three costs of war?
D. How did Hoosiers at home help the war effort?

SKILLS CHECK

MAP SKILL

Look at the map on page 205. Name six states that stayed in the Union and six states that left the Union. In total, did more states leave the Union or stay in the Union? Write your answers using complete sentences.

THE RICHARD OWEN MEMORIAL

While many terrible things happened during the Civil War, there were also some good results. The slaves were freed. The Union stayed together. Black Americans began to win their rights. These included the right to vote and the right to equal education. It is sad to think of the death and destruction that the war brought. Yet individual people also showed kindness, even to those who were their enemies during the war.

Few Confederate soldiers came to Indiana except as prisoners. Camp Morton in Indianapolis held many Confederate prisoners. Richard Owen, son of Robert Owen of New Harmony, was in charge of that prison camp. Knowing that the prisoners had fought bravely for their cause, Owen treated them with respect. After the war, a memorial was built in Richard Owen's honor. You can see this memorial in Indianapolis.

COLONEL RICHARD OWEN
COMMANDANT
CAMP MORTON PRISON 1862
TRIBVTE BY CONFEDERATE PRISONERS
OF WAR AND THEIR FRIENDS
FOR HIS COVRTESY AND KIND

Understanding Source Material

1. What does this memorial tell you about how the prisoners at Camp Morton felt about Richard Owen?
2. How is this different from the way that you think most prisoners feel about their commandant, or prison camp leader?
3. In what ways do you think Richard Owen was similar to his father, Robert Owen?

After the War

THINK ABOUT WHAT YOU KNOW
Think about a time when your parents allowed you a new freedom you had not had before. What kinds of feelings did you have at that time?

STUDY THE VOCABULARY
assassinate   sharecropper
fairness   depression
discrimination

FOCUS YOUR READING
What kinds of changes came to Indiana after the Civil War?

A. Continued Bitter Feelings

Death of a President On April 19, 1865, the Civil War ended. Slavery was forbidden. The Southern states came back into the Union. However, the bitter feelings between the North and the South did not end. Anger and hatred left over from the war hung on for many years.

President Lincoln never got the chance to rebuild the nation he worked so hard to save. He was **assassinated** (uh SAS un ayt ed), or killed, just six days after the war ended. His killer was an actor named John Wilkes Booth. Booth had very strong feelings for the South and for slavery. Booth wanted to get even with the North.

The Funeral Train Lincoln's body was taken by train from Washington, D.C., to Springfield, Illinois. He was buried there. It was night as the train approached Indianapolis. Some people lit bonfires along the tracks. Many just stood tearfully and watched the train roll by.

The funeral train stopped in Indianapolis. Thousands of people walked through the capitol building to view Lincoln's body. How very sad the people were!

This painting shows some Civil War soldiers during a break in the fighting.
▶ Where did they sleep?

Booker T. Washington was an important black leader in education.
▶ How did the government help in the education of freed slaves?

B. Adjusting to Freedom

After the war, the nation faced many problems. The slaves had been given their freedom. They needed jobs and places to live. It would not be easy to find either. Many former slaves had not been allowed to learn to read and write.

The government set up a special department to help. Teachers were sent to start schools for the freed slaves. They were finally given a chance to learn. Freedom and the chance to learn were some of the first steps in treating black people with **fairness.** Fairness involves treating all people equally.

A black leader named Booker T. Washington wrote, "Few people can imagine how much the people of my race wanted education. It was a whole race trying to go to school. Few were too young and none too old to make the attempt to learn."

C. North to Indiana

Unfair Treatment Before the Civil War, only 1 of every 100 people in Indiana was black. The Constitution of 1851 kept black people out of the state. It said that no black people could come into or settle in Indiana. This is an example of **discrimination** (dih skrihm ih NAY shun). Discrimination involves treating certain groups of people unfairly. Sometimes there is discrimination because of a person's religion. Here, it was because of race. One year after the Civil War, in 1866, the constitution was changed. Black people could then settle in Indiana.

Three years later they were given the right to go to public schools in the state. These were separate schools, however, and very poor. At that time, though, any chance to learn was taken. It meant blacks could one day find good jobs.

A New Beginning Many black people came to Indiana hoping to find work on farms. Some were like Elijah James. "After I was freed," Elijah said, "I went north to Indiana. I met Robert Wells, a white farmer. His farm had grown over the years, and one son had been killed in the war. So he needed help. The problem was, Wells had very little money to pay me with. So Wells shared what he *did* have — land for growing crops. He built a small house for my family and me. At last we had a place to live! I could grow food for my family and crops to sell. The money I made from selling crops I shared with Robert Wells."

Little Work and Less Money People like Elijah were called share-croppers. After they paid money to the landowners, most did not have enough money left to buy their own farms. In fact, back then few Hoosiers had much money!

Before the war, Indiana products and goods had been sold to storekeepers and businesses in the South. After the war, the Southern merchants had no money to buy these goods. Also, the stores and businesses where they would resell

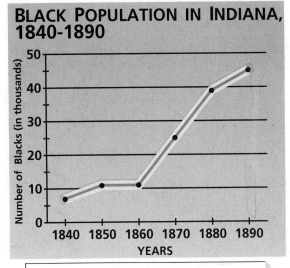

BLACK POPULATION IN INDIANA, 1840-1890

The black population in Indiana increased between 1840 and 1890.
► What was the main reason for this increase?

the goods had been destroyed in the war. Everybody suffered through a long period called a **depression** — a time when there was little work and little money.

D. Trying to Stop Change

A Secret Group After the war, a secret group started in the South. It was called the Ku Klux Klan, or the KKK. Members wore white robes and hoods. This group began to grow in Indiana in the years after the war. The KKK in Indiana tried to frighten black people coming from the South. The KKK did not want black people to have their rights.

A Time of Hate Much later, after World War I, the KKK became very

The Civil War caused much destruction throughout the South. After the war, the whole country entered a depression.
▶ What is a depression?

strong in Indiana. These people did not like the changes that new people brought to Indiana. It was not only the black people they were against. They did not like any of the new immigrants. They forgot that their families were once immigrants too. They refused to see that all people should have the same rights.

This time was known as the Wave of Hate. In spite of it, changes did come to Indiana.

LESSON 2 REVIEW

THINK AND WRITE

A. Why did John Wilkes Booth kill Abraham Lincoln?
B. What problems did freed slaves face after the war?
C. How did the Civil War help lead to the depression?
D. What did the KKK in Indiana try to do after the Civil War?

SKILLS CHECK

THINKING SKILL

Look at the map on page 205. Notice Indiana's location as compared with that of the states that seceded from the Union. Why do you think no major battles were fought in Indiana? Write your answer to this question using complete sentences.

LESSON 3

Indiana's Many Changes

THINK ABOUT WHAT YOU KNOW

When you make one change, usually other things change too. Think of one kind of change that could bring about many changes.

STUDY THE VOCABULARY

interdependent   **victory**
suffrage   **garden**

FOCUS YOUR READING

What changes have made Indiana the way it is today?

A. Changes in the Way People Live and Work

Moving to Cities   After the Civil War, life was hard. Even so, a new Indiana was taking shape. More and more people from other countries came to America. Many chose to settle in Indiana. They settled in towns and worked in shops and mills. As more and more people came, towns grew into cities where many people worked and lived.

Before the Civil War, nine out of ten people in Indiana lived and worked on farms. Indiana was mostly rural at that time. By 1900, only about six out of ten people were still living on farms. After that, even more Indianans moved to cities. Indiana's urban population was growing steadily. Hoosiers also moved northward, where the larger towns and cities were. Southern Indiana no longer had the most people.

During the early 1900s, many Indianans moved to cities.
▶ What was Indiana's urban population in 1940?

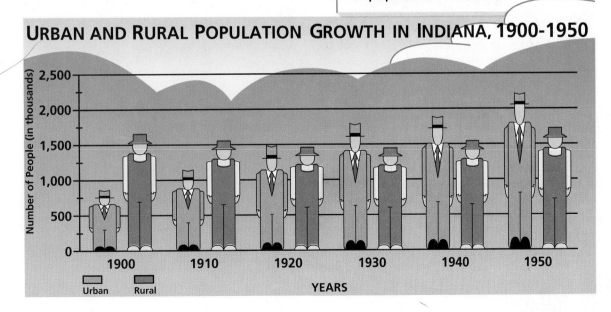

URBAN AND RURAL POPULATION GROWTH IN INDIANA, 1900-1950

Number of People (in thousands)

2,500 · 2,000 · 1,500 · 1,000 · 500 · 0

1900   1910   1920   1930   1940   1950

YEARS

Urban   Rural

213

Products for Sale As Indiana became more urban, more products were made to be sold. Fewer people grew their own food. Grain and corn were still very important, but they were used in different ways. Hoosier grain was fed to cattle and hogs. Farmers then sold these farm animals to meat packers. Meat from the animals was prepared and preserved for sale. Many meat-packing plants grew up along the Ohio River and the Wabash River. These were good locations, because from them the meat could easily be shipped to many other places.

Of course, Indiana farms were still important, even though fewer people were working on farms.

Those who stayed on farms had better seeds and tools than pioneer farmers. They could produce larger and better crops with less work.

At this time, the business of furniture making began in Indiana. Hoosiers had always made their own furniture. They began to make it to be sold. The furniture makers got their lumber from Indiana forests. Forests have always been important to Indiana workers.

B. Changes in Thinking

Depending on Others As time went on, Indiana shifted from a rural

This chart shows the process by which farm animals are raised and then sold in the market.
▶ What is the second step?

MEAT: FROM FARM TO MARKET

1. Farmers grow grain in Indiana fields.
2. Grains are fed to young animals. Pigs particularly like corn.
3. The pigs are shipped to meat packers.
4. The meat travels in refrigerated trucks to grocery stores. Your family can buy it there.

way of life to an urban way of life. Hoosiers found themselves depending on many other people. In other words, they became interdependent (ihn tur dee PEN dunt). People in cities and towns needed products from farms. Farmers, on the other hand, began to buy products made in cities and towns.

Sometimes the people who made these products needed supplies they could get only outside of Indiana. Then people became even more interdependent. When Hoosiers started depending on other people for things, they began to understand more about other people and their needs.

Voting Rights for Women Hoosiers became very interested in people's rights. Voting rights were very important. Black men had won the

More than half of the women who could vote did not vote in 1920.
▶ Why do you think so many women did not vote?

PERCENTAGE OF VOTING–AGE WOMEN IN THE UNITED STATES WHO VOTED, 1920

35%   65%

☐ Percentage of women of voting age who voted
◼ Percentage of women of voting age who did not vote

right to vote in 1870. Women were still not able to vote. Suffrage (SUF-rihj) groups formed. These were groups that worked for voting rights. The suffrage groups wanted to make sure that women were given their rights. They wanted to amend, or change, the United States Constitution. In 1920, after 40 years of hard work by suffrage groups, women were given the right to vote.

C. Changes Brought by War

The Great War In 1914 another war broke out. This time it was across the Atlantic Ocean, in Europe. At the time, people called it the Great War. Later it became known

Many women's suffrage groups worked to get voting rights.
▶ When did women finally get the right to vote?

215

as World War I. World War II followed in 1939. Again, it started in Europe. These two wars made the people of Indiana think about people in other parts of the world. After all, the Hoosier heritage was linked to many countries.

At first, our country tried to stay out of both wars. Finally, though, the United States entered each of the wars to help its friends.

Fighting for America During World War I, more than 100,000 Hoosiers served their country. About three times that many fought in World War II. These were costly wars. Even so, fewer Hoosier soldiers died in both world wars together than in the Civil War alone.

Today, visitors to Indianapolis are reminded of those who were killed in the wars. On and near Monument Circle stand memorials to Hoosiers who fought for freedom.

The Home Front Throughout both world wars, Indiana workers made airplane parts, tanks, guns, gunpowder, and radios. Farmers raised large crops to feed soldiers. Even urban people planted small gardens to grow their own food. These were called **victory gardens.**

Special groups organized programs to help with the war effort. Even schoolchildren were asked to help. Listen in on a wartime conversation at a Hoosier supper table.

"Today Miss Oates told us we could be good citizens by joining the Junior Red Cross, Mama," said Susannah. "Do you know what? Because my grades are so good, I can stay home and help Papa during the planting and harvesting this year!" Susannah felt proud to help with such an important job.

Her brother Tom was in high school. He was always trying to put Susannah in her place. "Well, Sue," he said, "you're not the only person in this family who is helping with the war. I saved five dollars and bought war stamps. It's like I'm giving a loan to the government to help pay for the war. And what about your new crop, Papa?" Tom asked.

During both world wars, women were an important part of the war effort on the home front.
▶ What are these women doing?

People at home helped the war effort in many ways. They bought government bonds, canned foods, and planted victory gardens.
▶ What is a victory garden?

Their father nodded slowly. "There isn't enough sugar around, that's a fact. I've been asked to plant sugar beets this year, and I'm very glad to do it."

Susannah broke in excitedly, "It seems like almost everything we do has *something* to do with the war." Susannah was right. Hoosiers at home and overseas were helping the war effort.

D. Equal Rights for Blacks

During the world wars, southern black people found work in Indiana mills, factories, and shops. They moved to cities along the Ohio River, Great Lakes, and also to Indianapolis. Black men and women provided much-needed labor to help the war effort. Black people also fought as members of the armed forces during both world wars.

The black population grew in Indiana, but there was still discrimination. Besides having separate schools, black people had separate places to live. They had to eat in special restaurants and sit in separate parts of movie theaters. At last, after World War II, black people were no longer required to be separate.

Black people were required to be separate from white people.
▶ What type of building is shown in this picture?

217

E. Changes Brought by Steel

One new industry made a big difference in Indiana. With better roads, people wanted better ways of travel. That meant that cars, trains, and buses needed to be made. These were made of steel, a very hard metal. Since people were beginning to travel by air, airplanes and airplane parts had to be made. These were also made of steel. By now most people had electricity in their homes. So they wanted refrigerators, stoves, and radios. All of these had steel parts. These parts, along with the steel itself, were made in Indiana. New machines to make these parts had to be made. New farm machinery was being produced. Indiana was on its way to becoming an important state for making steel and steel products.

F. Things That Do Not Change

The Changing Landscape With more people and trade, more roads and schools were needed. Indiana's land started looking different. People began seeing changes they did not like. They wanted to preserve the natural beauty of the state.

After World War II, Indiana began to develop state parks and forests. In fact, Indiana became a leader in building state parks. Today, Indiana has 20 state parks.

A Love for Nature Much of the work in preserving trees and plants was done by one man. Charles C. Deam was born the year the Civil War ended. He grew up on a farm in Wells County. He was a hard-working boy who loved nature. His love

Many products are made from steel including those shown here.
▶ What are some other products made from steel?

PRODUCTS MADE FROM STEEL

Bridges

Airplanes

Cars

Tools

Frying Pans

Deam Lake State Recreation Area is named after Indiana's first state forester, Charles Deam.
▶ What did Deam do for Indiana?

for nature never changed. Charlie Deam became Indiana's first state forester. He traveled to every part of the state in his Ford Model T truck. It was both his home and his office. On his travels he identified and listed more than 78,000 plants and trees. Just imagine that!

Today, the Deam Lake State Recreation Area in Clark County bears his name. There is also the Charles Deam National Wilderness Area. It covers 13,000 acres (5,265 ha) in Jackson, Brown, Lawrence, and Monroe counties. These are ways of remembering and thanking Charlie Deam for having a dream and for preserving Indiana's natural beauty for everyone.

LESSON 3 REVIEW

THINK AND WRITE

A. After the Civil War, how did the way people live change?

B. Why did Hoosiers become more interdependent?

C. How did Indiana workers help with both World War I and World War II?

D. When did black people in Indiana gain the right to use the same places as white people?

E. Why did steel making become such an important activity?

F. Why should the people of Indiana be thankful to Charles Deam?

SKILLS CHECK

WRITING SKILL
Study the graph on page 213. When were the urban and rural populations about equal in Indiana? Write your answer in a complete sentence.

USING THE VOCABULARY

Union	Confederacy
slavery	fairness
free state	discrimination
civil war	sharecropper
secede	victory garden

On a separate sheet of paper, write the best word to complete each sentence below. Choose your answers from the vocabulary words above.

1. The 11 Southern states that decided to leave the Union were known as the _____.
2. During World War I, a person who lived in the city might help by planting a _____.
3. Treating all people equally is called _____.
4. The early United States was known as the _____.
5. A person who worked the land but did not own it was called a _____.
6. Treating certain groups of people unfairly is called _____.
7. The practice of owning people is called _____.
8. War between groups of people in the same country is called _____.
9. To leave a group is to _____.
10. In a _____, the practice of slavery was not allowed.

REMEMBERING WHAT YOU READ

Write your answers in complete sentences on a separate sheet of paper.

1. What was the Union?
2. What were the two main causes of the Civil War?
3. When was the Civil War fought?
4. What were two ways that Indiana was involved in the Civil War?
5. How did the United States government help freed slaves?
6. What were the causes of the depression in Indiana?
7. What happened to Indiana's urban population after the Civil War?
8. What does *interdependence* mean?
9. What were suffrage groups?
10. What important industry grew in Indiana during and after the two world wars?

TYING MUSIC TO SOCIAL STUDIES

Slaves often expressed their feelings about slavery through music. Many songs sung by slaves are still sung today. Go to the library and find the words to at least three spirituals. (Examples include "Go Down Moses," "Steal Away," and "Walk With Me.") Study the words and then tell how you think these songs might have expressed the feelings of the slaves.

On some early roads, travelers had to stop and pay a toll. Even today, there are many toll roads.
▶ How did early toll roads work?

placed across roads. Travelers stopped to pay tolls at the pikes. Then the pikes were turned aside, and the traveler passed through.

The National Road was a very fine highway. An endless line of wagons and stagecoaches streamed along it. Riders carrying mail raced on horseback. Farmers used the new road to drive cattle, hogs, and even turkeys to market. They also used it to send wagonloads of grain. Inns grew up along the way. Towns sprang up too.

The old National Road ran through Indianapolis along Washington Street. It continued to Terre Haute and beyond. Today, Highway 40 and Interstate 70 follow the old route. Another highway, the Michigan Road, was important for early travel from north to south. It is now Highway 421.

D. Covered Bridges

Crossing Rivers The rivers of Indiana were a valuable means of transportation for early travelers. People traveled on them in boats. But crossing from one side of a river to the other was not always easy. Building bridges, of course, was the answer to the problem.

Like early roads, the first bridges were built of logs or boards. These soon rotted or were washed away by high waters. Then new bridges had to be built. Crossing bridges was always an adventure. They creaked and swayed. Boards sometimes broke. Then travelers and their wagons were dumped in the often icy rivers. Builders soon found that they could use stones to make the base of the bridge stronger. They put a roof over the bridge to keep it from rotting. Soon covered bridges popped up all over

227

Indiana. These bridges looked like long houses open at each end.

Payment and Uses A toll was sometimes collected to pay for the bridge. A rider on a horse might pay 6 cents to cross. A farmer had to pay 2 cents for each person in the wagon and 13 cents for the horses pulling the wagon. Tolls are still collected at some bridges today. However, they are much higher!

Covered bridges had many uses. In them, a traveler could find shelter from bad weather conditions such as rain and snow. The walls inside the bridge served as a kind of bulletin board. Papers were posted there that told of community news. But covered bridges could be scary too. Robbers sometimes waited in the darkness for travelers.

Warnings to Users Most covered bridges had warning signs like this one. Why, do you think, were the signs needed?

$5 FINE FOR RIDING OR DRIVING OVER BRIDGE FASTER THAN A WALK
$20 FINE FOR DRIVING OVER THIS BRIDGE WITH MORE THAN 20 HORSES OR CATTLE AT ONCE
$5 FINE FOR CARRYING FIRE OVER OR UNDER THIS BRIDGE IN AN UNCLOSED VESSEL

Covered bridges were often built across Indiana's rivers. Many of the bridges still exist in Indiana today.
▶ What were some uses for covered bridges?

Many covered bridges remain today. Parke County alone has 34 covered bridges. That is why it is known as the Covered Bridge Capital of America. Every year in October, Parke County holds a Covered Bridge Festival in Rockville.

E. The Horseless Carriage

In the mid-1800s, Indiana was a leader in making horse-drawn wagons. Hoosier-built wagons could be found all over the United States. In time, change came. Automobiles, called horseless carriages, replaced travel by wagon and stagecoach. The state and the country would never be the same again.

One of the first cars was built by Elwood Haynes in Kokomo. At one time more than 200 makes of autos were being built in Indiana! Many were just carriages with engines.

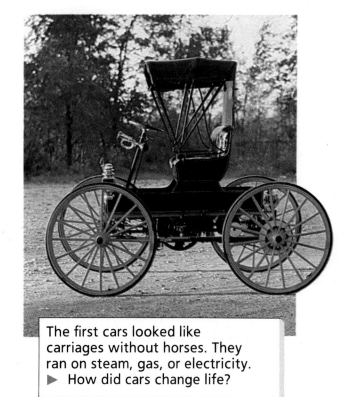

The first cars looked like carriages without horses. They ran on steam, gas, or electricity.
► How did cars change life?

Most soon disappeared. Still, Indiana was an important leader in the early days of the automobile. You can see many of the old cars in a museum in Auburn.

LESSON **1** *REVIEW*

THINK AND WRITE

A. How would you describe the trails that early people in Indiana traveled on?
B. How did early Hoosiers improve on wooden roads?
C. How did turnpikes get their name?
D. Why were covered bridges built?
E. What is another name for the horseless carriage?

SKILLS CHECK

MAP SKILL

Look at the map on page 356. Each large highway has a number that gives a clue to its direction. List the numbers of five roads that go north and south and of five roads that go east and west. Look at the last number in each one. How are the numbers in each group alike?

Traveling by Water and Rail

THINK ABOUT WHAT YOU KNOW

What problems did early Hoosiers have with water transportation?

STUDY THE VOCABULARY

flatboat	canal
keelboat	tow
freight	lock

FOCUS YOUR READING

In what ways have both water and rail transportation helped Indiana grow?

A. Ways of Travel Along Indiana's Rivers

One Way Only   Jeremy Smith loved to hear his father tell about moving to Indiana. His father had been 16 years old in 1810. In that year his family had come down the Ohio River on a flatboat. The base of this boat was shaped like a rectangle. On top of that was a rough cabin. The family ate, slept, and worked on the boat. It was their home until they built a log house on the banks of the Ohio River.

Then they used the flatboat to ship grain and hogs to market. The flatboat had one problem. It could only travel downstream. After finishing a trip, the flatboat was broken up and sold for wood. The family had to build another one when they had another shipment ready.

Transporting Freight   After a few years, the Smiths built a keelboat to haul their freight, or goods. The keelboat was long and narrow and easier to steer than the flatboat. It had another advantage over the flatboat. Keelboats could travel upstream — with the help of sails and poles. Jeremy's father said, "I was one of the eight pole men. There were four on each side. We each had a pole that reached the river bottom.

A flatboat had a rectangular base with a cabin on top.
▶ What was the major disadvantage with flatboats?

We placed one end of the pole on the river bottom. We then pushed the top of the pole with our shoulders as we walked down the deck. This moved the boat upstream. Then my father would yell 'Shift!' Quickly we all had to run back up the boat. We were supposed to get our poles down before the boat floated back downstream. It was hard work!"

Jeremy rubbed his arms, imagining the ache after a hard trip up the river. His father continued, "Our farm was very close to the river. For several years, our crops were washed out when the river overflowed its banks. Then we decided to move inland."

Jeremy broke in eagerly. "That's when you married Mother and bought this farm just south of Brookville, right?"

His father smiled. "Yes. The new land was very rich. We grew much more than our family needed. We wanted to sell some of our crops. But we had no way to get them to market except by wagon. Bridges washed out. Wagons became stuck in the mud. And tolls were high on the turnpikes."

"Did you ever think about giving up, Papa?" asked Jeremy.

"Oh, no! We were pioneers. We didn't run away from our problems. We looked for ways to solve them."

Keelboats were a big improvement over flatboats. Keelboats could travel upstream.
▶ How were keelboats propelled?

B. Digging the Canals

Jeremy's father said, "We farmers began to complain. We wanted easier, cheaper, and faster ways to ship our products to market. Merchants (MUR chunts), or storekeepers, joined us. They wanted an easier way to get products to their stores. The state decided to solve the problem by building canals (kuh-NALZ)." A canal is a narrow, water-filled ditch that people have dug across land. It often connects large natural waterways, such as rivers. Canals would allow the farmers and merchants who did not live along rivers to send and receive their goods by water.

Jeremy's father smiled. "Jeremy, you already know the story of *our* canal."

Yes, Jeremy remembered well. He was only six years old when he watched the men dig the big ditch close to the Smith farm. He had heard that soon Indiana—north to south and east to west—would be connected with four long canals. Not all of the canals were actually built, but those canals that were built moved people and goods.

C. Canals Carrying People and Freight

Travel on the Canal Months went by. In 1839 Jeremy and his father

Canal boats were pulled by horses that walked alongside the canal.
▶ Why were canals important to farmers and merchants?

watched excitedly as the first canal boat came into view! Horses **towed,** or pulled, the flat-bottomed boat along the canal. The horses walked along tow paths beside the canal. On the boat were people and freight. This was a happy day for farmers and merchants!

One day Jeremy and his father were among the people on the canal boat. Jeremy studied the mills and large storehouses that had been built along the canal banks. The most exciting part of the trip on the canal was going through the **locks.** Locks are gates that help boats go up and down as the land becomes higher or lower.

Jeremy and his father were going south, in the direction of the Ohio River. The elevation, or height, of the land gets lower as you approach the river. Father and son watched their boat float up to a gate. A man collected the toll at the gate. Then a gate behind the boat closed. Suddenly, Jeremy was aware that the water level was going down. It stopped at a certain point. Then the front gate opened. The canal boat floated out on the new, lower level of water. This happened several times during the trip.

"Papa, how do you think the boat will get up when we come back?" Jeremy asked.

HOW A LOCK WORKS

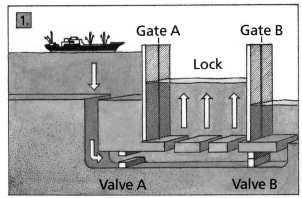

Water moving through Valve A raises the water level in the lock.

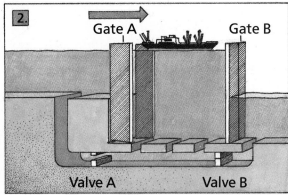

Gate A opens, and the ship moves into the lock.

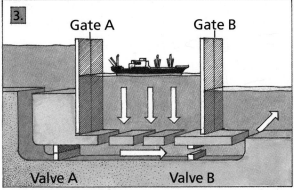

After Gate A closes, water is drained from the lock through Valve B.

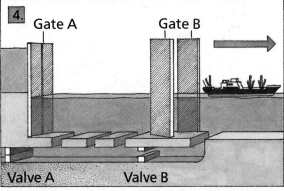

Gate B opens, and the ship leaves the lock.

This diagram shows how canal locks operate. The water level in the lock is raised and then lowered as the ship moves through.
▶ Why are canal locks necessary?

"Everything will work in reverse, Jeremy. We will go into a lock. The gate will close, and the water will rise. When the water has risen enough, the front gate will open. The boat will float out onto the higher water level." Jeremy could hardly wait to go back up the canal!

The End of Canal Travel Sadly, the canals were not a success. In winter the water froze. The wooden locks rotted. Tow paths along the banks washed away. Tolls alone could not pay for repairs. The state of Indiana was in debt from having built the canals. When Jeremy stood by the big ditch some years later, he saw no boats, no horses, no freight, and no people. But canals have not been forgotten. Each year, the people in Wabash hold a Canal Days Festival in July.

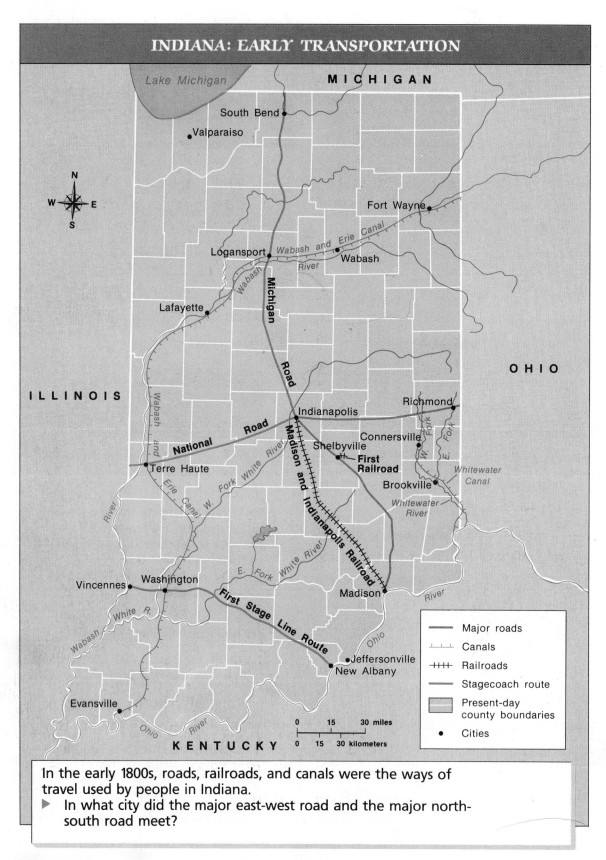

INDIANA: EARLY TRANSPORTATION

MICHIGAN

Lake Michigan

South Bend
Valparaiso

Fort Wayne

Logansport · Wabash and Erie Canal · Wabash
Wabash River

Lafayette

OHIO

ILLINOIS

Michigan Road

Richmond

Indianapolis
Connersville
Shelbyville
National Road
First Railroad
Terre Haute
Brookville

Madison and Indianapolis Railroad

W. Fork White River

W. Fork

E. Fork

Whitewater Canal

Whitewater River

Wabash and Erie Canal River

E. Fork White River

Vincennes Washington
First Stage Line Route

Madison

River

Wabash White R.

Ohio

Jeffersonville
New Albany

Evansville

Ohio River

KENTUCKY

Legend	
———	Major roads
⊢⊥⊢	Canals
┼┼┼┼	Railroads
———	Stagecoach route
▧	Present-day county boundaries
•	Cities

0   15   30 miles
0   15   30 kilometers

In the early 1800s, roads, railroads, and canals were the ways of travel used by people in Indiana.

▶ In what city did the major east-west road and the major north-south road meet?

234

D. The Age of Steam

Building Steamboats In the 1800s, the cheapest way to travel was by water. But flatboats, keelboats, and canal boats were slow-moving. There was another kind of boat that was powered by steam. In 1811, even before Indiana became a state, the first steamboat appeared on the Ohio River.

The steamboat did not help people like Jeremy's family. This is because it was a "high-river" boat. Unlike earlier flat-bottomed boats, the steamboat could sail only in deep water. The two largest rivers within Indiana—the Wabash and the White rivers—were not deep enough. Therefore, the Ohio River became the steamboat river.

Two Indiana towns on the Ohio River became famous for building steamboats. The fastest and most beautiful steamboats were built in New Albany and Jeffersonville. Jeffersonville alone built more than 2,000 steamboats. Between 1830 and 1860, New Albany also built many boats. One of them was the famous *Robert E. Lee*.

Regular steamboat service was established on the Ohio and Mississippi rivers around 1817.
▶ How did these boats move through the water?

Steamboats could go upstream as well as down. Big paddles on the sides or back pushed the steamboat through the water. The paddle wheels were turned by steam.

Floating Hotels Steamboats carried passengers and freight from Pittsburgh, Pennsylvania, to New Orleans, Louisiana. Some steamboats were like beautiful floating hotels. These were richly decorated with tall mirrors, velvet carpets, and beautiful wood carvings. Others were showboats. These were like floating theaters. People who lived along the river rushed to see the shows when they heard the boat whistle blow. The arrival of a steamboat was always an exciting event.

Every September, the people of Jeffersonville celebrate this exciting way to travel with the Steamboat Days Festival. You can learn many interesting things about old steamboats in the Howard Steamboat Museum in Jeffersonville.

E. New Ways to Travel on Land

Travel Problems Traveling on the early roads was difficult. Early boats were difficult to operate. What was the answer for cheap and easy transportation? Railroads!

The first railroad in Indiana was opened on July 4, 1834. It was located near Shelbyville, southeast of Indianapolis. The tracks were only a little more than a mile long, and they went nowhere. A horse pulled the one car along the small track. This little railroad was built for fun. Yet it was the start of something bigger.

A Steam Engine in Indiana Four years later, a real railroad was started. It took nine years to lay the tracks between Madison and Indianapolis. Finally, in 1847, a steam engine puffed into the capital. There was much celebrating in Indianapolis! The trip by stagecoach from Madison to Indianapolis took four days. The train had made it in five hours! During the 1850s, 2,000 miles (3,218 km) of tracks were laid across Indiana. Still, the building of railroads also had problems.

Some steamboats had many rooms that were beautifully decorated.
▶ What do you think this room was used for?

F. Working Together to Build Railroads

Building Railroads Building railroads costs a lot of money. Indiana had lost money on canals. The state was afraid to start spending more money for railroads. Companies started their own railroads. A company is a group of people who work together for a common purpose. Companies also find sources of money. Railroad companies paid for rails, engines, and boxcars. They paid workers to lay tracks. Many people from Germany and Ireland came to work on the railroads. Some of your ancestors may have come to Indiana at that time.

Some farmers wanted to be part of the railroad companies. They helped lay tracks and cut wood for fuel. Early engines needed a lot of wood to heat water for steam. Engines had to stop often to take on water and wood. Stations grew up at these stops. Soon many people were part of the railroad companies.

The Great Union Station During the week, trains hauled chickens, pigs, horses, and cattle. On the weekends, benches were placed on the cars so that people could ride. Soon railroads grew. Tracks reached out from Indiana to the east, west, north, and south. A great station for all railroad companies was built in

The city of Indianapolis is home to Union Station. This station was opened in 1853.
▶ Why was Union Station built?

East view of Union Station, Indianapolis, in the late 1850's

Trains are celebrated during the annual Iron Horse Festival.
▶ Why do you think the early trains were called iron horses?

Indianapolis. It was called Union Station. It opened in 1853. Union Station was the first station in the United States to unite all companies.

People and freight were carried to many places from Union Station.

By now you know that Hoosiers love festivals. There is one for railroads too. It is the Iron Horse Festival, held in Logansport in July. People called the train the iron horse in the early days of railroads.

LESSON *2* REVIEW

THINK AND WRITE

A. In what way was a keelboat better than a flatboat?

B. In what ways does a canal differ from a river?

C. Why do some canals need locks?

D. Why did the Ohio River become the steamboat river?

E. How were railroads better than stagecoaches for travel?

F. Why were companies needed to build railroads?

SKILLS CHECK

THINKING SKILL

Look over the story of the Smith family in this lesson. Then use the map on page 234 to figure out the name of the canal built near the Smith farm.

Traveling Around and Above the Earth

THINK ABOUT WHAT YOU KNOW

From what you have learned about the geography of Indiana, how can Indiana be called a great seaport state?

STUDY THE VOCABULARY

international   **maritime**

FOCUS YOUR READING

Why have Indiana and its capital become transportation centers for the nation and the world?

A. A Crossroads of America

Transportation Hub Indianapolis, the capital city, has become a city where many roads meet. Indianapolis can be reached easily from any direction, since it is in the center of the state. It is located on a flat plain. Therefore, roads and railroads can be built easily. Indianapolis is known as America's Interstate Capital. You have learned about its first two interstates—the Michigan Road and the National Road. Today, Interstates 65, 69, 70, 74, and 465 cross and circle the city of Indianapolis. Airplanes fly in and out of Indianapolis's **international** (ihn tur-NASH uh nul) airport. *International* means "between nations."

Transportation Center The capital city has become a main transportation center for people traveling by land and air. Indianapolis is not a water transportation center. The White River is not deep enough for large ships. But the state of Indiana does have three very important centers that are located on bodies of water. These bodies of water are connected to oceans.

B. Indiana Seaports

Large oceangoing ships carry freight to and from Indiana all the time. How is that possible? Indiana

The international airport in Indianapolis connects Indiana to the rest of the world.
► Why are airports near cities?

is in the middle of the United States and does not touch an ocean. Look at Lake Michigan on the map on pages 354–355. From the Atlantic Ocean trace the route ships would take to Lake Michigan.

At the southern tip of Lake Michigan is Burns Harbor. It is near the Indiana Dunes National Lakeshore. This deep-water port is located where Native Americans and the French once traded furs. Today, people of Indiana trade there with all parts of the world.

Indiana has two more harbors —both in the southern part of the state. Southwinds **Maritime** Center is near Evansville. **Maritime** means "near the water." This port is on the Ohio River, but oceangoing ships can reach the ocean by way of the Mississippi River and the Gulf of Mexico. The ships carry grain, coal, and oil products.

Near Jeffersonville is Indiana's third and newest port—Clark Maritime Center. This port is also on the Ohio River. Today, boats and barges are built there. Many kinds of products and goods—from grain to auto parts—are loaded on ships to be sent to other places.

C. Air and Space Pioneers

Indiana has always been proud of its pioneers. These also include pioneers of air and space travel. Wilbur Wright was born in 1867 on a small farm near New Castle. Two years later, the Wright family moved to Dayton, Ohio.

Burns Harbor lets oceangoing ships travel to and from Indiana.
▶ On what body of water is Burns Harbor located?

Wilbur and his brother Orville began building gliders as well as airplanes with motors. They tried out their inventions on the dunes at Kitty Hawk, North Carolina.

It was 10:35 in the morning on December 17, 1903. Orville Wright was lying on his stomach in a plane named the *Flyer*. The tips of his shoes were hooked over one edge of the lower wing. He wore very ordinary clothing on this special day. He had on a business suit, a tie, and a cap. The first airplane flight in history was recorded by camera. Orville flew 120 feet (37 m) for 12 seconds. It was a small beginning, but the brothers did not give up. They built model after model. After much work, they flew for over half an hour. Their first plane is now in the National Air and Space Museum in Washington, D.C. Indiana is proud of its first air pioneers. There is a Wilbur Wright State Memorial at his birthplace near New Castle.

Gus Grissom was the second American to orbit the earth.
▶ What happened to his capsule on his first flight?

D. The Boy Who Wanted the Moon

Space Pioneer Indiana's space pioneer was Virgil Ivan Grissom. Everyone called him Gus. He was born in Mitchell, a small town in southern Indiana. It is near Spring Mill Park.

As a boy, Gus was curious about anything that could fly. He liked to read about the Wright brothers. Sometimes he was late for school when he stopped to watch birds in the sky above.

Gus did not always get everything he wanted. Like many Hoosier boys and girls, he always wanted to play basketball. However, Gus was too small to play.

Test Pilot Grissom Gus joined the Air Force and became a test pilot. That is, he flew planes to see whether they were safe. About this time, a space program was started by a group in the government called National Aeronautics and Space Administration (NASA). Good pilots were needed to fly in space. They were called astronauts. In many ways, these astronauts were like the pioneers of early Indiana. They were to explore space by flying a spaceship, or capsule, to the moon.

Gus wanted to be one of the astronauts who would go to the moon. He was just one of hundreds of pilots who wanted the same thing. Seven men were chosen. Gus was one! He started training to fly the capsule.

Gus was now glad to be small. He could easily fit into the space capsule. He was very careful when testing the capsules. If they were not just right, he said so. He wanted the moon trip to be safe.

Space Flights   Finally, the day came when Gus flew high above the earth. Then he landed in the ocean just as planned. Suddenly, he was in trouble. The capsule was sinking.

Gus escaped, but he lost his capsule in the ocean. Gus never gave up. He gave his next capsule the nickname of *Unsinkable Molly Brown*. He orbited, or flew around, the earth in it three times. When it landed in the ocean, *Molly Brown* did not sink.

A Tragedy   On January 27, 1967, Gus and two other astronauts were testing the capsule that was to go to the moon. It was called *Apollo I*. Gus did not feel that *Apollo I* was safe. He was right. Suddenly, someone yelled, "Fire!" In 20 seconds, the three astronauts were dead in their space capsule.

Other spaceships were tested again and again. More than two years after the fire, *Apollo II* took the

Gus Grissom spent 15 minutes in space on his first flight.
▶ Why do you think capsules were landed in the ocean?

first team of astronauts to the moon. Gus Grissom did not make that trip, but he had helped others take their first steps there safely.

E. Remembering a Special Space Pioneer

People in Indiana wanted Gus Grissom to be remembered. A state memorial was built in Spring Mill Park. In the memorial stands the *Unsinkable Molly Brown*. Beside it is Gus's space suit. Nearby in Mitchell is another memorial. Children of Indiana gave their money to pay for it. The memorial is shaped like a spaceship. It is cut from Indiana limestone. It sits on eight tablets of stone. Each tablet tells part of the story of Gus's life.

Gus Grissom has been remembered in other ways too. An air force base was named after him. Indiana

This memorial to Gus Grissom is located in Mitchell. It is shaped like a spaceship.
▶ Who paid for the memorial?

astronomers discovered a small planet and named it Grissom for Indiana's first space pioneer.

LESSON **3** REVIEW

THINK AND WRITE

A. Why is Indianapolis called a transportation center?

B. What are the names of the three Indiana harbors?

C. Why do Hoosiers honor air pioneer Wilbur Wright?

D. In what way did Gus Grissom help the United States send astronauts to the moon?

E. What are two ways Hoosiers remember Gus Grissom?

SKILLS CHECK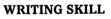

WRITING SKILL

Look at the time line on page 224. When did Gus Grissom make his first space flight? How many years later did he orbit the earth? Write your answers in complete sentences.

243

AIR TRAVEL THROUGH THE TIMES

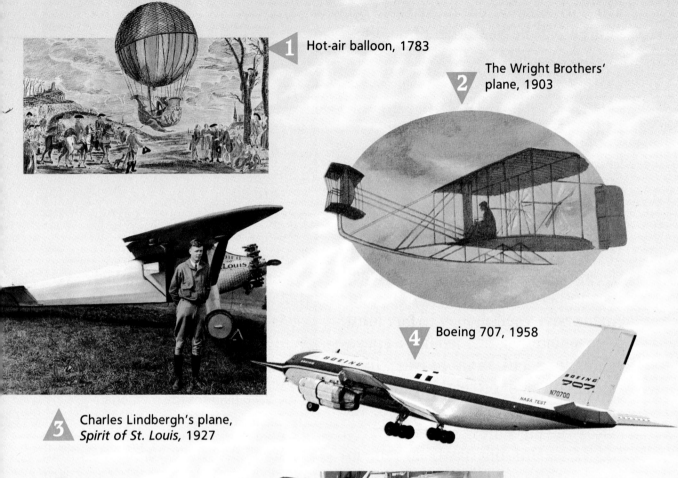

1 Hot-air balloon, 1783

2 The Wright Brothers' plane, 1903

4 Boeing 707, 1958

3 Charles Lindbergh's plane, *Spirit of St. Louis,* 1927

5 Gus Grissom's space capsule, *Liberty Bell,* 1961

6 Space shuttle, 1981

Compared with some types of transportation, air travel is relatively new. It has developed over the last 200 years. These pictures show how air travel has changed in many ways. Indiana is the birthplace of two important pioneers in air travel—Wilbur Wright and Gus Grissom.

▶ What are some of the ways in which air travel has changed?

USING THE VOCABULARY

transportation	freight
corduroy road	canal
plank road	lock
interstate	international
toll	maritime

On a separate sheet of paper, write the word that best matches each definition below. Choose your answers from the vocabulary words above.

1. money paid by travelers for the use of a road
2. a road made of flat boards
3. a narrow, water-filled ditch dug across land
4. ways of travel
5. near the water
6. between states
7. goods
8. one of a series of gates in a canal that help boats go up or down as land becomes higher or lower
9. a road made by laying logs side by side across a trail
10. between nations

REMEMBERING WHAT YOU READ

Write your answers in complete sentences on a separate sheet of paper.

1. Who or what made the very first trails across Indiana?
2. Why were gravel roads better than corduroy and plank roads?
3. How did turnpikes get their name?
4. How was Indiana a leader in land transportation in the mid-1800s?
5. What is the difference between a flatboat and a keelboat?
6. Why was the canal system in Indiana unsuccessful?
7. What two Indiana towns became famous for building steamboats?
8. What was special about Union Station in Indianapolis?
9. How can Indiana, an inland state, have three harbors?
10. Who was Virgil I. Grissom?

TYING LANGUAGE ARTS TO SOCIAL STUDIES: WRITING TO LEARN

Many important inventions have changed the way people travel. Look back through this chapter to find out about these inventions. Choose one invention to research. Go to your school library and use encyclopedias or other books to find out things that you have not learned before. Write a paragraph in which you describe at least two interesting facts about the invention. Share what you learned with the class.

THINKING CRITICALLY

Write your answers in complete sentences on a separate sheet of paper.

1. How did the National Road help people in Indiana?
2. Why did Indiana farmers and merchants want canals to be built?
3. Why could steamboats not travel on the Wabash and White rivers?
4. What were some ways that the railroads changed Indiana?
5. What are some of the reasons why Lake Michigan and the Ohio River are important to Indiana's trade with other nations?

SUMMARIZING THE CHAPTER

On a separate sheet of paper draw a graphic organizer that is like the one shown here. Copy the information from this graphic organizer to the one you have drawn. Under the main idea for each lesson, write three statements that support it. The first one has been done for you.

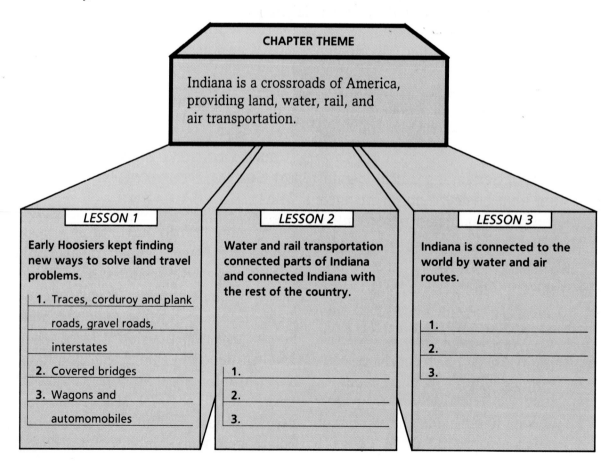

CHAPTER THEME

Indiana is a crossroads of America, providing land, water, rail, and air transportation.

LESSON 1

Early Hoosiers kept finding new ways to solve land travel problems.

1. Traces, corduroy and plank roads, gravel roads, interstates
2. Covered bridges
3. Wagons and automomobiles

LESSON 2

Water and rail transportation connected parts of Indiana and connected Indiana with the rest of the country.

1.
2.
3.

LESSON 3

Indiana is connected to the world by water and air routes.

1.
2.
3.

UNIT 4 INDIANA TODAY AND TOMORROW

The many varied industries in Indiana help keep the state growing. A bright and promising future lies ahead for Indiana.

▲ Education has always been important to the people of Indiana.

▲

There is something enjoyable for everyone to see and do in Indiana.

CHAPTER 10

THE RICHNESS OF INDIANA

*I*ndiana has good soil and valuable mineral resources. These things have allowed it to become an important farming and manufacturing state. Indiana has enough water for the needs of the state.

Farms and Farm Animals

THINK ABOUT WHAT YOU KNOW

Make a list of some foods you eat that may have been grown in Indiana.

STUDY THE VOCABULARY

natural resource   **cultivate**
fertile   **erosion**
organic

FOCUS YOUR READING

Why is Indiana a rich and productive state?

A. The Riches of Indiana

Rich in Many Ways "Are we rich, Mom?" Megan asked her mother this question as they hiked through the woods that were near their home in Brown County.

Her mother looked puzzled, then smiled. "Well, that depends on what you mean, Megan. Maybe you are asking if we have a lot of money. The answer to that is no, although we have enough. But we are rich in other ways. Your father and I love you very much. We enjoy living here, where we can hike through the hills whenever we want. We have good food to eat and many good friends. There are many different ways to be rich."

Indiana's Resources Indiana is a rich state. This does not mean that everyone in Indiana has lots of money. But Indiana is rich in **natural resources**. A natural resource is something that is useful to people and is provided by nature. Natural resources are found on and beneath the surface of the earth.

People use natural resources to grow food and make goods. The soil and the water are natural resources. The forests that provide timber and the coal that is used for fuel are also natural resources. There are many others too. The rocks that make up

The soil in Indiana is good for growing crops. Soil is an important natural resource.
► What is a natural resource?

the land are also natural resources. Some of them, such as limestone, are used for building. Clay from the earth is used for making pottery, bricks, and cement.

B. Soil for Farming

The soil has always been one of Indiana's most important natural resources. The soil allows farmers to grow good crops that keep people healthy. Almost all of our food comes from the soil.

Indiana has a great deal of rich, fertile soil. Fertile soil is soil that is good for growing crops. Soil is made up of tiny pieces of rock, rotting plants, and water. Fertile soil has a lot of plant waste. We call this plant waste organic (or GAN ihk) matter. Indiana also has some poor soil that is not often cultivated (KUL tuh vayt ed). To *cultivate* means "to prepare the land for growing crops."

The best soil in Indiana lies in the region called the Till Plains. This region contains the largest farming area in Indiana. Turn to the map of the regions of Indiana on page 47 and find the Till Plains. Another place with fertile soil is the Wabash lowland, found in the region called the Southern Hills and Lowlands. The Wabash lowland is in the southwestern corner of that region along the Wabash River.

C. Farming in Indiana

Agricultural Giant   Farmers in Indiana today grow some of the same crops as the first settlers did. Today, however, their tools are very different. The first farmers used only a simple plow pulled by a horse or a mule. Most farmers today use tractors. Their crops are gathered in by machines. Because of better farming methods, farmers can grow bigger and better crops than in the past. That is why Indiana can help feed people in the rest of the country and all over the world.

What crops do you find in the fields of Indiana? Corn is the most important crop. Farmers plant corn in May, when the frosts are over. They harvest it in the fall. Most of the corn is fed to cattle and hogs.

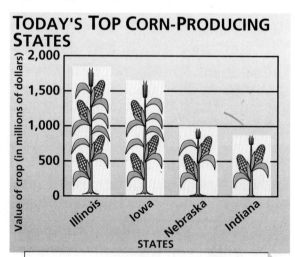

TODAY'S TOP CORN-PRODUCING STATES

Indiana is one of the four top corn-producing states.
▶ What is the value of the corn crop in Indiana?

Indiana is the fourth largest grower of corn in the United States.

The Popcorn Capital One of the products made from corn is a popular snack—popcorn. Several places in Indiana are famous for their popcorn. Orville Redenbacher is known as the Popcorn King. He was born on a farm in Brazil, Indiana. Today, his special brand of popcorn is made in Valparaiso (val puh RAY zoh). It is the best-selling brand in the United States. The town of Van Buren is also known for making popcorn. Every year in Van Buren there is a Popcorn Festival. During the festival, there is even a special football game called the Popcorn Bowl!

Hoosier farmers also grow soybeans. Soybean meal is used to feed farm animals and pets. Soybean oil

Soybeans are a very important crop in Indiana.
▶ What is Indiana's rank in soybean production?

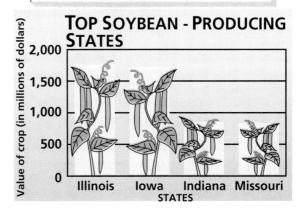

TOP SOYBEAN - PRODUCING STATES

is used to make candles and soap. Indiana is third in the production of soybeans in the country. Wheat and hay for animals are other important crops grown in Indiana.

Soybeans are used to make many different products, including those shown here.
▶ What else is soybean used for?

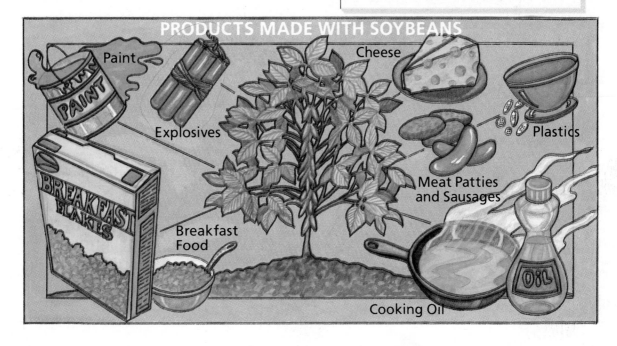

PRODUCTS MADE WITH SOYBEANS

Paint

Cheese

Explosives

Plastics

Meat Patties and Sausages

Breakfast Food

Cooking Oil

D. Taking Care of the Soil

Soil takes a very long time to form, but it can be destroyed quickly. It can be washed away by the rain and blown away by the wind. The loss of soil in these ways is called **erosion** (ee ROH zhun). Erosion is the biggest danger to soil resources. People can do things to help prevent erosion.

Matthew's parents own a grocery store. They get some of their fresh vegetables from Anna's father. He is a farmer. Let's listen in on a conversation taking place between Matthew and Anna.

"My mother says that your father is one of the best farmers in the county," Matthew said. "Why do you think she says that?"

"It's because my dad protects the soil. For example, he doesn't grow the same crop in one field year after year. He rotates the crops. That way, the parts of the soil that feed the plants don't get used up."

Matthew thought for a moment. "But I notice that he always has *something* planted in each field. Sometimes it's just grass."

"Dad does that to prevent water and wind erosion. The leaves of the plants break the fall of the rain. The roots drink in the rain and hold the soil together. Then water can't wash the soil away and wind can't blow it away," Anna said.

"I bet that's why he plows the way he does, too," said Matthew eagerly. "He never plows up and down a slope. I guess that would allow rain to wash the soil away. He always plows across the slope." What Matthew is talking about is called contour plowing.

"You're exactly right, Matthew!" Anna said with a grin. "Hey, you just might make a good farmer. My dad sure could use some help with the crops!"

Soil can be destroyed through erosion. However, farmers can prevent soil erosion in several ways, including contour plowing.
▶ What is contour plowing?

E. Indiana Farm Animals

Indiana Livestock Indiana farmers not only grow crops. They also raise cattle and hogs. Indiana is a very important state for farm animals. What are some food products that come from cattle? The most important foods are milk and meat.

You know that milk comes from the dairy cow. Many farms in Indiana are dairy farms. Milk from these farms is shipped to plants where it is made ready to be sold in local stores. Some of the milk is used to make butter and cheese.

Products from Livestock Cattle also provide us with beef. Many beef cattle are fed on corn grown in Indiana. Other farmers raise hogs. Hogs also eat corn and provide bacon and ham. You can see that Indiana is an important farm state.

There are many dairy farms found in Indiana.
▶ What are some products made from milk?

LESSON **1** *REVIEW*

THINK AND WRITE

A. What are two natural resources found in Indiana?
B. Which of the regions of Indiana has the largest area of land that is good for farming?
C. How is farming today different from the way that it was in pioneer times?
D. How can farmers prevent erosion?

E. What foods come from Indiana's farm animals?

SKILLS CHECK

THINKING SKILL

What do you think might happen to the soil if Indiana farmers did not protect it? Write your answer using complete sentences.

259

Water Resources and Mineral Resources

THINK ABOUT WHAT YOU KNOW

Think about all the things you did yesterday. Make a list of all the ways you used water.

STUDY THE VOCABULARY

irrigation	mine
reservoir	surface mining
seam	quarry

FOCUS YOUR READING

How are Indiana's water and mineral resources used for living and working?

A. Water for Home and Work

Water Needs   Water is one of Indiana's most important resources. Besides its rivers, the state has many, many lakes. When rain falls, it helps keep the lakes and rivers at a good level. Sometimes you may think that we have too much rain, especially if you have to cancel a picnic or baseball game. In most years, however, Indiana's farms, industries, and people need every inch.

Without rain, the land would become so dry that crops could not grow. To be sure that their crops get enough water, farmers in Indiana use irrigation (ihr uh GAY shun).

Irrigation is a way of bringing water to the fields through pipes and canals. You have probably seen irrigation sprinklers at work in the fields. These irrigation sprinklers help water the crops.

Water Supplies   Hoosiers need water in their homes and in the places where they work. How much water do you think you use in a day? Think about taking showers or baths, washing clothing, and washing dishes. Believe it or not, you probably use about 70 gallons (265 liters) each day!

This irrigation system brings water to the fields. The water is carried through pipes and canals.
► Why is irrigation important?

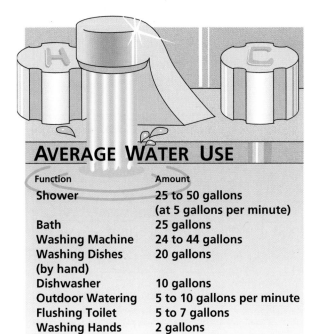

AVERAGE WATER USE

Function	Amount
Shower	25 to 50 gallons (at 5 gallons per minute)
Bath	25 gallons
Washing Machine	24 to 44 gallons
Washing Dishes (by hand)	20 gallons
Dishwasher	10 gallons
Outdoor Watering	5 to 10 gallons per minute
Flushing Toilet	5 to 7 gallons
Washing Hands	2 gallons
Brushing Teeth	2 gallons
Drinking	2 to 3 quarts
Average Amount Used Per Person Each Day: About 70 gallons	

Each person uses about 70 gallons of water in one day.
▶ How much water do you use when you take a bath?

Where does all this water come from? Some of it comes from wells sunk deep into the earth. But most of it is brought by pipes from **reservoirs** (REZ ur vwahrz). A reservoir is a place where water is stored before it is needed. Then the water can be pumped to cities and towns and into people's homes. Everyone wants to have enough water to use every day. And, of course, everyone wants the water to be clean. It is up to all Hoosiers and all Americans to avoid wasting water and making our streams and lakes dirty.

B. Coal Under the Ground

Mineral Resources The United States produces many valuable mineral resources. Two of them are found in large quantities in Indiana. They are coal and limestone.

Mineral resources are different from soil. If farmers take care of the soil, it will go on producing crops forever. But once a mineral resource is taken from the earth and used, it cannot be replaced. There is less coal left in Indiana this year than there was last year. How long will the coal in Indiana last? The answer depends on how much coal is in the earth and on how much of it is dug out each year.

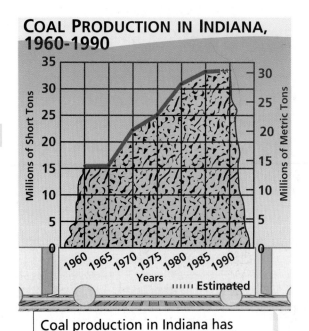

COAL PRODUCTION IN INDIANA, 1960-1990

Coal production in Indiana has increased over the years.
▶ About how much coal was produced in Indiana in 1985?

261

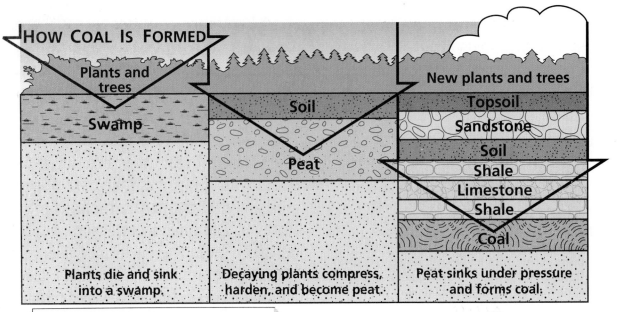

HOW COAL IS FORMED

Plants and trees

Swamp

Plants die and sink into a swamp.

Soil

Peat

Decaying plants compress, harden, and become peat.

New plants and trees

Topsoil
Sandstone
Soil
Shale
Limestone
Shale
Coal

Peat sinks under pressure and forms coal.

Decaying plants and trees form peat. This is an early stage in the formation of coal.
▶ What happens next?

How did coal get in the ground in the first place? It began to form many millions of years ago. Today, coal is found in **seams**. Seams are level bands of coal under the earth. The seams may be a few inches thick or many feet thick. Some seams have to be reached by **mines**. These are tunnels or pits that go deep into the earth. Mining is dangerous. Today, mine owners, workers, and the government work together to try to make mining safer.

Mining Indiana Coal In Indiana much of the coal lies close to the surface. Large power shovels remove the soil and then dig out this coal. This is called **surface mining**.

The coal is put into railroad cars and taken away. Then it can be used for power and heating.

In the past, surface mining harmed the land. The top layers of soil were taken away and not replaced. Erosion took away any soil that was left there. Nothing was able to grow where surface mining had taken place.

Surface mining is now less harmful to the land. The soil is replaced after the coal is removed.
▶ Why is the soil replaced?

Today, most mining companies are much more careful. When they begin to work in a place, they save the soil. Then, after they have removed the coal, they put the soil back. The companies plant trees, bushes, or grass in the soil to keep rain and wind from carrying it away. Careful mining companies work to avoid wasting one of Indiana's most valuable resources — soil.

C. The Best Limestone

Building Blocks Indiana has a huge supply of building stone called limestone. Much of it is found in Monroe and Lawrence counties in southern Indiana. Indiana limestone is one of the finest building stones found in the United States. Limestone from Indiana was used to build the Empire State Building in New York City! Although limestone is easy to carve, it is very hard and lasts for a long time.

Cut from Quarries Like coal, limestone comes from the remains

Limestone is mined from pits in the earth. Indiana limestone has been used for many buildings, including the Empire State Building.
▶ Where is most of Indiana's limestone?

PRODUCTS MADE FROM LIMESTONE

Bricks

Ceramics

Toothpaste

Rubber

Glass

Materials for Highways

There are many different uses for limestone besides buildings. Indiana limestone is used to make glue, glass, and rubber.
▶ What are some other products made from limestone?

of plants and animals that lived long ago. The plants and animals that formed limestone lived in the water. Water covered this area long ago. Today, limestone is taken out of **quarries**, which are large pits in the earth. Indiana quarries produce about three fifths of the limestone in the United States. Besides being used for buildings, limestone is used to make cement, glass, and road coverings. Indiana limestone is shipped to places all over the United States and to other countries as well.

LESSON 2 REVIEW

THINK AND WRITE

A. Why do Indiana farmers use irrigation in their fields?

B. How would you compare old ways of surface mining with modern ways?

C. Why is Indiana limestone so widely used?

SKILLS CHECK

MAP SKILL

Look at the map on page 356. Name two rivers that are within Indiana or lie along its border. Then name five lakes that are in Indiana or that border the state.

Forests and Wildlife

THINK ABOUT WHAT YOU KNOW

Make a list of the kinds of trees that grow near your school or home. How many of these trees remain green all through the year? How many of these trees shed their leaves each fall?

STUDY THE VOCABULARY

deciduous   **migrate**
evergreen   **conservation**

FOCUS YOUR READING

Why are Indiana's forests one of the state's important resources?

A. Indiana's Forests

Into the Woods The Colby family's flatboat floated down the Ohio River in 1815. The Colbys settled in southwestern Indiana. They found their new home covered with forests. Soon the Colbys and their neighbors cut down trees and used the wood to build homes, wagons, furniture, and tools. Where they had settled, the land was fertile. They plowed the land and grew crops.

Not all the land in southern Indiana was fertile. In areas where the soil was not good for crops, forests were left untouched. That is why large areas of southern Indiana still have many forests.

Types of Trees Most of the trees in Indiana are **deciduous** (dee SIHJ oo us). That means they lose their leaves in the fall. The most common deciduous trees in Indiana are the oak, maple, hickory, and poplar. When the Colbys and others began settling in Indiana, the tulip tree was common. It is the state tree of Indiana. Today it is rather rare.

The lumber from deciduous trees is mostly hardwood. Hardwoods such as oak and maple are used for making furniture. Indiana is known for its furniture making.

Evergreen trees stay green year-round. Pine and fir trees are evergreens. The Colbys did not find evergreens when they came to settle. In recent years, evergreens have been planted in Indiana. They grow quickly, and when they are cut down, they provide softwood lumber. This is lumber that can be

Each fall, deciduous trees lose their leaves. Evergreen trees stay green all year.
► What is a type of evergreen?

cut easily. It is used in building homes and furniture.

The largest forest in Indiana is the Hoosier National Forest. It is cared for by the United States government. Indiana's 13 state forests are protected by the state.

B. Indiana Wildlife

Forest Homes Many kinds of wild animals make their homes in the forests of Indiana. Have you ever wondered how Turkey Run State Park got its name? In pioneer days, there were large flocks of wild turkeys. This bird was a delicious part of the pioneer family's diet. Turkey Run State Park was named for the large number of wild turkeys that were once found there. Today, some people are becoming worried that too few wild turkeys are left. They are finding ways to increase the numbers of wild turkey flocks.

Wildlife Patterns Indiana forests are home to other wild animals too. They include deer, foxes, raccoons, squirrels, opossums, woodchucks, and rabbits. There are brightly colored birds such as blue jays and cardinals. Indiana's state bird is the cardinal. In the fall many birds **migrate** (mye grayt), or leave the area to spend the winter in a warmer place. They return in the spring.

Then they build their nests and raise their young. There are also many snakes and lizards. These animals are called reptiles.

Indiana rivers and lakes are filled with fish. Many people fish for pike, sunfish, catfish, and bass.

C. People as Resources

You may not have thought of it, but people are resources too. They farm the soil, cut the forests, and mine the coal. People make things using natural resources. As you learned in Chapter 8, people use the wood from Indiana's forests to

Indiana forests are filled with many kinds of wildlife, including raccoons, squirrels, and rabbits.
▶ What animals are shown here?

make furniture. People also make steel, automobile parts, televisions, school buses, recreational vehicles, and many other things. Indiana sells these goods to people in other parts of the United States. Indiana also sells its goods to many nations around the world.

People use natural resources to make things for themselves and others. They also have the skills needed to make sure resources are used wisely and not wasted.

Many people make things from natural resources. This man is making a piece of furniture.
▶ What else do people make?

D. Conserving Our State's Natural Resources

Many people in Indiana and in our nation are interested in **conservation** (kahn sur VAY shun). Conservation means keeping natural resources from being wasted or destroyed. When farmers protect their soil from erosion, they are practicing soil conservation. When people try to keep lakes and streams clean, they are practicing water conservation. All kinds of natural resources need protection.

Indiana has a special program for this purpose. It is called the Indiana Natural Heritage Program. Its goal is to protect rare animals, plants, and the places where they live and grow. These places include forests, prairies, and marshes.

LESSON 3 REVIEW

THINK AND WRITE

A. Why are some parts of southern Indiana still heavily forested?
B. Why do some birds migrate from Indiana in the fall?
C. What are some reasons why people are a valuable resource?
D. What is the Indiana Natural Heritage Program?

SKILLS CHECK

WRITING SKILL

Look at the graph on page 42. How is the greatest amount of land in Indiana used? What takes up the next greatest amount of land? Write your answers to these questions using complete sentences.

RECYCLING ALUMINUM

Aluminum is a lightweight, silver-colored metal. It is easy to shape and has many uses. Many parts for automobiles, airplanes, and boats are made from aluminum. Many household items, such as refrigerators, toasters, air conditioners, pots and pans, and lawn furniture, have some aluminum in them. Aluminum is also used to make beverage cans, bottle caps, wrapping foil, and frozen food trays.

Some items that contain aluminum are used for long periods of time. Other items, such as beverage cans and frozen food trays, are used only once and thrown away. People throughout the world throw away thousands of tons of used aluminum every day. As a result, the environment has become polluted. At the same time, more aluminum must be produced to meet people's needs.

Aluminum is produced from a mineral called bauxite, which is found in the earth. The process by which we get aluminum from bauxite requires large amounts of electricity. In order to save bauxite and electricity and to keep the environment from being polluted, aluminum is now being recycled. To recycle something means to process it so that it can be used again. Used aluminum items, such as cans, are melted down and made into new items. In some communities, laws now require that residents recycle aluminum cans and other items. In this way, we are saving natural resources and energy. We are also helping to keep our environment clean.

Thinking for Yourself

On a separate sheet of paper, answer the questions in complete sentences.

1. Why is recycling used aluminum so important?
2. What are some ways in which individuals can help recycle aluminum?
3. What other items, besides aluminum cans, can you think of that can be recycled?

USING THE VOCABULARY

natural resource	reservoir
fertile	surface mining
organic	deciduous
cultivate	evergreen
irrigation	conservation

On a separate sheet of paper, write the best ending for each sentence below. Choose your answers from the vocabulary words above.

1. One way to get coal from the earth is through _____ .
2. To be sure their crops get enough water, Indiana farmers bring water to their fields through _____ .
3. Something useful to people and provided by nature is called a _____ .
4. Trees that lose their leaves in the fall are called _____ .
5. People who help keep natural resources from being wasted or destroyed are practicing _____ .

REMEMBERING WHAT YOU READ

Write your answers in complete sentences on a separate sheet of paper.

1. What are four natural resources found in Indiana?
2. Where is the best soil in the state of Indiana found?
3. What is the most important crop grown in Indiana?
4. What is erosion?
5. What is a reservoir?
6. Why is surface mining widely used in Indiana?
7. What is limestone used for?
8. Which of the two groups of trees provides hardwood?
9. What is special about Indiana's Brown County?
10. What does it mean to cultivate?

TYING SCIENCE TO SOCIAL STUDIES

Collect at least eight different leaves and needles from trees near your home or school. Use encyclopedias or other library books to identify the tree from which each sample came. Use your samples to make a chart. You may either draw the leaves and needles or paste them on your chart. Your chart should show the samples that came from deciduous trees and the samples that came from evergreen trees.

THINKING CRITICALLY

Write your answers in complete sentences on a separate sheet of paper.

1. How can natural resources be used to improve people's lives?

2. Why do people need water?
3. How do modern coal mining companies help to conserve soil?
4. In what way are coal and limestone similar to one another?
5. Why is conservation important?

SUMMARIZING THE CHAPTER

On a separate sheet of paper, draw a graphic organizer that is like the one shown here. Copy the information from this graphic organizer to the one you have drawn. Under the main idea for each lesson, write three statements that support it. The first one has been done for you.

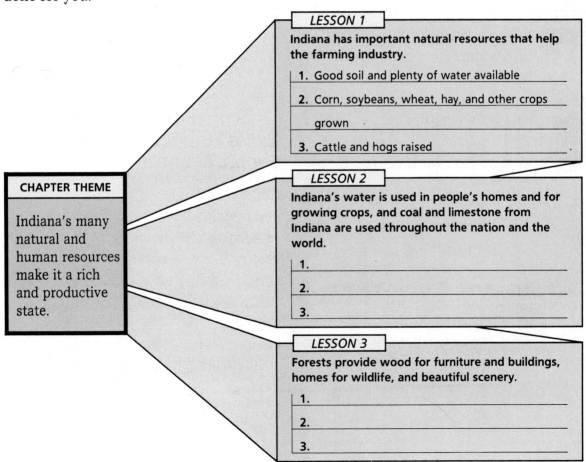

CHAPTER THEME

Indiana's many natural and human resources make it a rich and productive state.

LESSON 1

Indiana has important natural resources that help the farming industry.

1. Good soil and plenty of water available
2. Corn, soybeans, wheat, hay, and other crops grown
3. Cattle and hogs raised

LESSON 2

Indiana's water is used in people's homes and for growing crops, and coal and limestone from Indiana are used throughout the nation and the world.

1.
2.
3.

LESSON 3

Forests provide wood for furniture and buildings, homes for wildlife, and beautiful scenery.

1.
2.
3.

11

MANUFACTURING
IN INDIANA

The first factories in Indiana made goods that helped farmers. Then other industries came to Indiana. But industries need energy to run. Some forms of energy can harm the air, water, plants, and wildlife in Indiana.

were no airplanes at that time. Hammond had to find a way to keep the meats cold during the long trip. He came up with the idea of using refrigerated railroad cars to keep the meat from spoiling.

Hammond, Indiana Hammond chose the northwestern corner of Indiana for his meat-packing factory. It was near Lake Michigan. Ice could be taken from the lake. It was also near the cattle stockyards of Chicago, Illinois. Hammond's business was a big success. The Indiana town that grew up around his factory was named after him.

George Hammond used the railroads to ship his meat. The railroads also helped many other kinds of manufacturing to grow. People set up factories in Indiana because they knew that railroads linked Indiana to cities in the East. It was an easy way for them to send goods back and forth.

C. The Automobile Industry

A Partnership Did you know that Indiana was once the leading automobile-manufacturing state in the country? Some pioneers of the auto industry were Hoosiers.

Elwood Haynes lived in Kokomo in the late 1800s. He got tired of bumpy rides in his buggy. In 1891, Haynes started planning to build a horseless carriage. Near the end of 1893, Haynes took his plans to Elmer and Edgar Apperson. These brothers built bicycles for a living. They began to assemble Haynes's car in their shop.

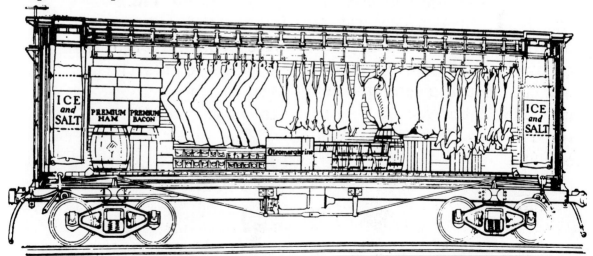

The refrigerated railroad car allowed meat to be taken long distances without spoiling. This was an important advance in meat packing.
▶ Who first thought of using refrigerated cars?

It was the Fourth of July 1894. Elwood Haynes towed his strange-looking machine out of town behind a horse and buggy. Out in the country, Haynes and Elmer Apperson got into the machine. The car moved off at a speed of about 7 miles (11 km) per hour. On the way into town the car approached a small hill. Apperson turned to Haynes and said, "I wonder if the little devil can make the hill?" Both laughed with relief as the car chugged up the hill successfully. As they entered Kokomo, people lined the streets and cheered.

Haynes's car was not the first automobile ever built. But it was the first one to have an engine much like those that are in cars today. Soon Haynes and the Apperson brothers became partners. Together they made cars to sell.

Elwood Haynes built an early automobile. Its engine was similar to that of today's car engines.
▶ How fast did this car travel?

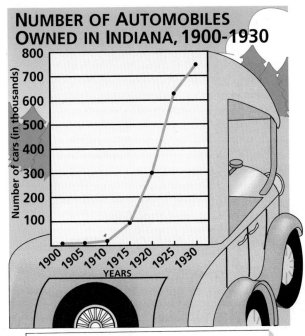

NUMBER OF AUTOMOBILES OWNED IN INDIANA, 1900-1930

Number of cars (in thousands): 800, 700, 600, 500, 400, 300, 200, 100

YEARS: 1900, 1905, 1910, 1915, 1920, 1925, 1930

In the early 1900s, the number of cars in Indiana rose steadily.
▶ About how many Indianans owned cars in 1925?

ideas. He had seen an automobile in New York City. Clem, Jr., felt that if the Studebakers did not produce a car, their company would be left behind. At first his father called the idea nonsense. But soon he changed his mind about it.

On July 22, 1904, the first automobile left the Studebaker factory. A man from South Bend, Mr. H. D. Johnson, paid $2,000 cash for the car. That was a lot of money!

The Indy 500 Five years later, in 1909, the famous Indianapolis Motor Speedway was built. The Speedway began as a place for car manufacturers to test and improve the cars they had made. The first Indianapolis 500 race was held on May 30, 1911. The race, now called the Indy 500, still takes place in May every year.

In 1963, almost 60 years after it produced its first car, the Studebaker factory closed. At one time, the Studebaker was just one of many cars made in Indiana. Others included the Auburn, the Cord, the Duesenberg (DOOZ un burg), the Overland, and the Stutz.

The Move to Detroit Today, most American automobiles are made in Detroit. Why did the center of the United States auto industry move from Indiana to Michigan? The

The Studebaker Brothers In South Bend, about 80 miles (129 km) north of Kokomo, other transportation pioneers were at work. In the 1800s, five brothers were well known for their wagons. The brothers were Henry, Clement, J. M., Peter, and Jacob Studebaker (STOOD uh bay kur). Studebaker wagons had carried many pioneers across the West.

In 1895 Peter and Clem Studebaker were talking together about their business. In addition to wagons, they wanted to make harnesses and saddles for horses. Clem's son, Clem, Jr., had other

answer lies in one man, Henry Ford. He lived and worked in Detroit, Michigan. There, he made small, simple cars. He was the first person to **mass-produce** cars. This means that he made them quickly, cheaply, and in large numbers. People began to buy the cheaper Detroit cars instead of the more expensive cars from Indiana.

Indiana still makes **components** (kum POH nunts) for cars.

Components are parts that are used in making something else. Examples of components are engines, headlights, and door handles. Automobile components are taken to Detroit and other cities, where they are put into cars. Many cities in northern Indiana make car components. Most American cars have some part that was made in Indiana.

Perhaps you came to school this morning in a school bus. If you

TOP FIVE PRODUCERS OF RECREATIONAL VEHICLES

Indiana | California | Florida | Pennsylvania | Iowa

🚐 = 5% of the total number of recreational vehicles produced

important industry. Skilled crafts workers cut the wood and assemble the pieces into tables, desks, chairs, and other items. They work in large factories. The pieces of furniture they make are shipped to many parts of the country.

D. Other Early Industries

From Injury to Invention Another famous Indiana industry is the making of band instruments. This industry began in Elkhart in 1875. Charles G. Conn was a grocer who loved to play the cornet. The cornet is like a small trumpet. When Conn hurt his lip one day, he found that he could not play his cornet. So he designed a mouthpiece that would

did, you probably rode in one that was made in Indiana. Your local fire company may have fire engines that were made in Anderson, Indiana. Indiana also produces recreational vehicles, or RVs.

You read in Chapter 8 that the people of Indiana began to make furniture to sell in the early 1900s. They used wood from Indiana's forests to make the furniture. The forests of Indiana still supply wood for this

Making musical instruments is an important industry in Indiana.
▶ What musical instrument is South Whitley known for making?

allow him to play, even with his hurt lip. Soon his friends and their friends wanted the same mouthpiece. He began to manufacture them in his home. As business grew, he rented a building and made not only mouthpieces but cornets as well.

Music, Music, Music In 1900, over half of all band instruments made in this country came from northern Indiana. Today, Elkhart supplies musical instruments to many parts of the world. Other places in Indiana make musical instruments too. Many musicians feel that the town of South Whitley makes the finest

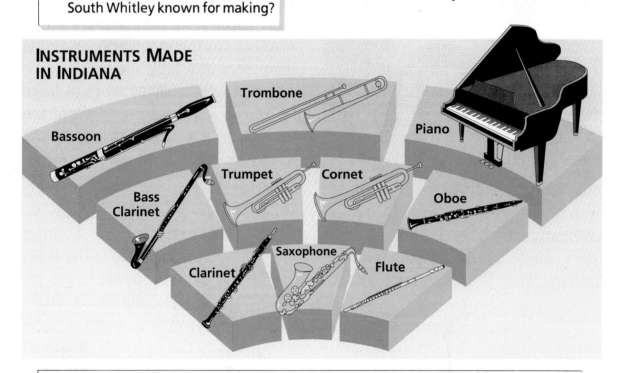

INSTRUMENTS MADE IN INDIANA

Bassoon
Trombone
Piano
Bass Clarinet
Trumpet
Cornet
Oboe
Clarinet
Saxophone
Flute

This picture shows the different musical instruments that are played in a band. Many of these instruments are made in Indiana.
▶ Which of these instruments have you heard being played?

Many prefabricated homes are made in Indiana.
► How do they get to where people will live in them?

bassoons in the country. A bassoon is another musical instrument. Study page 282 to learn what different musical instruments look like.

Indiana also makes prefabricated (pree FAB rih kayt ed) homes.

Prefabricated homes are partly or entirely made in a factory. They are then taken by truck to the place where people will live in them.

LESSON *1* REVIEW

THINK AND WRITE

A. What are three service industries?
B. In what way did farming help the state of Indiana become important in manufacturing?
C. How did mass production in Detroit affect auto production in Indiana?
D. What kind of manufacturing is Elkhart known for?

SKILLS CHECK

WRITING SKILL

Each of the following cities is known for an invention or a special product: Kokomo, Elkhart, South Bend. Use the Gazetteer on pages 357–364 to find another fact about each city. Write your answers on a separate sheet using complete sentences.

AUTOMOBILES THROUGH THE TIMES

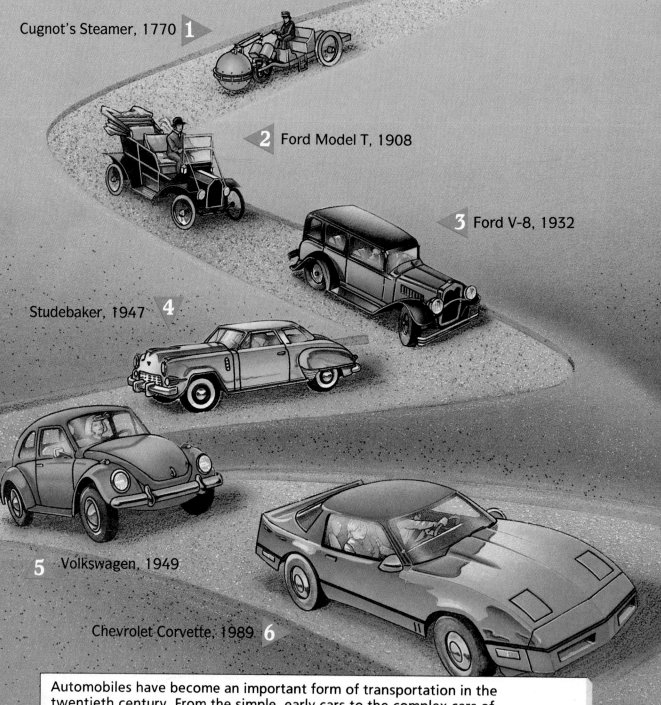

Cugnot's Steamer, 1770 **1**

2 Ford Model T, 1908

3 Ford V-8, 1932

Studebaker, 1947 **4**

5 Volkswagen, 1949

Chevrolet Corvette, 1989 **6**

Automobiles have become an important form of transportation in the twentieth century. From the simple, early cars to the complex cars of today, automobiles have improved greatly over the years. Indiana played an important role in the early days of automobile manufacturing.
► How do you think cars will look in the future?

New Industries in Indiana

THINK ABOUT WHAT YOU KNOW

Make a list of ways that manufacturing has made your life more pleasant or comfortable.

STUDY THE VOCABULARY

ore   smelting
coke   laboratory
blast furnace

FOCUS YOUR READING

What new industries have come to Indiana, and why are they located here?

A. Mighty Iron and Steel

Making Steel The most important product made in Indiana's factories today is steel. Steel is made from iron ore. Ores are natural resources from which we get metals, such as iron and copper. These ores are found below the ground. Iron ore was once mined in Indiana. But the supply has been exhausted. That means none is left. However, iron ore from Minnesota and Canada can easily be brought to Indiana in large ships called ore carriers. These ships sail on the five Great Lakes. They bring iron ore to Gary and East Chicago. These cities are located on Lake Michigan in northern Indiana.

Gary, Indiana The Gary steel factory and the city of Gary have an interesting history. Elbert H. Gary was a judge who became a leader in the steel industry in the early 1900s. He wanted to build a new factory for the United States Steel Company. He chose a stretch of land along the sand dunes and swamps of northwestern Indiana. It was a perfect site because the iron ore could be brought in on the Great Lakes. It was also near railroad lines. Coal had to be brought in by railroad. Coke, a fuel that is made from coal, is also used to make steel. Once he selected this place, Elbert Gary

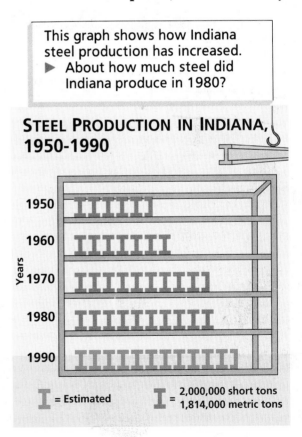

This graph shows how Indiana steel production has increased.
▶ About how much steel did Indiana produce in 1980?

STEEL PRODUCTION IN INDIANA, 1950-1990

Years

1950
1960
1970
1980
1990

I = Estimated

I = 2,000,000 short tons
1,814,000 metric tons

formed a company to build the steel factory in 1906.

But Gary did not build just a factory. He built a town too. He cared about his workers. He wanted to improve their lives both inside and outside the factory. He tried to create clean working conditions in the factory. His plan for the town included wide streets. One of the first buildings he had built was a schoolhouse. He even offered loans to workers so that they could buy homes. The town was named in his honor. Today, Gary is a major steel-producing city.

Steel Mills on the Lake   Other steel factories, or mills, were built at Indiana Harbor in East Chicago and in Calumet. The steel mills take up miles and miles of lakefront. They provide work for thousands of people of northern Indiana.

Steel from all these mills is used in Indiana for making products that our nation needs. Steel is also sent to other states in the Midwest and to other nations. A little more than one fifth of the steel made in the United States comes from northern Indiana. Steel is produced in some other parts of Indiana too.

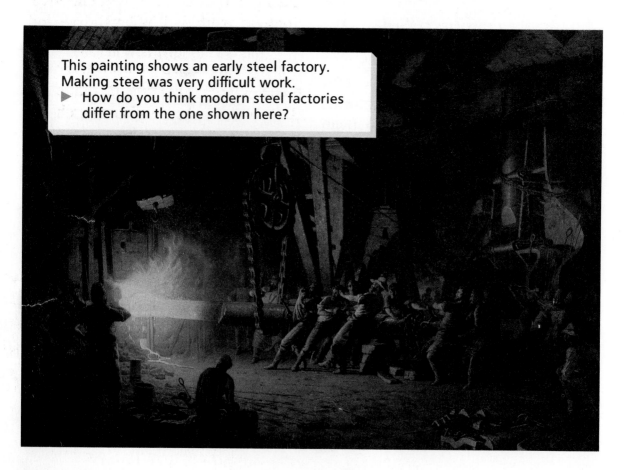

This painting shows an early steel factory. Making steel was very difficult work.
► How do you think modern steel factories differ from the one shown here?

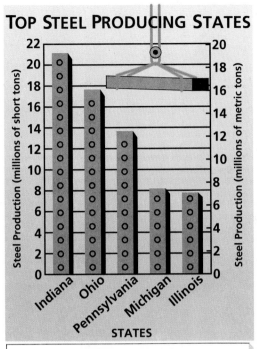

TOP STEEL PRODUCING STATES

Steel Production (millions of short tons) / Steel Production (millions of metric tons)

States: Indiana, Ohio, Pennsylvania, Michigan, Illinois

Indiana is the top steel-producing state in the country.
▶ What state follows Indiana in steel production?

B. The Story of Steel

Look at the drawing on page 288. This shows the steps that make iron ore into steel. Follow the ore from the quarry to the ore carrier. The ore is unloaded from the carrier at Gary or at Indiana Harbor. It is then put into a furnace called a **blast furnace.** In a blast furnace the iron is melted out of the ore. This process is called **smelting.**

Iron is a hard metal, but it is brittle. This means that it breaks easily. It has to be turned into steel, which is much stronger. This is done in the steelworks. They are close to the blast furnaces. In the steelworks the steel is formed into sheets and bars. These are loaded onto trucks and taken to factories that make automobiles, washing machines, and other products.

C. Keeping People Well

Curing Illness Most people need medicine at one time or another. Medicines help cure many sicknesses. They may even keep some sicknesses from happening.

The manufacturing of medicines in the United States started during the War for Independence. Soldiers wounded in battle needed medicine. That is when the first **laboratory** was set up. A laboratory is a place where medicine is made. In laboratories people also search for new drugs to cure sicknesses.

Making Pills One of the leading laboratories in the United States is located in Indianapolis. A man named Eli Lilly was an officer in the Civil War. After the war he bought a cotton plantation in Mississippi. But the plantation failed. Lilly had to do something else for a living. In 1876 he started a company that made pills covered with a powder that made them easier to swallow. Soon the company was making many other kinds of medicines. His son, Josiah,

287

THE STORY OF STEEL

1. At the quarry, machines dig iron ore from the ground. Iron ore is a rock that contains iron.

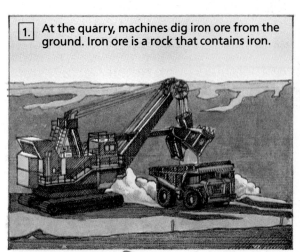

2. Ships carry the iron ore to steel mills.

3. Iron ore is put into a blast furnace. It smelts the iron out of the ore at 2100°F (1150°C).

4. In the steel-works, the iron is mixed with other metals in an oxygen furnace.

5. Machines cool and press or roll the steel into sheets or bars.

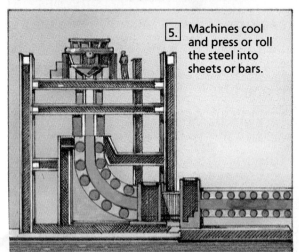

6. The steel is taken to factories to make many kinds of products.

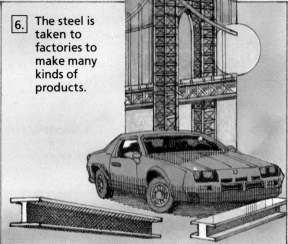

This flow chart shows the process by which iron ore is turned into steel. There are many steps in this process.
► What happens when the iron ore is put into a blast furnace?

Workers at this Indiana factory make different kinds of medicine.
▶ Why do you think the workers are dressed this way?

followed him in the business. Members of the Lilly family still run this business today. Eli Lilly and Company has played an important role in making medicines for the nation and for people around the world.

D. Other New Industries

Many other industries have started in Indiana. Televisions and elevators are made in Bloomington. They are sold all over the United States. Large engines that drive factory machines are made in Columbus. Evansville is known for manufacturing refrigerators. Washing machines are made in South Bend, La Porte, and Fort Wayne. Fort Wayne is also well known for making tools that are used to cut diamonds. Indianapolis is a center for the making of telephones.

All of the major city areas have many service industries. These include hotels, motels, restaurants, and amusement parks.

LESSON *2* REVIEW

THINK AND WRITE

A. Why did the northwestern corner of Indiana become important in steel manufacturing?

B. How is steel made?

C. How does Indiana help keep people well?

D. Other than steel and medicines, what are three present-day industries in Indiana?

SKILLS CHECK

MAP SKILL

You read that iron ore is brought to Indiana from Minnesota. Look at the map of the United States on pages 354–355. On which of the Great Lakes would a ship have to travel to get from Minnesota to Gary, Indiana?

Some Problems of Modern Industry

THINK ABOUT WHAT YOU KNOW

What machines do you use every day? How do you think they get their power?

STUDY THE VOCABULARY

energy	nuclear power
petroleum	refine
power station	solar energy
hydroelectric power	pollute
	acid rain

FOCUS YOUR READING

What are some problems that manufacturing in Indiana faces?

A. Energy to Get Work Done

Power to Work "Mom, I just can't seem to get this sink clean," Andy complained. He threw down the scrubbing pad in disgust.

Andy's mother shook her head. "That's hard to believe, Andy. I think you need to put as much energy into cleaning the sink as you do into playing basketball!"

Without energy, nothing gets done. Energy is power that can be used to do work — or play. Andy and his friends get their energy from the food they eat. Energy is also what makes the machines in Indiana's factories work.

Energy Sources Indiana's factories get their energy from many sources. They get it by burning coal, natural gas, or petroleum (puh TROH lee um). Petroleum is an oily substance that can be pumped up from within the earth. When people talk about "oil," they mean petroleum. Gasoline, fuel oil, and many goods are made from petroleum. Natural gas also comes from deep within the earth.

Coal, oil, and natural gas are burned in buildings called power stations. Power stations turn the energy in fuel into electricity. Electricity is much easier to use than

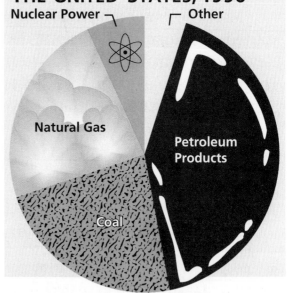

SOURCES OF ENERGY USED IN THE UNITED STATES, 1990

Nuclear Power

Other

Natural Gas

Petroleum Products

Coal

This pie graph shows the different sources of energy that are used in the United States.
▶ Which source is used the most?

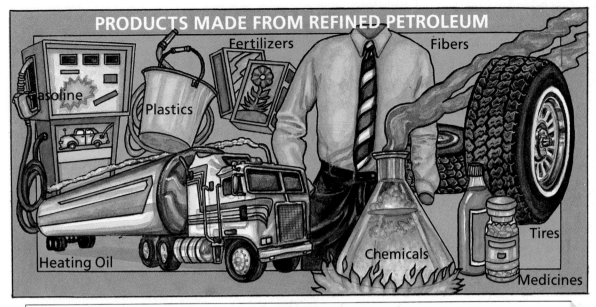

PRODUCTS MADE FROM REFINED PETROLEUM

Gasoline

Fertilizers

Fibers

Plastics

Heating Oil

Chemicals

Tires

Medicines

Refined petroleum is used to make many different products, including those shown here. One of the most important uses for petroleum is as an energy source.

▶ Which of the products shown are energy sources?

coal or oil. Electricity moves through cables. Cables are wires laid underground or hung between posts. Electricity can be used to drive machines as small as a toaster and as large as a railroad train.

There are other ways of making electricity for homes and factories. One is called **hydroelectric** (hye droh ee LEK trihk) **power.** This is power from running water. Do you remember Spring Mill from Chapter 6? The mill wheel used the power of running water to grind corn. This same idea is used in making hydroelectric power. Hydroelectric plants use the power of mighty rivers to create electricity.

A New Energy Source Another way of making electricity is through **nuclear** (NOO klee ur) **power.** Certain kinds of substances give out heat as they break up into other substances. This heat can be used to generate power. Not all people agree that this way of making electricity is safe. Because of safety fears, not many nuclear power plants are being built anymore.

B. Refining Petroleum

Petroleum is a very important source of energy. Indiana is a center for **refining** petroleum. Refining means turning petroleum into gasoline and fuel oil. Indiana was once an

PETROLEUM: FROM CRUDE OIL TO CONSUMER PRODUCTS

1. A drill is built to find oil, and then a well collects the oil.

2. Crude oil and natural gas are pumped from the well to the surface and into gathering lines.

3. Crude oil and natural gas travel through gathering lines into storage tanks. They are then moved to refineries through underground pipelines.

4. Crude oil is refined, or made usable.

This chart shows the steps through which crude oil is taken to become a usable product.
▶ What is the first step in this process?

important source of oil. But today oil is brought into Indiana from western states. It comes through a pipeline. A pipeline is a large steel pipe that oil flows through.

In Indiana there is a very large oil refinery at Whiting. Refineries there and in other places make gasoline and send it to gas stations all over the Midwest. The refineries also make fuel oil to supply energy for machines in factories. Fuel oil is also used for heating homes.

C. Using Up Our Resources

Every time you put gasoline in the car, you use up part of the earth's resources. The supplies of coal, oil, and natural gas are getting smaller and smaller. There may be a time when there are none left. That is why people are looking for other forms of energy.

Anything in nature that moves can be used to create energy. As long as rain falls and rivers flow, people will be able to use the power of running water. The wind is another source of energy. Perhaps you have seen windmills on farms in Indiana. They turn in the wind and raise water from deep underground. The heat you feel from the sun is another form of energy. It, too, can be used. Energy from the sun is called **solar energy.**

D. Pollution Problems

Spoiling the Environment "What do you think you're doing, Lisa?" Five-year-old Lisa was startled at her grandfather's shout. She spilled the water she was holding in her cupped hands all over herself and the ground.

"I heard you telling Daddy how you used to drink from this stream when you were a boy," Lisa said tearfully. "I was just trying to do the same thing."

Lisa's grandfather took her in his arms with a big sigh. "That was a long time ago, Lisa. Now this stream is **polluted** (puh LOOT ed). That means that people have put things

Windmills are a source of energy used on some farms in Indiana.
▶ Why are people looking for other forms of energy, such as the wind?

into it that have made it dirty or dangerous. Today, this water has to be cleaned before we can drink it."

Kinds of Pollution Lisa's grandfather is talking about a serious problem — pollution. There are many kinds of pollution. The kind of pollution Lisa's grandfather is talking about is water pollution. Some factories empty their waste into streams and rivers. There it kills fish and makes the water unfit to drink. Water pollution affects rivers, lakes, streams, and even the world's oceans.

Another kind of pollution is air pollution. What happens when coal is burned? There is a lot of heat and smoke. The heat is used to make energy, but what happens to the smoke? It rises into the air. Sometimes it forms a dark cloud. People who live where a lot of coal is burned have to breathe that smoke. The smoke harms their health. Smoke also makes things dirty.

Finding Solutions Air pollution can also create other problems. Our cars burn gasoline, and the gases that come out of the exhaust go into the air. These gases are blown around by the wind and are brought down to the earth when it rains. We call this **acid rain.** Acid rain kills plants and trees. It gets into streams and lakes and kills fish. Acid rain is also caused by substances sent into the air by factory smoke.

Pollution is dangerous. We must do all that we can to prevent

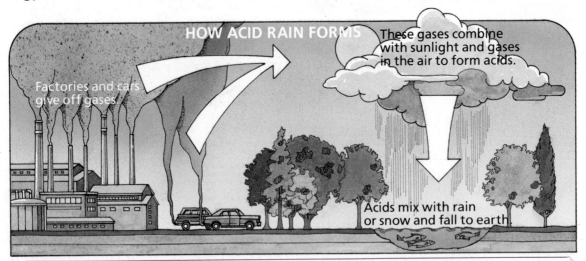

HOW ACID RAIN FORMS

These gases combine with sunlight and gases in the air to form acids.

Factories and cars give off gases.

Acids mix with rain or snow and fall to earth.

Acid rain is a very serious problem for our environment. It kills plants, trees, and fish. However, there are things that we can do to help prevent acid rain from occurring.
▶ What are the two main causes of acid rain?

Indianans can do many things to help keep our state beautiful.
▶ How are these children helping their community?

pollution. We can drive cars that burn less fuel and that do not give off as many dirty substances. We can look for ways to keep factory smoke from passing into the air. We can find places to put the waste from our factories where it can do no harm.

Individuals and companies can help to cut down on pollution. If people work together, Indiana can be a clean and beautiful place to live. Each person must do his or her part to keep Indiana that way.

LESSON 3 REVIEW

THINK AND WRITE

A. What things are burned to produce energy?

B. How do Indiana's refineries help people run their cars and heat their homes?

C. Why are people searching for new forms of energy?

D. Why do people need to worry about pollution?

SKILLS CHECK

THINKING SKILL

Write a paragraph that talks about the good things and the harmful things that industry can bring.

USING THE VOCABULARY

industry	smelting
component	energy
ore	power station
coke	refine
blast furnace	pollute

On a separate sheet of paper, write the best word or words to complete each sentence below. Choose your answers from the vocabulary words above.

1. To turn petroleum into gasoline and fuel oil is to _____ it.
2. A business or trade that provides goods or services is an _____.
3. To put dirty or dangerous things into the air or water is to _____ it.
4. A part that is used to make something else is called a _____.
5. Iron is melted out of iron ore when it is heated in a _____.
6. The process of melting iron out of ore is called _____.
7. A building in which fuel is burned to make energy is a _____.
8. A natural resource from which we get metals is an _____.
9. Machines work because of the power of _____.
10. _____ is a type of fuel that is made from coal.

REMEMBERING WHAT YOU READ

Write your answers in complete sentences on a separate sheet of paper.

1. Why are there fewer farmers in Indiana today than in the past?
2. What is manufacturing?
3. What two industries started in Indiana were related to farming?
4. What did Elwood Haynes do in 1894 in Kokomo?
5. How did the band instrument business start in Indiana?
6. Why was Elbert Gary important to the state of Indiana?
7. What is smelting?
8. What is energy?
9. What happens in a refinery?
10. What are two kinds of pollution?

TYING SCIENCE TO SOCIAL STUDIES

Research the subject of the pollution and damage caused by acid rain. Using books, magazine articles, and newspapers, tell about the effects of acid rain on such things as crops, livestock, bodies of water, forests, and wildlife. Use pictures from old magazines or newspapers to illustrate your report.

THINKING CRITICALLY

Write your answers in complete sentences on a separate sheet of paper.

1. How do machines make work easier for farmers?

2. How did railroads help Indiana's industries to grow?

3. What are some ways that Indiana's industries help people?

4. What might happen if people do not try to conserve resources?

5. How is pollution harmful?

SUMMARIZING THE CHAPTER

On a separate sheet of paper draw a graphic organizer that is like the one shown here. Copy the information from this graphic organizer to the one you have drawn. Under the main idea for each lesson, write three statements that support it. The first one has been done for you.

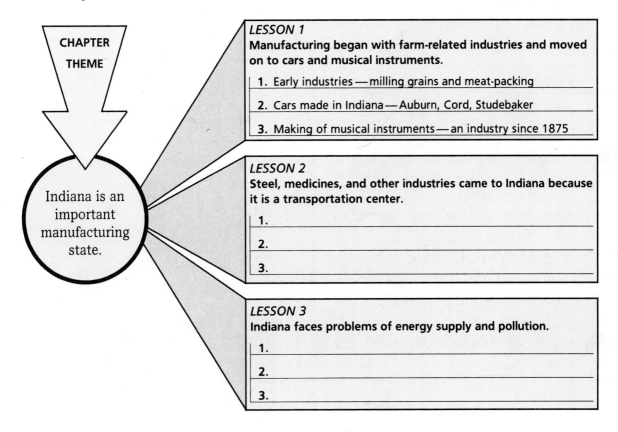

CHAPTER THEME

Indiana is an important manufacturing state.

LESSON 1
Manufacturing began with farm-related industries and moved on to cars and musical instruments.

1. Early industries—milling grains and meat-packing

2. Cars made in Indiana—Auburn, Cord, Studebaker

3. Making of musical instruments—an industry since 1875

LESSON 2
Steel, medicines, and other industries came to Indiana because it is a transportation center.

1.

2.

3.

LESSON 3
Indiana faces problems of energy supply and pollution.

1.

2.

3.

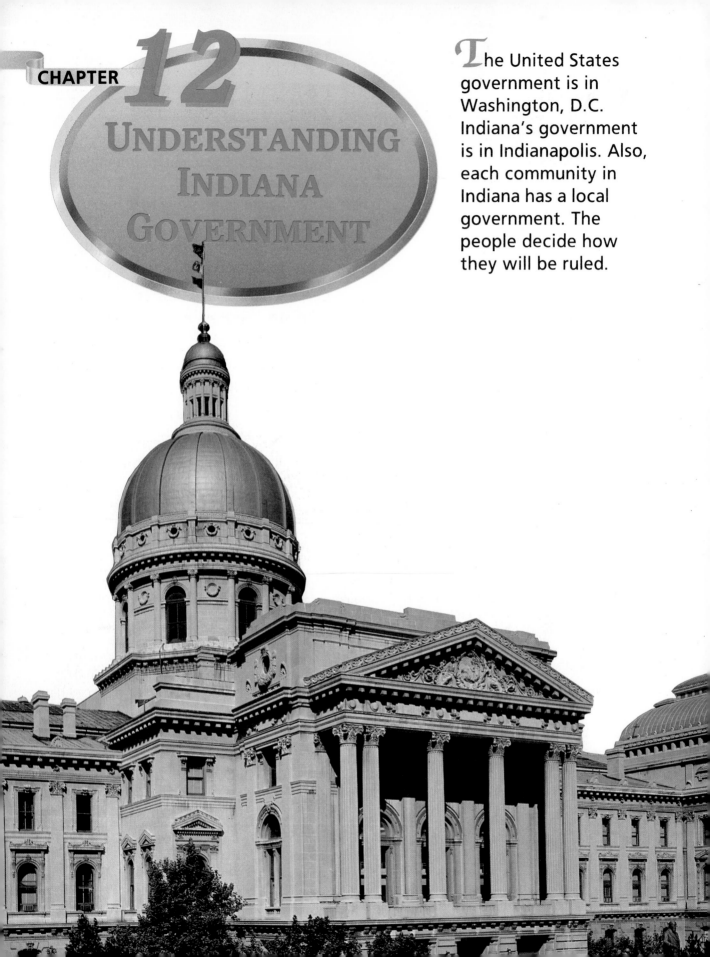

CHAPTER **12**

UNDERSTANDING INDIANA GOVERNMENT

The United States government is in Washington, D.C. Indiana's government is in Indianapolis. Also, each community in Indiana has a local government. The people decide how they will be ruled.

Types of Government

Why do you think a nation needs to have a government to run the country?

federal	**councilor**
elect	**UNIGOV**
term	**democracy**
capitol	

How do national, state, and local governments differ?

A. The Government of the United States

Indiana is one of 50 states that make up the United States. Our nation's government is based in Washington, D.C. We call this city the capital of the United States.

Do you know what *D.C.* stands for? It means "District of Columbia." This is a small area of land in the eastern part of the country. It is not part of any state. It is there only as a place for the **federal** government to do its work. The federal government is another name for the national government.

The leader of our federal government is the President. He lives in Washington, D.C., in a house called the White House. The President is **elected,** or chosen, by the citizens (SIHT uh zunz) of the United States. People have to be of voting age in order to vote in elections and choose our nation's leaders.

Each state is represented in Washington, D.C., by members of Congress. The people of each state elect their state's members of Congress. The members of Congress who are chosen meet together in Washington, D.C. There they make important decisions about laws for the entire country.

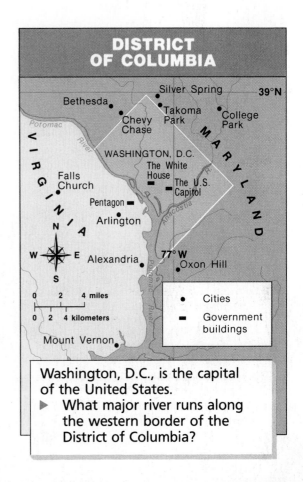

DISTRICT OF COLUMBIA

Washington, D.C., is the capital of the United States.

▶ What major river runs along the western border of the District of Columbia?

B. The Government of Indiana

Governing the State Indiana, like all of the 50 states, also has its own government. It is in Indianapolis, the state capital.

The head of Indiana's state government is the governor. Indiana's governor is elected by the people of the state. In 1988 Evan Bayh (bye) was elected governor. His **term** began in January 1989. A term is the period of time for which a person is elected. Like the President of the United States, the governor serves a term of four years. Like the President, the governor can be elected for a second term, but not for longer.

The governor makes decisions about how the state should be run. He decides on such things as new laws and how to spend state money. He also appoints people to certain positions in the government.

Indiana also has a lieutenant (loo TEN unt) governor. Frank O'Bannon was elected lieutenant governor in 1988. He took office in January of 1989. The lieutenant

In 1988 George Bush was elected President of the United States. Dan Quayle was elected Vice President.
► Who elects the President?

In 1988 Indianans elected Governor Evan Bayh and Lieutenant Governor Frank O'Bannon.
▶ How long is a governor's term?

governor helps the governor run the state. He also leads the meetings of the state senate. Like the governor, the lieutenant governor is elected for a term of four years.

Representing the People The people of Indiana also elect people to represent them in the state government. Hoosiers elect a total of 50 state senators and 100 state representatives. All the state senators and state representatives meet in Indianapolis at the beginning of each year. They meet in a building called the capitol. There, the state senators

and state representatives make laws for the state. The flow chart on page 302 shows how a new law is made.

Indiana's capitol is a very beautiful building with a golden dome. It looks something like the nation's capitol in Washington, D.C. It is not as large, however. You might be interested in reading what one traveler, writing in the late 1800s, said about the state capitol building. This description comes from *Travel Accounts of Indiana 1679–1961*. As

HOW A BILL BECOMES A LAW

1. A member of the House of Representatives or Senate writes a bill.

2. After being discussed, the bill must be approved by a majority vote in each house.

3. If the governor signs the bill, it becomes a law.

4. If the governor vetoes, or rejects, the bill, it may be returned to the House and Senate.

5. If each house again approves the bill by a majority vote, it becomes a law.

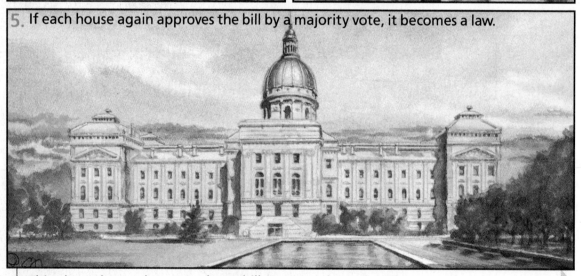

This chart shows the steps that a bill must go through before it can become a law.
▶ What happens if the governor vetoes the bill?

you will read here, another name for a capitol is a state house.

There are in the state house beautiful pillars of pink granite, fine paintings on the ceilings, and a large library. In one room hang, in heavy frames, the portraits of every governor of the state. Every state in the United States has this kind of state house in its capital. The state senate convenes [meets together] there. . . . This building is usually the pride of the state. . . . Of course, it is open to everyone and its library may be used by all. In its halls one can meet people of all kinds: small boys . . . , men . . . , schoolgirls, tourists, college students, and women dressed in silk.

Capital or Capitol Today, more than 100 years later, you can probably meet some of the same kinds of people. Have you ever been inside Indiana's state capitol building?

You have probably noticed that the words *capital* and *capitol* look almost the same as each other. Yet they mean different things. A capital is a city. But a capitol is a building. One way to remember the difference is by remembering that our state capitol building has a dome. Both the words *capitol* and *dome* have the letter *o* in them!

Indiana's capitol in Indianapolis has a beautiful dome.
▶ What building does Indiana's capitol look like?

303

State representatives and state senators meet in the capitol.
▶ How many state senators does Indiana have?

But they make rules about different kinds of things.

This is a little bit like national and state governments. Both have the task of governing, or making rules. But like the jobs of your parents and your teachers, their jobs are quite different.

Federal Law   Our country is governed according to a constitution. You learned in Chapter 5 that a constitution is a set of laws describing how a country or state is to be governed. The United States Constitution was signed in 1787. Since then,

C. State and Federal Governments Working Together to Govern

Making Rules   You would not ask your teacher if you could play at your friend's house after school, would you? And you would not expect your parents to give you your homework assignment for tonight. Both your parents and your teachers make certain rules that you follow.

only 26 changes, or amendments, have been made to it.

The United States Constitution says what our federal government can do and what our state government can do. The federal government is allowed to collect certain taxes. It can have an army and a navy. It can talk to the governments of other countries, control trade, and do many other things. But other jobs are left up to the states.

This painting shows the scene at the signing of the United States Constitution.
▶ How many amendments have been made to the Constitution?

State Law Each state has a constitution as well. This describes what the duties of the state government are. Indiana's first constitution was written in 1816. The constitution Indiana now has was accepted in 1851. Since then, many amendments have been made to it.

State governments are very interested in education in the state's schools. The Indiana state government has decided that all pupils should study the history and geography of their state.

The state government is also allowed to collect taxes. It has the power to protect the health and safety of its citizens. The state government also has charge of the state police, takes care of the state parks, manages the state forests, and builds the state highways.

D. Local Governments in Our Daily Lives

A Neighborhood Pool "Yippee!" said Christine and Jason. "We are going to have a swimming pool!"

"Wait just a minute, kids," Mrs. O'Connor said. "I said *maybe.*"

Mrs. O'Connor had just told her ten-year-old twins that the city might build a new public swimming pool. The recreation committee was going to suggest that it be built.

305

"You see, children, our committee is just one part of the local government. We have studied the city's needs. We think a pool would be a good idea. We know about how much it will cost. And we know where we want to build it. But we have to present our idea to the mayor and the **councilors**. They have been elected to run our city. They will make the final decision."

"Oh, yes," Jason answered. "Katie's father, Mr. Schwartz, was elected a councilor."

"So is Mrs. Moore, Tim's mother," Christine piped up. "Tim

Local Government Every county and every city has its own local government. The government of each of Indiana's 92 counties is located in the county seat. Where is the county seat in your county? In addition, each city has a government like the one in the O'Connors' city. It is made up of a mayor and a number of councilors.

In one place, local government leaders joined together a county and a city government. They did this to combine services and save money. The city of Indianapolis was a good place to try this. The city takes up a large part of Marion County. It

says they have to go to meetings in the evening."

"That's true," said Mrs. O'Connor. "They have to meet at night because they are at work during the day at their own jobs. We owe a lot to these people who give so much of their time to help us all."

Town meetings are an important part of local government. People discuss the community's needs.
► What might they talk about?

307

seemed wasteful to have separate governments. The united government of city and county is called **UNIGOV** (YOO nuh guv). It has been very successful. Cities in other states may follow this example.

UNIGOV has helped Indianapolis become the fine city that it is today. The work of UNIGOV is carried on in the 25-story City-County Building in the heart of Indianapolis.

Government Services People in local government take charge of many local services. These include police, fire protection, public libraries, and some roads. Local governments decide where traffic lights are to be placed. They organize how trash will be collected. They decide how to dispose of the trash. They choose where to open a new park or open a new road. They decide whether to build a new public swimming pool! All of these things are matters for local government. Life would be much less comfortable without our local governments.

E. Three Levels of Government

So far you have studied three levels of government: national, state, and local. As you just read, each level has different tasks and duties. But all levels have one very important thing in common. They are run by leaders who have been

This modern City-County Building in Indianapolis is home to UNIGOV. UNIGOV has been very successful.
▶ What is UNIGOV?

Local governments are very important. They provide many needed services to their citizens.
► What are some of the jobs being done here?

elected by the voters. In this way, *all* the people have a say in what government does. Government leaders, whether local, state, or federal, represent the people who voted for them. They are elected to carry out the wishes of the people. This type of government is called a **democracy**. Democracy means that the people govern themselves.

LESSON 1 REVIEW

THINK AND WRITE

A. What is Washington, D.C.?

B. How are the terms of office of the governor of Indiana and of the President of the United States similar?

C. What are two jobs of the national government and two jobs of the state government?

D. Why did UNIGOV come about?

E. How does a democracy work?

SKILLS CHECK

MAP SKILL

Look at the map of Washington, D.C., on page 299. Which two states surround the District of Columbia?

YOU DECIDE: PUBLIC OR PRIVATE?

If you are like most students, you probably visit your local public library from time to time. You probably use the reference books there for homework assignments. You may also check books out and bring them home to read. And it costs you nothing!

Have you ever wondered who paid for all the books at the library? Who pays the librarians' wages? Who pays for the library's heating and lighting?

The answer is that everyone in your community pays. The money for public libraries comes from the local taxes that homeowners and wage earners pay. Local taxes are also used for such services as road maintenance and repair, street lighting, and other services that benefit everyone. However, not everyone benefits directly from the public library.

Some people whose money is used for funding the library never even set foot inside the building. Some simply do not read books. Other people prefer to buy their own books.

Do you think it is right that everyone should contribute to a service that is not used by everyone? What if libraries were made into private institutions instead of public ones? Then they would be funded only by the people who choose to give them money. Private libraries could only be used by those who gave money for them. They would probably have less money — and fewer books and services to offer. But people who did not want to use them would not be paying for them.

You decide — should libraries be public or private? The questions should guide you in reaching your decision.

Thinking for Yourself

On a separate sheet of paper, answer the questions in complete sentences.

1. What services does your local public library offer?
2. In what ways does a community benefit from having a public library?
3. What would be the advantages of making libraries private?
4. What would be the disadvantages of making libraries private?
5. Overall, what do you think is best for a community —public or private libraries?

Indiana and the National Government

THINK ABOUT WHAT YOU KNOW

Name some activities carried on by the national government.

STUDY THE VOCABULARY

federation   executive
legislative   judicial

FOCUS YOUR READING

What part does the state of Indiana play in the government of our country?

A. The Federal Government

The United States of America is a **federation** (fed ur AY shun). This means that it is made up of separate states. Each state governs itself in some ways. In other ways, however, the states are controlled by the federal government.

There are several other federations in the world today. Canada and West Germany are both examples of federations. They, too, are made up of separate states.

Indiana is represented in the Senate by two senators. Richard Lugar is shown on the left, and Dan Coats is shown on the right.
▶ What is the other house of Congress called?

B. The Legislative Branch

Senators in Washington The federal government has three branches. The **legislative** branch makes the laws for the country. When people talk about Congress, they are talking about the legislative branch of government. Another name for Congress is the legislature.

Congress has two houses. One is called the Senate, and the other is

called the House of Representatives. Each of the 50 states is represented in the Senate by two senators. Indiana has two senators. Each of Indiana's neighbors has two. A state with very few people, such as Alaska, has the same number of senators as a state with many people, such as California or New York.

Representatives in Washington

The House of Representatives is

made up differently. There, the number of representatives that each state has depends on the number of people in the state. Alaska and Delaware each have only 1 representative. California has 45. Indiana has 10. If the population of Indiana increased greatly, the number of representatives would also increase.

Each of the ten Indiana representatives in Congress is chosen by voters in areas that are called congressional districts. There are ten congressional districts in Indiana.

Jill Long is one of Indiana's representatives in Congress.
▶ How many representatives does Indiana have?

Indiana's state government also has a legislative branch. The state government is divided in the same ways as the federal government. The diagram on page 315 shows the different branches of the Indiana government.

C. The Executive Branch

The President of the United States is head of the **executive** branch. The duties of this branch are to see that the laws are carried out.

The Vice President is also a member of the executive branch. The Vice President takes over all of the duties of the President if the President dies or leaves office.

Many departments, or parts, of government help the President carry out the laws. The State Department deals with the governments of other countries. The Department of Defense makes sure that the nation is safe. The Department of Agriculture helps farmers. The Department of Commerce manages trade.

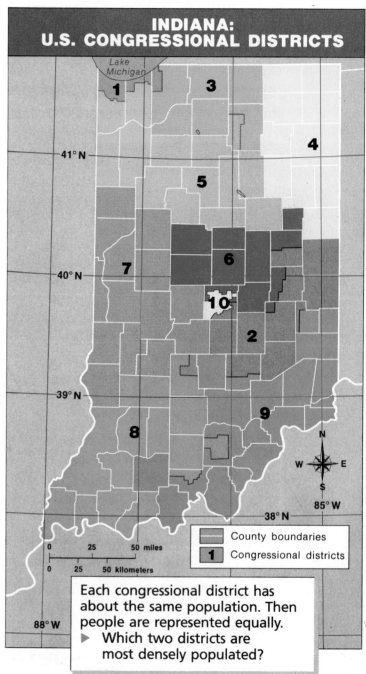

INDIANA: U.S. CONGRESSIONAL DISTRICTS

County boundaries
1 Congressional districts

Each congressional district has about the same population. Then people are represented equally.
▶ Which two districts are most densely populated?

D. The Judicial Branch

In addition to the legislative and executive branches, there is the judicial branch. It is made up of judges, and its duty is to explain the laws and to judge cases that are brought before it. Although our United States Constitution tells what the federal and state governments can do, there are sometimes arguments between them. These are settled by the judicial branch.

The head of this branch is the chief justice. This judge is appointed by the President and Congress together. The judicial branch is the only branch of government that is not elected by the people.

E. Three Branches of Government in Indiana

The government of Indiana is set up like the government of the United States. Its legislative branch has two houses, just like Congress. It has an executive branch whose chief is the governor. There is also a judicial branch of government to explain the laws made by the legislature of Indiana.

BRANCHES OF THE INDIANA GOVERNMENT

Legislative Branch

Senate (50 members)

House of Representatives (100 members)

Executive Branch

Governor → Lieutenant Governor → Cabinet (Governor's Top Advisors)

Judicial Branch

Supreme Court (5 members)

Court of Appeals (*12 members)
*to be changed in 1991

Indiana's state government is divided into three branches.
▶ Who makes up the executive branch of Indiana's government?

LESSON 2 REVIEW

THINK AND WRITE

A. What is a federation?

B. What makes up the legislative branch of our national government in Washington, D.C.?

C. What is the job of the executive branch of government?

D. How is the judicial branch different from the legislative and executive branches?

E. In what ways is the Indiana state government like the national government?

SKILLS CHECK

WRITING SKILL

Study the flowchart on page 302. In your own words, explain how a bill becomes a law. Write in complete sentences.

Choosing a Government

THINK ABOUT WHAT YOU KNOW

Can you remember the last national or local election? Who ran for office? Who won?

STUDY THE VOCABULARY

election	register
campaign	policy
candidate	polls

FOCUS YOUR READING

How do we choose the people who will represent us in government at all levels?

A. Holding an Election

Electing Our Leaders At **election** time, voters choose the people who will represent them in the United States Congress and in the state Senate and state House of Representatives. Every four years, Hoosiers help choose the President of the United States. Members of the nation's House of Representatives are chosen every two years and senators are chosen every six years. Indiana state representatives are elected every two years. State senators are elected every four years.

A Practical Campaign Before every election there are many months of **campaigning** by those who hope to be elected. To campaign is to travel around, trying to influence people to vote for you. During their campaigns, **candidates** make speeches saying what they will do if they are elected. A candidate is someone who is running for public office. Candidates shake hands with people and ask for their votes. Have you ever seen posters in shop windows or on billboards that tell you to vote for someone? Perhaps you have seen a candidate talking to people in a shopping center or around the town square. This is part of the candidate's campaign.

Elections for the federal government take place in the first week

During election campaigns, candidates make many speeches.
► Why do candidates campaign before elections?

of November, always on a Tuesday. That is a very busy time for people who work in government. Because November is so busy, local elections are sometimes held during other months of the year.

B. Running for Office

Some of you may someday decide that you want to run for public office. You may decide to become a candidate for election at the local, state, or national level.

Would you make a good candidate? Good candidates enjoy discussing problems and are able to make decisions. They should always want to do what is best for the people. They must also be ready to spend time meeting and talking with people. Good candidates must be willing to listen to the concerns of others and act to solve problems.

C. Voting at Elections

Voter Registration   Scott was upset. "Dad, if you go to vote now, you'll miss the beginning of my game. I'm the starting pitcher. What difference will it make if you don't vote? You're just one person."

"I know you're upset, Scott," said his father. "Your games are important to me. I'll get there as soon as I can. But, you see, voting is important to me too. Not every country

Voting is an important right. It lets us choose our government.
▶ At what age will you be eligible to vote?

in the world allows its citizens to choose the government. My vote *is* important. It's my way of making my voice heard."

When you reach the age of 18, you will be eligible (EL ih juh bul), or able, to vote. But first you must **register** as a voter. That means you must get your name on the list of voters. The list is called a register.

As a registered voter, you will listen to the candidates and learn about their **policies.** Their policies are what they want to do if they are elected. You can do this by reading the newspaper, listening to the radio, watching television, or going to hear candidates speak in person. Then you must choose which of the candidates you will vote for.

Election Day Let's follow Scott's father as he goes to vote in this election. First he goes to the polls. This is the place where he votes. For his district, the polls are located in a local high school. He sees tables with people sitting behind them. In front of each person is a large book. In it, the person checks Scott's father's name in the register of voters. Then he waits his turn to go to the voting machine.

He steps up to the voting machine and pulls a lever. This causes a curtain to surround him so that he can vote privately. On the voting machine he sees the names of all the candidates who are running for office in that election.

Now he is ready to cast his vote. Voting machines differ slightly from place to place. On this machine, Scott's father moves a little switch next to the name of each person he wants to vote for. Once he has voted, he pulls the lever again. That records his vote. It also opens the curtain so that the next person can go in.

Counting the Votes At the end of the day, the voting machine will be checked. It will tell how many votes each candidate has received. But it

These pie graphs compare the percentage of registered voters with that of actual voters.
▶ Why do you think such a high percentage did not vote?

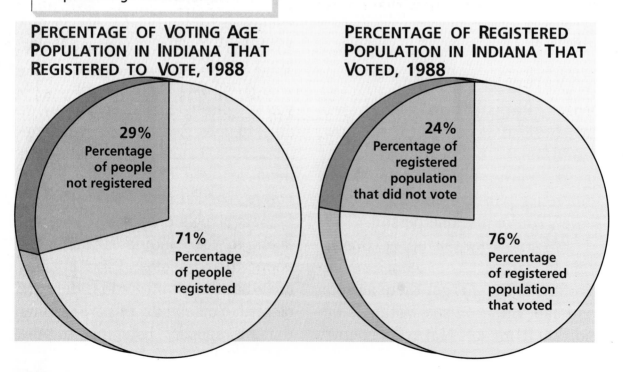

PERCENTAGE OF VOTING AGE POPULATION IN INDIANA THAT REGISTERED TO VOTE, 1988

29% Percentage of people not registered

71% Percentage of people registered

PERCENTAGE OF REGISTERED POPULATION IN INDIANA THAT VOTED, 1988

24% Percentage of registered population that did not vote

76% Percentage of registered population that voted

Some schools hold classroom elections. Students campaign for different offices. Then students vote for class leaders.
► What might a classroom election help students learn about?

will not tell how Scott's father voted. No one will know that unless he tells them.

As Scott's father pointed out, not every country in the world holds elections. In some countries, you would not be allowed to run for office. You would not be allowed to say what you believe or to ask people to vote for you. In the United States we are very lucky. We are free to do all these things. The government we get is the government we choose. In this way, we all contribute to solving the problems of our city, county, state, and country.

LESSON **3** *REVIEW*

THINK AND WRITE

A. What does a candidate do during a campaign?
B. How can a person be a good candidate in a campaign?
C. Why should people vote?

SKILLS CHECK

THINKING SKILL
Write a paragraph that tells how being a leader in your school might be like being a leader in government.

USING THE VOCABULARY

federal	executive
term	judicial
capitol	election
democracy	campaign
legislative	polls

On a separate sheet of paper, write the word that best matches each definition below. Choose your answers from the vocabulary words above.

1. the place where people go to vote
2. the form of government in which people govern themselves
3. the branch of government that makes the laws
4. the period of time for which a person is elected
5. the time when voters choose representatives in government
6. the building in which senators and representatives make laws for the people of the state
7. the branch of government that explains the laws and judges cases brought before it
8. another name for the national government of our country
9. to travel around, trying to influence people to vote for you
10. the branch of government that sees that laws are carried out

REMEMBERING WHAT YOU READ

Write your answers in complete sentences on a separate sheet of paper.

1. What is another name for the federal government?
2. How long is the term for which Indiana's governor is elected?
3. What is the job of the mayor and councilors of a city?
4. Where is the government of each Indiana county located?
5. What is the name of the combined government of Indianapolis and Marion County?
6. What are the three branches of the federal government?
7. How many senators does Indiana have and how many representatives in the federal government?
8. What is the job of the judicial branch of government?
9. What is a candidate?
10. What are a candidate's policies?

TYING LANGUAGE ARTS TO SOCIAL STUDIES: WRITING TO LEARN

Choose one branch of the federal government. Imagine that you work in that branch. Write a paragraph in which you tell what kind of work you do.

THINKING CRITICALLY

Write your answers in complete sentences on a separate sheet of paper.

1. What are some ways that our government representatives serve us?
2. Why do cities and counties need local government?
3. Why does Indiana have ten representatives but only two senators?
4. Why is voting a good way for people to choose who will represent them?
5. Why should voters be familiar with each candidate's policies?

SUMMARIZING THE CHAPTER

On a separate sheet of paper draw a graphic organizer that is like the one shown here. Copy the information from this graphic organizer to the one you have drawn. Under the main idea for each lesson, write three statements that support it. The first one has been done for you.

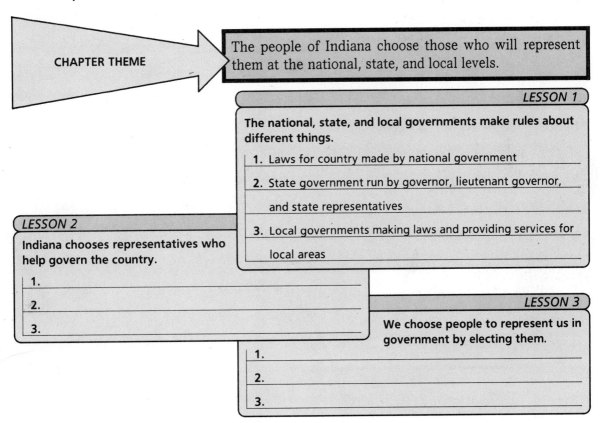

CHAPTER THEME

The people of Indiana choose those who will represent them at the national, state, and local levels.

LESSON 1

The national, state, and local governments make rules about different things.

1. Laws for country made by national government
2. State government run by governor, lieutenant governor, and state representatives
3. Local governments making laws and providing services for local areas

LESSON 2

Indiana chooses representatives who help govern the country.

1.
2.
3.

LESSON 3

We choose people to represent us in government by electing them.

1.
2.
3.

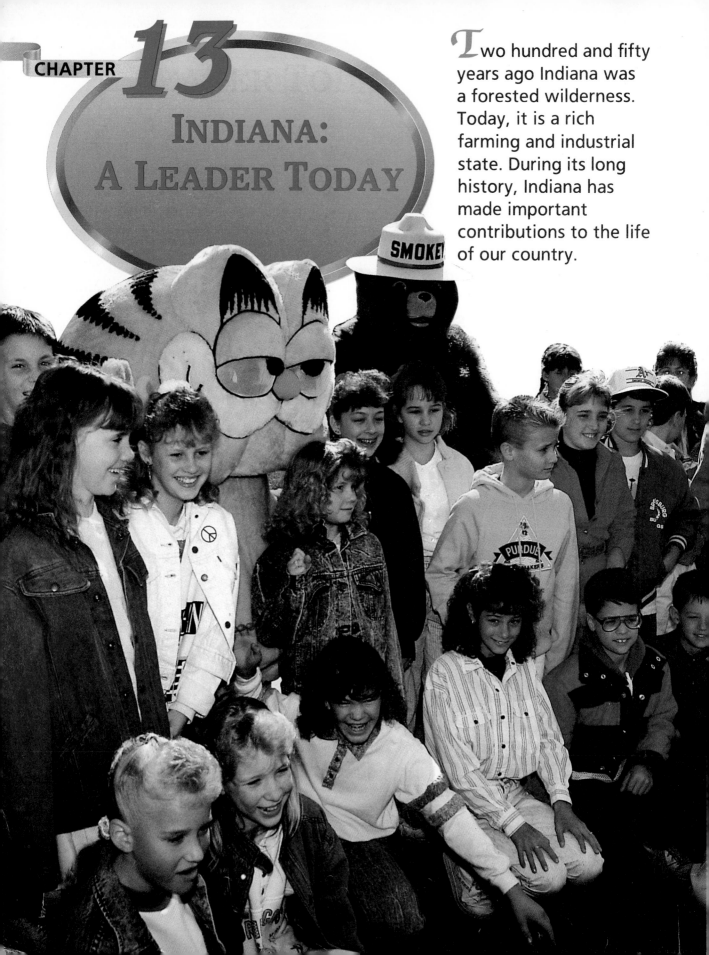

13

INDIANA: A LEADER TODAY

*T*wo hundred and fifty years ago Indiana was a forested wilderness. Today, it is a rich farming and industrial state. During its long history, Indiana has made important contributions to the life of our country.

SMOKEY

A Leader Among States

THINK ABOUT WHAT YOU KNOW
Think back over what you have studied so far in this book. Name one way that Indiana has helped the United States to develop.

STUDY THE VOCABULARY
ambassador   **gallery**
correspondent   **museum**

FOCUS YOUR READING
What contributions have Indiana's government, artistic, and sports leaders made to the United States?

A. Indiana Leaders in Government Positions

Heads of Government   Indiana has produced its share of national government leaders. From Indiana have come some candidates for President as well as Presidents and Vice Presidents. The ninth President, William Henry Harrison, had been a territorial governor of Indiana. The twenty-third President, Benjamin Harrison, although born in Ohio, studied law and lived in Indianapolis. He led an Indiana regiment during the Civil War.

You have read that Abraham Lincoln grew up in Indiana. Wendell L. Willkie grew up in Elwood in Madison County. Willkie ran for President in 1940. He lost to the very popular Franklin D. Roosevelt. In 1989 Indiana Senator J. Danforth Quayle became Vice President of the United States.

Lawmakers and Leaders   Indiana has provided other leaders as well. Charles A. Halleck was from DeMotte in Jasper County. Halleck served in the United States House of Representatives for many years. Paul V. McNutt was another Hoosier who brought honor to Indiana. First he served as governor of Indiana. Then, in 1937 McNutt became

Vice President Dan Quayle was born in Indianapolis.
▶ Which Presidents lived or studied in Indiana?

the high commissioner (kuh MIHSH uh nur) to the Philippines. This means that he was a representative of the United States government there. Later, he became an advisor to President Franklin Roosevelt. Eugene Debs from Terre Haute was an important political leader. He served in the Indiana legislature from 1885 to 1892. In 1893 he formed the American Railway Union.

A Popular Mayor The city of Gary, in northwestern Indiana, elected one of the first black mayors of a major American city. Richard Hatcher was elected mayor in 1967. Mayor Hatcher improved housing, started job training programs, and did many other good things for the city of Gary. City voters liked him so much that they reelected him in 1971, 1975, 1979, and 1983. Indiana has helped to lead the nation.

Richard Hatcher was an important leader in Indiana government.
▶ How many years did he serve as mayor of Gary?

B. Indiana Writers

Authors Everywhere There is a legend told of a man named Opie Read. He made a speech in Fort Wayne. Mr. Read began his speech by saying that he knew Indiana was famous for having many writers. Read suggested that anyone in the audience who was an author should stand up. Everyone in the audience stood up! Everyone, that is, except one older man. Opie Read pointed to the man, saying that there was at least *one* Hoosier who was not an author. "Oh, no," a member of the audience spoke up, "he writes too. He just didn't hear the question."

Writing Poetry This funny legend probably did not really happen. But it points to something true. Many writers have been born in Indiana or have lived in the state. One of the most famous was James Whitcomb Riley, who was born in Greenfield in 1849. Riley wrote many poems about children. Both children and adults enjoy them even today.

Riley liked to write about everyday Indiana people. Hoosiers are proud of Riley. In Greenfield there is a statue of the Hoosier Poet, as he is often called.

Writing Fiction Edward Eggleston was born in southeastern Indiana in 1837. He wrote several novels.

These children are admiring the statue of James Whitcomb Riley. Riley was born in Greenfield.
► What did Riley like to write about?

Novels are long stories. His most famous novel is called *The Hoosier Schoolmaster*. In this book, he tells about the early settlers in Indiana.

Theodore Dreiser was born in Terre Haute in 1871. He went to Indiana University for one year. Dreiser was a well-known novelist. *Sister Carrie* and *An American Tragedy* are his most important works.

Have you ever seen the movie *Ben Hur?* It was about life in ancient Rome. The movie was made from the book *Ben Hur*, written by Lew Wallace, a Hoosier. Lew Wallace is sometimes called General Wallace.

This is because he served as a general in the Civil War. In 1878 he became the governor of the New Mexico Territory. Then, in 1881 President Garfield made Wallace ambassador to Turkey, a foreign country. That means that he represented the United States in Turkey.

Another very well known Hoosier writer was Booth Tarkington. He was born in Indianapolis in 1869. Tarkington wrote novels, plays, short stories, and essays. *Penrod* and *Penrod and Sam* are two famous collections of his stories about the joys of being a young boy. Booth

These pictures show works from famous Hoosier writers. The works include *Ben Hur* and *Penrod and Sam.*
▶ What other works are shown?

Tarkington was interested in everything that had to do with Indiana. He even served a term in the Indiana House of Representatives.

Almost everyone is familiar with the doll named Raggedy Ann™. Raggedy Ann's™ creator was Johnny Gruelle, a Hoosier. He wrote the original Raggedy Ann™ stories in about 1918. Raggedy Ann™ dolls soon followed, and they have been popular ever since. Gene Stratton Porter was a Hoosier novelist who wrote about the Indiana countryside and its people. A modern Hoosier novelist is William E. Wilson. His novels show what life used to be like in parts of southern Indiana. Another modern writer from Indiana is Kurt Vonnegut.

Writing About War   Ernie Pyle was from Vermillion County. He was a war **correspondent** during World War II. A correspondent is a person who describes events in writing. He or she writes these accounts for a newspaper. Ernie Pyle was so good at his job that he won a Pulitzer (POOL iht sur) Prize. Pulitzer prizes are given for the best writing in many different classes. Ernie Pyle won for newspaper writing. Ernie Pyle died doing what he loved best. He was observing on the battlefield when he was killed in 1945.

From: "LITTLE ORPHANT ANNIE"

By: James Whitcomb Riley

Setting: Indiana in the late 1800s

James Whitcomb Riley lived in Indiana from his birth, in 1849 until his death, in 1916. Riley wrote many poems about life in Indiana's small towns and farming communities. Often he tried to imitate the language of everyday Indiana people. He did this in one of his best-known poems: "Little Orphant Annie."

This poem tells the story of an orphan girl named Annie. In the late 1800s, an orphan would usually be taken in by relatives. In the new family, however, the girl or boy would have to work hard. He or she would be treated almost like a servant. The first stanza of the poem follows. It shows what a hard worker Annie is. But it also tells about one of Annie's special talents: telling ghost stories that everyone loves to hear.

*Little Orphant Annie's come to
    our house to stay,
An' wash the cups an' saucers up,
    an' brush the crumbs away,
An' shoo the chickens off the
    porch, an' dust the hearth, an'
    sweep,
An' make the fire, an' bake the
    bread, an' earn her board-an'-
    keep;
An' all us other childern, when the
    supper-things is done,
We set around the kitchen fire an'
    has the mostest fun
A-list'nin' to the witch-tales 'at
    Annie tells about,
An' the Gobble-uns 'at gits you
       Ef you
          Don't
            Watch
             Out!*

. . . .

Many people feel that this well-loved poem was the idea for the comic strip *Little Orphan Annie*. This popular comic strip has been in newspapers for more than 50 years!

C. Indiana Musicians

Famous Tunes   One of America's most famous songwriters was Cole Porter. He was born in Peru, Indiana, in the late 1800s. He wrote and sold his first song when he was only 11 years old! One of his best-known songs is "Night and Day." He went on to write musicals for the stage and for the movies. A musical is a play with music. Some of his musicals are *Kiss Me Kate, High Society,* and *Silk Stockings.*

Hoagy Carmichael was born in Bloomington in 1899. He studied law at Indiana University. But instead of being a lawyer, he became a famous songwriter. His most famous song is "Stardust."

Famous Brothers   Paul Dresser was Theodore Dreiser's brother. When Paul joined a traveling music show at 16, he changed his name to Dresser. Paul Dresser wrote the state song of Indiana, "On the Banks of the Wabash, Far Away." Some people think that this is one of the greatest folk songs in America.

Perhaps you are more familiar with two of Indiana's newer songwriters. One is Michael Jackson. He was born in Gary, Indiana. There, his family performed as a group and became famous. Today, Michael Jackson performs on his own. He has recorded many best-selling songs.

Songs about Struggles   Rock artist John Cougar Mellencamp was born in Seymour, Indiana, in 1951. His albums have been praised for both their music and their messages. Many of his songs talk about the struggles of ordinary people who face hard times. Today, Mellencamp lives with his family outside Bloomington.

Michael Jackson first sang with the Jackson Five. He has won many music awards.
▶ Where was Michael born?

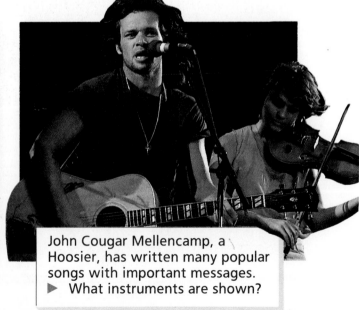

John Cougar Mellencamp, a Hoosier, has written many popular songs with important messages.
▶ What instruments are shown?

You should think of one Indiana songwriter whenever you go to a baseball game. Albert von Tilzer, a Hoosier, wrote "Take Me Out to the Ball Game." It is played thousands and thousands of times during each baseball season.

D. Indiana Artists

Many artists have lived and worked in Indiana. J. Otis Adams started an art school in Fort Wayne. William Forsyth started to paint while he was still a child. He, along with T. C. Steele and Will Vawter, painted the beautiful scenery of Brown County. Steele, in fact, started an artist's colony there.

The artist George Winter is known for his paintings of the Miami

This is Robert Indiana's famous word image *LOVE*.
▶ What was the artist's name before he changed it to Indiana?

and Potawatomi (paht uh WAHT uh mee) Indians. Robert Indiana is known for paintings called word images. This artist, who was born

This work, titled *Brown County Garden,* was painted by T. C. Steele.
▶ What other artists also painted scenery of Brown County?

329

Many people visit the Indianapolis Museum of Art. Beautiful artwork is kept here.
▶ What is a museum?

E. Indiana Athletes

Sports Fans Sports are so important to Indianans that their love of basketball is often called Hoosier Hysteria. Todd is typical.

"I *love* basketball! When I get to high school, I hope to be one of the stars of our team. Everyone in town comes out to see the games. My sisters and I started learning how to play when we were in elementary school. I guess that's why the high schools, colleges, and universities in Indiana have such good teams."

Robert Clark, took the name of the state he was born in. One of his word images is of the word *LOVE*.

All over Indiana there are **galleries** and **museums**. A gallery is a place where pictures are shown. A museum is a place where rare and valuable objects are kept. The Indianapolis Museum of Art includes many galleries where beautiful art can be enjoyed by all.

The Indiana State Museum recently celebrated the tenth birthday of a famous cartoon cat. The cat was Garfield. The creator of the *Garfield* comic strip, Jim Davis, is a Hoosier.

Basketball Is Best Indiana University has won the NCAA (National Collegiate Athletic Association) basketball tournament five times. The coach of Indiana University's basketball team is Bobby Knight. He is known throughout Indiana and throughout the country. He is a strict coach who wants his players

People across the country enjoy the adventures of Garfield, the famous cartoon cat.
▶ Who created Garfield?

Bobby Knight is the well-known coach of Indiana University's basketball team. Damon Bailey is a popular young basketball star from Indiana.
▶ What is Indianans' love of basketball sometimes called?

to do well on the basketball court and in the classroom too.

The Pacers Indiana's professional team is the Indiana Pacers. This team is a member of the NBA (National Basketball Association). Market Square Arena in Indianapolis, completed in 1974, is the home of the Pacers. The arena can seat over 18,000 people. It has no inside pillars to block the view of the game.

It should be no surprise that Indiana has a state Basketball Hall of Fame. Todd has been to this museum in Indianapolis.

Big Bird "It was great! The most interesting part for me was the display on Larry Bird. He's from my hometown—French Lick—in southern Indiana! Larry Bird has no trouble reaching the basket. He's 6 feet, 9 inches tall! Larry Bird played for Indiana State University. He led the team to a record number of victories. Then he went on to play for the Boston Celtics in the NBA. Maybe someday there will be a display about *me*!"

A Cycling Champ An important sports figure of Indiana's past was

Marshall "Major" Taylor was a top bicycle racer from Indiana.
▶ What Indianapolis sports arena was named after him?

Marshall "Major" Taylor. This black athlete was a top bicycle racer almost 100 years ago. He was the American Champion in 1899 and the World Champion in 1900. Today you can visit the Major Taylor Velodrome (VEE luh drohm) in Indianapolis. This bicycling arena honors a great Hoosier athlete.

A Famous Coach Football is also a very popular sport in Indiana. The state's NFL (National Football League) team is called the Indianapolis Colts. The Colts play in the spectacular Hoosier Dome, built in 1986. This sports arena seats over 60,000 fans. It holds the National Track and Field Hall of Fame Museum.

Both the Purdue University Boilermakers and the Indiana University Hoosiers belong to the Big Ten. This is a group of teams from the leading midwestern universities. The University of Notre Dame (noh truh DAYM), located in South Bend, has one of the best-known college football teams in the country. One of the greatest football coaches of all time was Knute Rockne (noot RAHK nee). He was head football coach at Notre Dame for many years. Notre Dame has been the national college football champion eight times.

The Indianapolis Colts play football in the Hoosier Dome.
▶ In what year was this sports arena built?

More than 300,000 people watch the Indy 500 each year. It is a very famous car race.
▶ When is the Indy 500 held?

The Great Race Another very famous sport in Indiana is auto racing. The Indy 500 is the most famous car race in the world. It is held every year over the Memorial Day weekend. On Saturday, the exciting 500 Festival Memorial Parade occurs. On Sunday, drivers race their cars for 500 miles (805 km) around the 2-1/2-mile (4-km) track at the Indianapolis Motor Speedway.

Other Indiana Sports Women's sports activities are an important part of university sports programs. Indiana University's women's tennis team has ranked high in the Midwest. At Notre Dame and Purdue, women's basketball, volleyball, tennis, and cross-country are popular.

Indiana University's swimming and diving teams are among the best in the nation. One Indiana University swimmer, Mark Spitz, set an Olympic record in 1972 by winning seven gold medals!

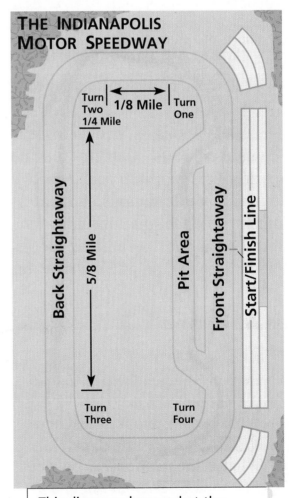

THE INDIANAPOLIS MOTOR SPEEDWAY

This diagram shows what the Indy 500 racecourse looks like.
▶ How long are the back and front straightaways?

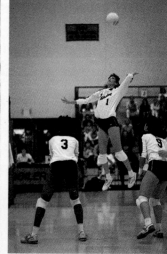

Indiana state universities and colleges offer students a wide variety of sports programs.
▶ What sports are shown in these photographs?

Indianapolis is known as the Amateur Sports Capital of the World. Its natatorium (nayt uh TOR ee um) is world-famous. A natatorium is a place that includes one or more indoor swimming pools. Swimming, diving, and other water sports are featured there. Indianapolis hosted the Pan-American games during the summer of 1987. The Pan-American games are something like the Olympics. But only countries that are in the Western Hemisphere attend.

LESSON *1* REVIEW

THINK AND WRITE

A. How has Indiana helped to lead the nation?

B. What two writers from Indiana wrote about life in Indiana?

C. What is the relationship between a famous Hoosier author and a famous Hoosier songwriter?

D. How has Indiana's geography influenced some of its artists?

E. What does the term *Hoosier Hysteria* mean?

SKILLS CHECK

THINKING SKILL

Why do you think it is important for athletes to do their best both in the classroom and on the playing field? Write your answer on a separate sheet using complete sentences.

334

A Pioneer in Education

THINK ABOUT WHAT YOU KNOW

Make a list of the colleges and universities in Indiana that you know about.

STUDY THE VOCABULARY

engineer   research
veterinarian   experiment
pharmacist

FOCUS YOUR READING

How has education developed in Indiana, and how does Indiana contribute to education today?

A. Elementary and High School Then and Now

Old and New Schools Indiana has always been concerned about education. The first Indiana constitution in 1816, said that the state had to provide money for schools.

Today's students are sometimes surprised to learn what the first schools in Indiana were like. Let's listen in on Molly as she discusses with her family what she has learned in class.

"Dad and Mom, did you know that the first schools in Indiana were log cabins? Abraham Lincoln went to one like that! A whole bunch of grades were in one room. It must have been noisy!" said Molly.

"That's really different from today, isn't it, Molly?" her mother said. "Of course, classes were a lot smaller then."

Molly nodded her head. "Sometimes children had to walk a long way to school. I can't imagine that. I ride the school bus every day."

"What did children study then?" asked her father.

"Let's see —" Molly tried to remember. "Reading, writing, arithmetic, history, and geography. But one teacher taught everything."

"And how is that different from your school?" asked her father.

"Well, we learn the things that they did. But we learn other subjects

Education has always been important to the people of Indiana.
▶ How is this classroom similar to or different from yours?

too. They didn't have science, music, art, physical education, or computer science. Also, some of my teachers teach only one subject. Mr. Spence teaches only music. Miss Ashton teaches only art."

"I bet I can think of another difference, Molly," said her mother. "I don't think the pioneer children had soccer, chorus, or scouting! I wonder what they would think of that?"

Better Schools   The lawmakers of Indiana have always done their best to provide the state with good schools and universities. In 1987 Governor Robert Orr brought the A+ Program to the Indiana public school system. The goal of this program was to make Indiana's public schools even better.

B. Universities and Colleges

First College   Universities and colleges are schools of higher education. That means that their studies are more advanced than those in high school. These schools also prepare students for careers in law, medicine, teaching, and other fields.

Ten years before Indiana became a state, a college was set up in Vincennes. This was the first college in what was then the western part of the country. That college still exists. It is called Vincennes University.

A Great Library   Indiana University, or IU as many people call it, began as a small school in Bloomington in 1820. The school became Indiana College in 1827, and it is now Indiana University. IU is still in Bloomington, and it has other campuses around the state in Indianapolis, Fort Wayne, Gary, Kokomo, Richmond, South Bend, and New Albany. A campus is the buildings and grounds of a college or university. Students go to IU to learn medicine, dentistry, nursing, science, art, music, and law. The IU library in Bloomington is one of the largest and best in the country.

Bloomington is Indiana University's largest and oldest campus. You can see some of the features of the campus in these pictures.
▶ What is a campus?

Begun in a Log Cabin In 1842 the Roman Catholic University of Notre Dame was founded at South Bend. Although Notre Dame is a Roman Catholic school, students of all faiths may go there. Students can learn to be scientists, lawyers, teachers, and engineers. An engineer is a person who studies the use of energy and the planning and building of engines, roads, canals, buildings, and bridges. There are more than 90 buildings at Notre Dame. The first building that was put up was a log cabin. This log cabin is still on the grounds of Notre Dame today.

Student enrollment in Indiana schools has risen steadily.
▶ How many students were enrolled in 1988?

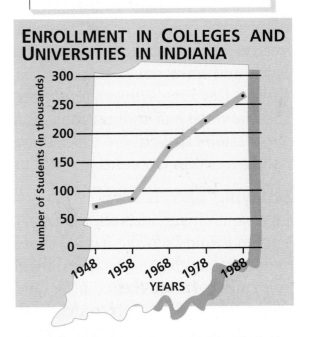

ENROLLMENT IN COLLEGES AND UNIVERSITIES IN INDIANA

Number of Students (in thousands)

300, 250, 200, 150, 100, 50, 0

1948, 1958, 1968, 1978, 1988

YEARS

Branch Campuses Purdue University was built in Lafayette in 1869. Today, the university has branch campuses in Indianapolis, Fort Wayne, Hammond, and Westville. Purdue is best known as an engineering school. Purdue also teaches methods of farming. It teaches students how to be veterinarians, or animal doctors. Pharmacists, or people who work with medicines, can also be trained at Purdue. Purdue is now one of the most famous universities in the world for these kinds of studies. Purdue's branch in Indianapolis has now joined with a branch of IU to form Indiana University–Purdue University at Indianapolis (IUPUI).

337

Colleges and universities in Indiana have grown quickly and now have about 300,000 students. Most of these students are at the state universities. The rest go to other colleges and universities in the state. Butler, DePauw, Wabash, Hanover, the University of Indianapolis, and Valparaiso are some of these colleges and universities.

Studying and Testing The colleges and universities of Indiana are known throughout the world. Thousands of students come to them from all parts of the country and from many foreign countries. A great deal of important research is done in their libraries and laboratories. Research is a careful hunting for and studying about facts or truths. In laboratories, people make experiments. An experiment is a test to find out facts. Experiments help people develop new medicines and new ways of doing things.

These Purdue students are finishing a mirror they made to be used on a research telescope.
▶ How do their reflections differ from their real faces?

LESSON 2 REVIEW

THINK AND WRITE

A. What is one way that schools in the 1800s were different from schools today?
B. How do Indiana colleges and universities help our country and the world?

SKILLS CHECK

MAP SKILL

Purdue University was started in Lafayette. Find Lafayette on the map on page 39. Using the map key, tell whether Lafayette is in an area of high population density.

At Home in Indiana

THINK ABOUT WHAT YOU KNOW

What are some of your favorite things to do in Indiana?

STUDY THE VOCABULARY

touring   recreation
scenic   seminary

FOCUS YOUR READING

Why is Indiana a good state for people to live in?

A. Beautiful Indiana

Loving Indiana Indiana's beauty and warm hospitality make it a great state for **touring**. Touring means traveling for pleasure. Indiana is **scenic**. That means it has beautiful areas. There is some especially beautiful natural scenery in the hilly southern part of Indiana.

The state government has set up state parks in some of the most beautiful areas of the state. The state parks provide **recreation**. Recreation is what people do for fun and exercise and rest.

For Tourists and Hoosiers There are many state parks in Indiana. The largest state park is Brown County State Park. This is a forested area of great beauty. Clifty Falls State Park is another. It lies near Madison, close to the Ohio River. Clifty Falls is Indiana's highest waterfall. The water plunges over 100 feet (30 m)! The falls attract many visitors throughout the year. Another very beautiful state park is Turkey Run State Park in Parke County.

Visitors to Indiana's state parks can enjoy beautiful scenery such as Clifty Falls.
▶ How high is Clifty Falls?

Indiana Dunes State Park is on the shore of Lake Michigan. Beside the lake are dunes, which are huge heaps of windblown sand. Also along Lake Michigan's shores is the Indiana Dunes National Lakeshore. This part of the shore is cared for by the federal government.

There are many lakes in Indiana. They are important for boating and fishing. Some fish that you may catch in these lakes are bass, catfish, and bluegill. Lake Monroe in Monroe and Brown counties is a favorite lake for sailing. In addition, Indiana has woods, prairies, and swamps to see and explore.

B. Historic Indiana

Indiana is a state that enjoys its history and traditions. Why else would Hoosiers celebrate so many yearly festivals?

Historic places in Indiana include the prehistoric Angel Mounds, Conner Prairie, New Harmony, and the restored fort at Fort Wayne. These places remind Hoosiers of the early days of Indiana. Other interesting places include the Studebaker National Museum with its exhibits of old cars and wagons, the John Dillinger Historical Museum, the

Indiana has many lakes for fun water activities, such as boating, swimming, and fishing.
▶ What kind of boats are shown in this picture?

This scene shows some of the fun at the annual circus festival in Peru. This festival is held every July.
▶ In what county is Peru located?

Levi Coffin house, and the Gus Grissom memorial.

The peaceful St. Meinrad's Archabbey in St. Meinrad is the oldest **seminary** in the United States. A seminary is a place where priests or other religious leaders are trained.

C. Fun Indiana

Things to Do Every person's favorite activity can be found somewhere in Indiana. There are many interesting things to do. There is fishing, boating, swimming, camping, tobogganing, picnicking, and even skiing. There are so many museums to be visited that it would take many trips to see them all.

Let's take a tour. The first stop is in Miami County. There, you will find a circus museum. Many famous American circuses spent their winters there. Every July, Peru holds a four-day circus festival. While you are there, visit Cole Porter's birthplace.

In April, spend some time at the Renaissance Fair in Terre Haute. The Renaissance occurred in Europe from about 1350 to 1600. You will see plays and eat food that is like what people ate at that time. Up in Fort Wayne, spend some time at the petting zoo as well as at the famous pioneer fort.

End your tour in Indianapolis. It is an exciting city to visit. Trains no longer bring people and goods to Union Station as they did 100 years ago. Now the huge building is filled with restaurants and shops. Save some time for the Children's Museum. It has five floors of exhibits just for children.

Modern buildings and skyscrapers form an impressive skyline in the city of Indianapolis.

▶ What type of transportation is shown in this picture?

Indianapolis Zoo
White River State Park

Visitors to the Indianapolis Zoo can see more than 500 different kinds of animals.
▶ In what park is the Indianapolis Zoo located?

and artifacts of Native Americans and the American West. You will see paintings, sculptures, costumes, masks, and other items that bring the West alive.

Take time to enjoy the White River Park promenade (prahm uh NAYD), or walkway, close to the zoo. The promenade is lined with giant

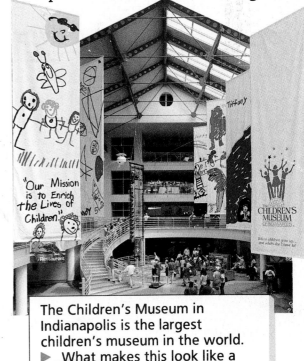

The Park in the City Do not miss the White River State Park! In this park is the new 65-acre (26-hectare) Indianapolis Zoo, with over 2,000 animals. You can see elephants, giraffes, and other animals living in natural settings.

Be sure to visit the Elteljorg Museum as well. It celebrates the art

The Children's Museum in Indianapolis is the largest children's museum in the world.
▶ What makes this look like a children's museum?

Indiana is a fun and exciting place to live.
▶ What do you like best about living in Indiana?

blocks of limestone. They remind you of the seas that covered the land hundreds of millions of years ago. Now look down at the White River. Close your eyes and pretend Native American tribes are still hunting and fishing as they did before Indianapolis became the state capital. Raise your eyes to the capitol building, skyscrapers, sports domes, and the rest of the beautiful city of Indianapolis. The limestone promenade is a walk into Indiana's far past, its proud history, its present, and its bright future.

LESSON 3 REVIEW

THINK AND WRITE

A. How has the state government helped Indiana to remain scenic?
B. How do Hoosiers show their interest in history?
C. Which of the different fun activities in Indiana would you most enjoy doing?

SKILLS CHECK

WRITING SKILL

Imagine that you are touring Indiana. Use the map on page 356 to tell about how many miles (kilometers) there are between the cities of Terre Haute and Indianapolis. Write your answer in a complete sentence.

B. Learning the Skill

One part of the library is the **reference section**. Here you will find encyclopedias, almanacs, atlases, dictionaries, and other books of general information. If you want to learn about a topic, an encyclopedia is a good place to start.

Many libraries have collections of pictures, maps, pamphlets, and articles. These are kept in a **vertical file**. Information in the vertical file is usually stored alphabetically by subject.

Another important section of the library is the **card catalog**. A card catalog is a list of all the books in the library. The books are listed on cards that are kept in drawers. Each book is listed alphabetically by title, author, and subject. The **librarian** will help you find information, too. Librarians are specially trained to find information. Although librarians are willing to help, you should first try to find the information on your own.

C. Practicing the Skill

Andrew Carnegie was a pioneer in the steel industry in the United States. Clara Ingram Judson, a native Indianan, wrote a book about him. Her book is called *Andrew Carnegie*. Think about how you would find this book in your library. Then think about how you would find additional information about Andrew Carnegie.

Read the following questions about the library. Write your answers on a separate sheet of paper.

1. What section of the library would you use to find Clara Ingram Judson's book about Andrew Carnegie?
2. What are three ways to find this book in the card catalog?
3. Where in the library might you find a pamphlet about Andrew Carnegie?
4. Which section of the library would you use to find general information about Carnegie's life?

D. Applying the Skill

Listed below are some topics about Indiana and some famous Indianans. Choose one topic or person from the list. Using the books and other materials in the library, write a short report on your topic. At the end of your report, list the books and materials you used.

Johnny Appleseed	Archaeology
Knute Rockne	Virgil Grissom
George Rogers Clark	Hoosiers
Indy 500	Amish

349

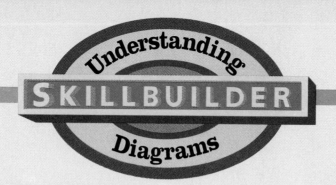

A. WHY DO I NEED THIS SKILL?

Diagrams are special drawings that show how things work or how things happen. Diagrams help us understand difficult ideas. Learning to read diagrams will help you in many subjects, including social studies.

B. LEARNING THE SKILL

Diagrams do not show exactly how something looks. They are sketches or drawings that help you picture how something might look. Diagrams use words, pictures, and other symbols to explain certain things.

Read the following paragraph about how coal is formed.

After trees and plants die, they begin to decay. The decaying plants and trees form a brown, woody substance called peat. The peat becomes buried under layers of rock, sand, and minerals. After thousands or millions of years, the weight of these layers presses the peat into coal.

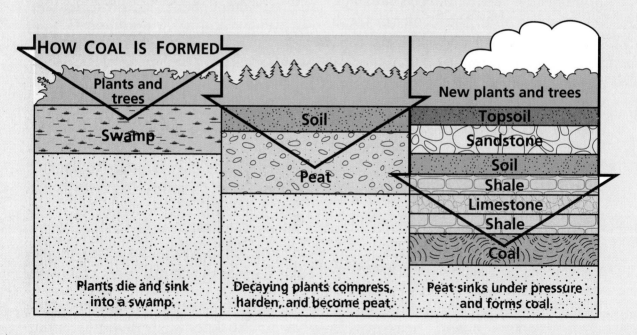

HOW COAL IS FORMED

Plants and trees / Swamp — Plants die and sink into a swamp.

Soil / Peat — Decaying plants compress, harden, and become peat.

New plants and trees / Topsoil / Sandstone / Soil / Shale / Limestone / Shale / Coal — Peat sinks under pressure and forms coal.

Now look at the diagram on the facing page. Like the paragraph, it explains how coal is formed. Each drawing in the diagram shows a different stage in the formation of coal.

C. PRACTICING THE SKILL

Use the diagram to answer the following questions about how coal is formed.

1. What is the subject of this diagram?
2. How many stages in the formation of coal are shown here?
3. What happens in the second stage?

4. How does the coal get so far under the ground?
5. What happens above the ground after the first plants and trees become peat?

D. APPLYING THE SKILL

Steel production is an important industry in Indiana. Use the library to find out how steel is made. Write a paragraph explaining what you learned. Then draw a diagram to show the information in your paragraph. Be sure to label your diagram for your readers.

ATLAS

THE WORLD: POLITICAL

Scale:
0 — 1,500 miles
0 — 1,500 kilometers

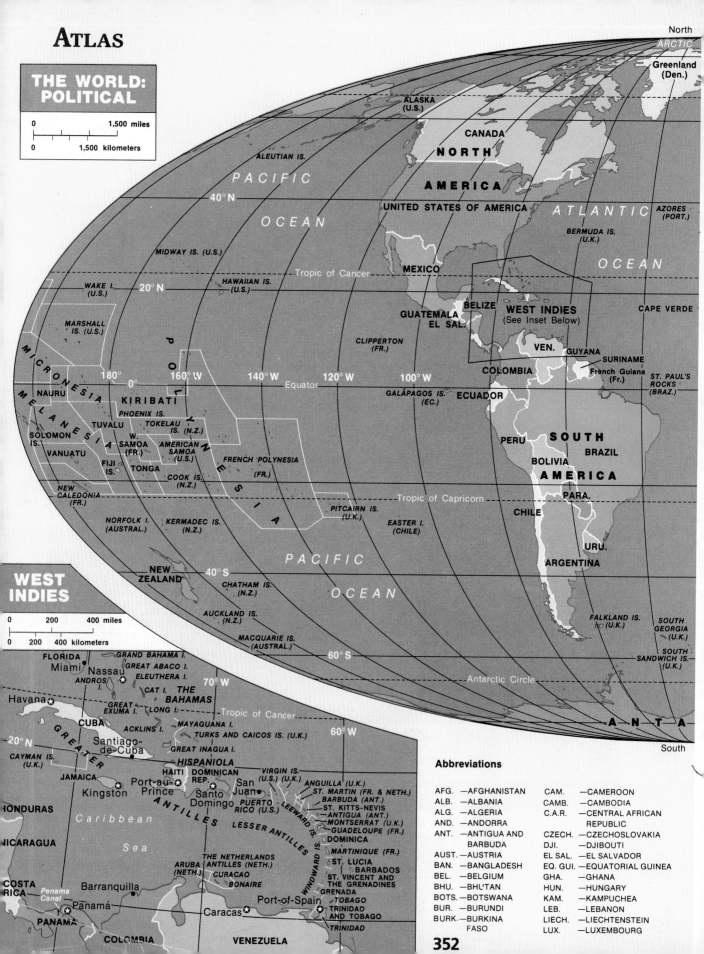

North
ARCTIC
Greenland (Den.)

ALASKA (U.S.)

CANADA

NORTH AMERICA

ALEUTIAN IS.

PACIFIC OCEAN

40° N

UNITED STATES OF AMERICA

ATLANTIC OCEAN

AZORES (PORT.)

BERMUDA IS. (U.K.)

MIDWAY IS. (U.S.)

Tropic of Cancer

MEXICO

WAKE I. (U.S.)   20° N

HAWAIIAN IS. (U.S.)

BELIZE

GUATEMALA
EL SAL.

WEST INDIES (See Inset Below)

CAPE VERDE

MARSHALL IS. (U.S.)

CLIPPERTON (FR.)

VEN.

GUYANA
SURINAME
French Guiana (Fr.)

ST. PAUL'S ROCKS (BRAZ.)

MICRONESIA
MELANESIA

180°   0°   160° W   140° W   Equator   120° W   100° W

COLOMBIA

NAURU

KIRIBATI

GALÁPAGOS IS. (EC.)

ECUADOR

PHOENIX IS.

PERU

SOUTH

BRAZIL

TUVALU

TOKELAU IS. (N.Z.)

W. SAMOA (FR.)

AMERICAN SAMOA (U.S.)

FRENCH POLYNESIA (FR.)

BOLIVIA

AMERICA

SOLOMON IS.

VANUATU

FIJI IS.

TONGA

COOK IS. (N.Z.)

Tropic of Capricorn

PARA.

CHILE

URU.

NEW CALEDONIA (FR.)

NORFOLK I. (AUSTRAL.)

KERMADEC IS. (N.Z.)

PITCAIRN IS. (U.K.)

EASTER I. (CHILE)

ARGENTINA

PACIFIC OCEAN

NEW ZEALAND   40° S

CHATHAM IS. (N.Z.)

FALKLAND IS. (U.K.)

SOUTH GEORGIA (U.K.)

AUCKLAND IS. (N.Z.)

MACQUARIE IS. (AUSTRAL.)

60° S

SOUTH SANDWICH IS. (U.K.)

Antarctic Circle

A N T A

South

WEST INDIES

Scale:
0 — 200 — 400 miles
0 — 200 — 400 kilometers

FLORIDA
Miami

GRAND BAHAMA I.
GREAT ABACO I.
ELEUTHERA I.

Nassau
ANDROS I.

CAT I.

70° W

THE BAHAMAS

Havana

GREAT EXUMA I.
LONG I.

Tropic of Cancer

CUBA

ACKLINS I.

MAYAGUANA I.

TURKS AND CAICOS IS. (U.K.)

60° W

20° N

Santiago-de-Cuba

GREAT INAGUA I.

CAYMAN IS. (U.K.)

HISPANIOLA

VIRGIN IS. (U.S.) (U.K.)

ANGUILLA (U.K.)

JAMAICA

HAITI

DOMINICAN REP.

San Juan

ST. MARTIN (FR. & NETH.)
BARBUDA (ANT.)
ANTIGUA (ANT.)
ST. KITTS-NEVIS
MONTSERRAT (U.K.)
GUADELOUPE (FR.)
DOMINICA

Kingston

Port-au-Prince

Santo Domingo

PUERTO RICO (U.S.)

LEEWARD IS.

HONDURAS

NICARAGUA

Caribbean Sea

ANTILLES

LESSER ANTILLES

MARTINIQUE (FR.)

ST. LUCIA
BARBADOS
ST. VINCENT AND THE GRENADINES
GRENADA

THE NETHERLANDS ANTILLES (NETH.)

ARUBA (NETH.)

CURACAO

BONAIRE

WINDWARD IS.

TOBAGO

TRINIDAD AND TOBAGO

COSTA RICA

Barranquilla

Port-of-Spain

PANAMA
Panama Canal
Panamá

Caracas

TRINIDAD

COLOMBIA

VENEZUELA

Abbreviations

AFG.	—AFGHANISTAN	CAM.	—CAMEROON
ALB.	—ALBANIA	CAMB.	—CAMBODIA
ALG.	—ALGERIA	C.A.R.	—CENTRAL AFRICAN REPUBLIC
AND.	—ANDORRA		
ANT.	—ANTIGUA AND BARBUDA	CZECH.	—CZECHOSLOVAKIA
		DJI.	—DJIBOUTI
AUST.	—AUSTRIA	EL SAL.	—EL SALVADOR
BAN.	—BANGLADESH	EQ. GUI.	—EQUATORIAL GUINEA
BEL.	—BELGIUM	GHA.	—GHANA
BHU.	—BHUTAN	HUN.	—HUNGARY
BOTS.	—BOTSWANA	KAM.	—KAMPUCHEA
BUR.	—BURUNDI	LEB.	—LEBANON
BURK.	—BURKINA FASO	LIECH.	—LIECHTENSTEIN
		LUX.	—LUXEMBOURG

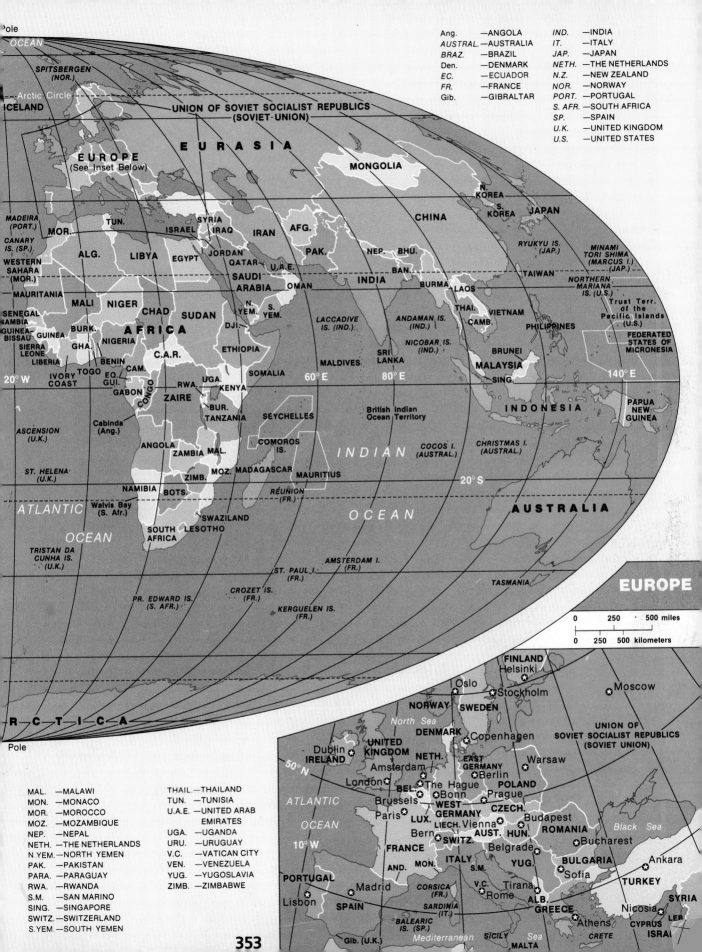

EUROPE

C A N A D A

Seattle
WASHINGTON
Olympia
Spokane
45° N
Portland
Columbia River
Salem
Great Falls
Missouri River
Grand Forks
Eugene
Helena
MONTANA
NORTH DAKOTA
OREGON
Bismarck
Fargo
IDAHO
Boise
Billings
Snake
Idaho Falls
SOUTH DAKOTA
River
WYOMING
Rapid City
Pierre
Pocatello
Sioux Falls
Great
Salt
Lake
Casper
NEVADA
West Valley
Salt Lake
City
Laramie
NEBRASKA
Reno
Provo
Cheyenne
Sacramento
Carson City
Grand Island
Omaha
Oakland
UTAH
Lincoln
San Francisco
San Jose
Denver
Aurora
Topeka
Fresno
COLORADO
Colorado
Springs
35° N
CALIFORNIA
Las
Vegas
KANSAS
Colorado River
Arkansas
River
Wichita
Los Angeles Anaheim
Riverside
Santa Fe
Tulsa
Long Beach
Santa Ana
ARIZONA
Albuquerque
OKLAHOMA
San Diego
Phoenix
NEW MEXICO
Oklahoma City
PACIFIC
Mesa
Lawton
Red River
OCEAN
Tucson
Las Cruces
Arlington
Dallas
30° N
Fort Worth
El Paso
Brazos
120° W
TEXAS
River

HAWAII
Kailua
Austin
Pearl City Honolulu
PACIFIC
20° N
OCEAN
U.S.S.R.
Houston
ARCTIC OCEAN
San Antonio
0   100 miles
0   100 kilometers
Yukon
River
Corpus
160° W   155° W
Fairbanks
Christi
180°
ALASKA
CANADA
MEXICO
55° N
Anchorage
0   200 miles
0   200 kilometers
Juneau
354
PACIFIC   OCEAN
170° W   150° W   140° W

CANADA

MINNESOTA
Duluth •

MICHIGAN

Minneapolis
St. Paul •

Green Bay •

WISCONSIN

MICHIGAN

Madison •

Grand
Rapids •

Lansing •

Detroit •

IOWA

Cedar
Rapids •

Rockford •

Milwaukee •

Chicago • Gary •

Toledo •

Akron •

Cleveland •

Fort Wayne •

INDIANA

Des
Moines •

Davenport •

ILLINOIS

Springfield •

Indianapolis •

Columbus •

OHIO

Wheeling •

Rochester •

Buffalo •

NEW YORK

Springfield •

Albany ✪

Worcester •

MAINE

Augusta ✪
Lewiston •

Montpelier ✪

Portland •

Burlington •

VERMONT

Rutland •

Concord ✪

NEW HAMPSHIRE

Manchester •

Nashua •

Boston ✪ **MASSACHUSETTS**

Pawtucket •
Providence ✪
Warwick •
RHODE ISLAND

Hartford ✪
New Haven •
Bridgeport •

CONNECTICUT

Jersey City •
Newark •
Trenton ✪
New York •

PENNSYLVANIA

Harrisburg ✪

Pittsburgh •

Philadelphia •
Wilmington •
Newark •

NEW JERSEY

Dover ✪
DELAWARE

Baltimore •

Rockville •

Washington,
D.C. ✪

Annapolis ✪

MARYLAND

ATLANTIC

OCEAN

Kansas City •
Kansas
City •
Jefferson City ✪
St. Louis •

MISSOURI

Springfield •

Cincinnati •

Louisville •
Frankfort ✪
Lexington •

KENTUCKY

Huntington •
Charleston ✪

**WEST
VIRGINIA**

Richmond ✪

VIRGINIA

Norfolk • • Virginia Beach

Raleigh ✪

Greensboro •

NORTH CAROLINA

Charlotte •

ARKANSAS

North
Little Rock •

Fort
Smith •

Little Rock ✪

Memphis •

Nashville ✪

Knoxville •

TENNESSEE

Columbia ✪

SOUTH CAROLINA

North Charleston •
Charleston •

Atlanta ✪

Birmingham •

MISSISSIPPI

ALABAMA

Columbus •

GEORGIA

Savannah •

Shreveport •

Meridian •

Montgomery ✪

Jackson ✪

LOUISIANA

Mobile •

Biloxi •

Baton Rouge ✪

New Orleans •

Tallahassee ✪

Jacksonville •

FLORIDA

Tampa •

St. Petersburg •

Miami •

Gulf of Mexico

**THE UNITED STATES
OF AMERICA**

〜 Rivers

✪ National capital

✪ State capitals

• Other cities

| 0 | 100 | 200 miles |
| 0 | 100 | 200 kilometers |

Tropic of Cancer

40° N

35° N

75° W

70° W

30° N

25° N

80° W

85° W

90° W

355

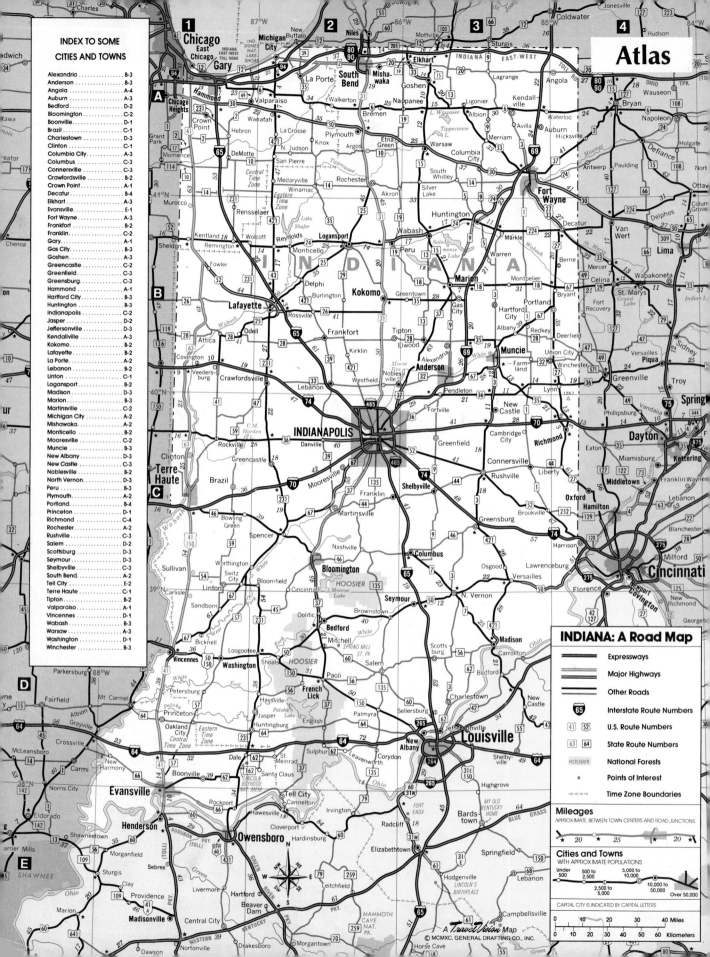

Atlas

INDIANA: A Road Map

- Expressways
- Major Highways
- Other Roads
- **65** Interstate Route Numbers
- **41** **52** U.S. Route Numbers
- **63** **64** State Route Numbers
- HOOSIER National Forests
- Points of Interest
- Time Zone Boundaries

Mileages
APPROXIMATE, BETWEEN TOWN CENTERS AND ROAD JUNCTIONS

Cities and Towns
WITH APPROXIMATE POPULATIONS

| Under 500 | 500 to 2,500 | 5,000 to 10,000 |
| 2,500 to 5,000 | 10,000 to 50,000 | Over 50,000 |

CAPITAL CITY IS INDICATED BY CAPITAL LETTERS

0   10   20   30   40 Miles
0   10   20   30   40   50   60 Kilometers

A Travel Vision Map
© MCMXC, General Drafting Co., Inc.

Some words in this book may be new to you or difficult to pronounce. Those words have been spelled phonetically in parentheses. The syllable that receives stress in a word is shown in small capital letters.

For example: **Chicago** (shuh KAH goh)

Most phonetic spellings are easy to read. In the following Pronunciation Key, you can see how letters are used to show different sounds.

PRONUNCIATION KEY

a	after	(AF tur)								ng	long	(lawng)
ah	father	(FAH thur)	y	hide	(hyd)	u	taken	(TAY kun)		s	city	(SIH tee)
ai	care	(kair)	ye	lie	(lye)		matter	(MAT ur)		sh	ship	(shihp)
aw	dog	(dawg)	oh	flow	(floh)	uh	ago	(uh GOH)		th	thin	(thihn)
ay	paper	(PAY pur)	oi	boy	(boi)	ch	chicken	(CHIHK un)		thh	feather	(FETHH ur)
e	letter	(LET ur)	oo	rule	(rool)	g	game	(gaym)		y	yard	(yahrd)
ee	eat	(eet)	or	horse	(hors)	ing	coming	(KUM ing)		z	size	(syz)
ih	trip	(trihp)	ou	cow	(kou)	j	job	(jahb)		zh	division	(duh VIHZH un)
eye	idea	(eye DEE uh)	yoo	few	(fyoo)	k	came	(kaym)				

The Gazetteer is a geographical dictionary. It shows latitude and longitude for cities and certain other places. Latitude and longtiude are shown in this form: (37°N/80°W). This means "37 degrees north latitude and 80 degrees west longitude." The page reference tells where each entry may be found on a map.

A

Africa. The earth's second largest continent. p. 7.

Allegheny Mountains. Part of the Appalachians. They extend from Pennsylvania to Virginia and West Virginia. p. 355.

Allen County. The largest Indiana county in area, located in the eastern part of the state. p. 37.

Anderson (40°N/86°W). County seat of Madison County. It is the eighth most populated city in Indiana. Located on the West Fork of the White River. Settled about 1823. p. 356.

Angel Mounds (38°N/87°W). Prehistoric Indian town near Evansville. Eleven prehistoric mounds have been found here. Today, Angel Mounds is part of a state park. p. 164.

Antarctica. The earth's third smallest continent. p. 7.

Arctic Ocean. Large body of salt water north of the Arctic Circle. p. 7.

Asia. The earth's largest continent. p. 7.

Atlantic Ocean. Large body of salt water separating North America and South America from Europe and Africa. p. 7.

Auburn (41°N/85°W). County seat of De Kalb County and location of an automobile museum. p. 356.

Australia. The earth's smallest continent. Also the name of the country that covers the whole continent. p. 7.

B

Bloomington (39°N/87°W) (BLOOM ing tun). County seat of Monroe County. It is the tenth most populated city in Indiana. Bloomington is the home of Indiana University. Settled in 1818.   p. 356.

Brown County.   A county located in south central Indiana and known for its beautiful scenery.   p. 37.

Burns Harbor (42°N/87°W).   A harbor on the southern tip of Lake Michigan.   p. 356.

C

Canada.   The largest country in North America and the northern neighbor of the United States.   p. 352.

Charleston (38°N/82°W).   Industrial city and capital of West Virginia.   p. 355.

Chicago (42°N/88°W) (shuh KAH goh).   City in Illinois. Located on Lake Michigan in the northeastern part of the state.   p. 355.

Cincinnati (39°N/84°W) (sihn suh NAT ee). City in Hamilton County, Ohio. Located in southwestern Ohio on the Ohio River. p. 355.

Clarksville (38°N/86°W).   Town in Clark County. Located just north of Louisville, Kentucky. It was started by George Rogers Clark. Settled about 1783.   p. 113.

Clinton (40°N/87°W).   City in Vermillion County. Located on the Wabash River. p. 356.

Columbus (39°N/86°W).   County seat of Bartholomew County. Located on the East Fork of the White River. Settled about 1819. p. 39.

Columbus (40°N/83°W).   Capital of Ohio. A commercial and manufacturing city. p. 355.

Conner Prairie (40°N/86°W).   In pioneer times, it was called William Conner's Fur Post.

Today, it is a reconstructed pioneer village in Noblesville. Men, women, and children play the parts of the pioneers to show us how settlers lived in the 1820s and 1830s. p. 164.

Corn Island.   An island located near Clarksville, Indiana. It is the site from which George Rogers Clark launched his campaign against the British forts in the area. p. 113.

Corydon (38°N/86°W) (KAWR uh dun).   County seat of Harrison County. In 1813 it became the second capital of the Indiana Territory. In 1816 it became the first capital of the new state of Indiana. It remained the capital until 1825. Settled about 1808.   p. 164.

D

Detroit (42°N/83°W) (dih TROIT).   One of eight cities in the United States with a population of more than 1,000,000. Located on the Detroit River in Michigan, near Lake Erie. Founded as a fort in 1701.   p. 355.

E

East Chicago (42°N/87°W).   City in Lake County. Located on Lake Michigan in the northwest corner of Indiana. Indiana Harbor, the state's largest port, is in East Chicago. Settled in 1888.   p. 39.

Eastern Hemisphere.   The half of the earth east of the Prime Meridian. It includes Australia and most of Europe, Africa, and Asia. p. 18.

Elkhart (42°N/86°W) (ELK hahrt).   City in Elkhart County. Located at the point where the Elkhart and St. Joseph rivers join. It is well known for the manufacturing of musical instruments. Settled in 1832.   p. 39.

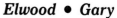

Elwood (40°N/86°W).   City in Madison County. Wendell Willkie was born here.   p. 356.

England.   A country located in Europe. The Prime Meridian passes through Greenwich, England.   p. 353.

Equator.   On a map, a line drawn that circles the earth halfway between the two Poles. It is labeled 0° latitude.   p. 17.

Europe.   The earth's second smallest continent.   p. 7.

Evansville (38°N/88°W) (EV unz vihl).   County seat of Vanderburgh County. It is the fourth most populated city in Indiana. Located on the Ohio River about 30 miles (48 km) from where it is joined by the Wabash River. Settled in 1817.   p. 39.

F

Fall Creek (40°N/86°W).   The original name of the city that today is our state capital—Indianapolis. Settled in 1819.   p. 164.

Florida.   A state in southeastern United States. Under the Treaty of Paris, Florida was the southern boundary of the United States.   p. 355.

Fort Cahokia (39°N/90°W) (kuh HOH kee uh).   In 1778 George Rogers Clark and 175 frontiersmen captured Fort Cahokia from the British. Today Cahokia is a village in St. Clair County, southwestern Illinois.   p. 113.

Fort Detroit (42°N/83°W).   Once called Pontchartrain, the fort was founded by Cadillac in 1701. It was founded on what now is the city of Detroit.   p. 113.

Fort Duquesne (40°N/80°W) (doo KAYN)   Fort built by the French. Today it is the site of Pittsburgh, Pennsylvania.   p. 102.

Fort Kaskaskia (38°N/90°W) (ka SKAS kee uh).   In 1778 George Rogers Clark and 175 men captured Fort Kaskaskia from the British. Kaskaskia is a village in Randolph County, southwestern Illinois. p. 113.

Fort Miami (41°N/86°W).   Fort built by the French on the Maumee River in 1721. p. 102.

Fort Ouiatanon (40°N/87°W).   Fort built by the French on the Wabash River in 1717. p. 102.

Fort Vincennes (39°N/88°W) (vihn SENZ).   Fort built by the French on the Wabash River in 1712. Called Fort Sackville by the British and captured by American George Rogers Clark in 1779.   p. 113.

Fort Wayne (41°N/85°W).   County seat of Allen County. It is the second most populated city in Indiana. Located at the point where the St. Joseph, St. Marys, and Maumee rivers meet. Started as a trading post in 1680. p. 20.

Fountain City (40°N/85°W).   Town in Wayne County. Levi Coffin, a Friend and the leader of the Underground Railroad in Indiana, lived here.   p. 195.

Frankfort (38°N/85°W).   Capital of Kentucky. Located in the north central part of the state.   p. 355.

French Lick (39°N/87°W).   Town in Orange County. It is the birthplace of basketball star Larry Bird.   p. 356.

G

Gary (42°N/87°W).   Industrial city in Lake County. It is the third most populated city in Indiana. Located on Lake Michigan. One of the most important steelmaking centers in the United States.   p. 39.

Great Lakes.   Five large lakes located in North America. One of them, Lake Michigan, is entirely within the United States. Part of the boundary between the United States and Canada passes through the other four lakes—Ontario, Erie, Huron, and Superior. p. 11.

Great Lakes Plains.   One of three regions in Indiana. It is north of the Till Plains. It is an important manufacturing area.   p. 47.

Greenfield (40°N/86°W).   County seat of Hancock County. Located on Brandywine Creek. James Whitcomb Riley was born here. Settled in 1828.   p. 356.

Greenland.   Large island between Canada and Iceland. Belongs to Denmark. Excluding the continent of Australia, it is the largest island in the world.   p. 352.

Greenwich (52°N/0° long.) (GREN ihch).   A place in London, England, designated as 0° longitude. The Prime Meridian runs from the North Pole through Greenwich to the South Pole.   p. 18.

Gulf of Mexico.   Body of salt water bounded by the United States, Mexico, and Cuba.   p. 11.

H

Hammond (42°N/88°W).   City in Lake County. It is the sixth most populated city in Indiana. Located near Lake Michigan on Grand Calumet River. Settled in 1851.   p. 39.

Harmonie (38°N/88°W) (HAHR muh nee).   Town founded in 1814 by George Rapp and the Rappites. In 1825 it was renamed New Harmony. Located on the Wabash River about 25 miles (40 km) from Evansville.   p. 164.

I

Illinois River.   Formed in northeastern Illinois. Flows southwest, joining the Mississippi River in southwestern Illinois.   p. 97.

Indian Ocean.   Large body of salt water bordered by Africa, Asia, and Australia.   p. 7.

Indiana Territory.   That part of the Northwest Territory from which Indiana, Illinois, Wisconsin, and parts of Minnesota and Michigan were formed.   p. 133.

Indianapolis (40°N/86°W) (ihn dee uh NAP uh lihs).   County seat of Marion County. Also the capital of Indiana. It is the most populated city in the state. Located on the West Fork of the White River. It was originally known as Fall Creek. Settled in 1819. p. 39.

J

Jeffersonville (38°N/86°W).   County seat of Clark County. Located on the Ohio River. It was an early steamboat-building center. Settled in 1802.   p. 356.

K

Kankakee River (kang kuh KEE).   Begins near South Bend. It joins the Des Plaines River near Kankakee, Illinois, to form the Illinois River.   P. 97.

Kentucky.   The state that borders Indiana to the south. The home state of Abraham Lincoln before he and his family moved to Indiana.   p. 355.

Kokomo (40°N/86°W) (KOH kuh moh).   County seat of Howard County. Located on Wildcat Creek. Settled about 1843.   p. 20.

L

La Porte (42°N/87°W).   County seat of La Porte County. Located on Pine Lake. Settled in 1830.   p. 356.

Lafayette (40°N/87°W). County seat of Tippecanoe County. Located on the Wabash River. Lafayette is the home of Purdue University. Settled in 1825. p. 356.

Lake Erie. Located along the border between Canada and the United States. Second smallest of the five Great Lakes. Has coastline in Michigan, Ohio, Pennsylvania, and New York. p. 11.

Lake Huron. Located along the border between Canada and the United States. Second largest of the five Great Lakes. The United States' portion of the lake is in Michigan. p. 11.

Lake Michigan. Located in the United States. Third largest of the five Great Lakes. Has coastline in Michigan, Wisconsin, Illinois, and Indiana. p. 11.

Lake Ontario. Located along the border between Canada and the United States. Smallest of the five Great Lakes. The United States' portion of the lake is in New York. The only one of the Great Lakes that does not have a coastline in Michigan. p. 11.

Lake Superior. Located along the border between Canada and the United States. Largest of the five Great Lakes. Has coastline in Minnesota, Wisconsin, and Michigan. p. 11.

Lawrence County. A county in southern Indiana where much of the state's limestone is found. p. 37.

Leningrad (60°N/30°E) (LEN un grad). Second most populated city in the Soviet Union. Located on the Gulf of Finland. p. 17.

Liberty (40°N/85°W). County seat of Union County. Located in eastern Indiana. p. 356.

Lincoln City (38°N/87°W). Village in Spencer County. Farm of Thomas Lincoln is located here. p. 356.

Logansport (41°N/86°W). County seat of Cass County. Located on a branch of the Wabash River. Settled about 1826. p. 356.

M

Madison (39°N/85°W). County seat of Jefferson County. Located on the Ohio River. Founded in 1823. p. 356.

Marion County. The most populated Indiana county. Located in the central part of the state. p. 37.

Martinsville (39°N/86°W). City in Morgan County in central Indiana. p. 356.

Maumee River (mau MEE). River in Indiana and Ohio. It is formed by the joining of the St. Joseph and the St. Marys rivers at Fort Wayne. p. 47.

Minnesota. Located in the north central United States. Part of Minnesota was included in the Northwest Territory. p. 355.

Mississippi River (mihs uh SIHP ee). The longest river in the United States. Rises in northern Minnesota and flows into the Gulf of Mexico near New Orleans, Louisiana. p. 11.

Missouri River. The second longest river in the United States. Rises in western Montana and flows into the Mississippi River near St. Louis, Missouri. p. 11.

Mitchell (39°N/86°W). City in Lawrence County. Spring Mill State Park is nearby. p. 356.

Monroe County. A county in southern Indiana where much of the state's limestone is found. p. 37.

Monroe Lake (39°N/86°W). Monroe Lake is located in Monroe and Brown counties, just south of Bloomington. p. 356.

Muncie (40°N/85°W) (MUN see).   County seat of Delaware County. Located on West Fork of White River. It is the home of Ball State University. Settled around 1827.   p. 39.

N

New Albany (38°N/86°W).   County seat of Floyd County. Located on the Ohio River opposite Louisville, Kentucky. Was an early steamship-building center. Settled about 1800.   p. 39.

New Castle (40°N/85°W).   County seat of Henry County. Located on Big Blue River. Wilbur Wright was born near here. Settled about 1820.   p. 356.

New Harmony (38°N/88°W).   Town in Posey County. Located on the Wabash River about 25 miles (40 km) from Evansville. It was founded in 1814 by George Rapp. Originally called Harmonie. Renamed New Harmony by Robert Owen in 1825.   p. 164.

New Orleans (30°N/90°W) (noo OR lee unz).   Most populated city in Louisiana. Located on the Mississippi River. One of the busiest ports in the United States. Settled around 1718.   p. 355.

New York City (41°N/74°W).   The most populated city in the United States. One of eight cities in the country with more than 1,000,000 people. Location of the Empire State Building, which was made from Indiana limestone.   p. 355.

North America.   The earth's third largest continent. Our country is in North America.   p. 7.

North Pole.   The most northern place on the earth.   p. 17.

Northern Hemisphere.   The half of the earth that is north of the Equator.   p. 17.

Northwest Territory.   Area of land north of the Ohio River. The states of Ohio, Illinois, Michigan, Wisconsin, and Indiana and parts of Minnesota were once part of the Northwest Territory.   p. 133.

O

Ohio.   The state that borders Indiana on the east. One of the six states that made up the Northwest Territory.   p. 355.

Ohio River.   Formed at Pittsburgh, Pennsylvania, by the joining of the Allegheny and Monongahela rivers. Flows into the Mississippi River at Cairo, Illinois. It forms part of the boundary of Indiana and four other states.   p. 355.

P

Pacific Ocean.   The earth's largest body of water. It stretches from the Arctic Circle to Antarctica and from the western coast of North America to the eastern coast of Asia.   p. 7.

Paris (49°N/2°E).   National capital and most populated city in France. Located on the Seine River. In 1783 the United States and England signed a treaty here that ended the War for Independence.   p. 353.

Parke County.   A county in western Indiana and location of Turkey Run State Park.   p. 37.

Peru (41°N/86°W).   County seat of Miami County. Located on the Wabash River. Winter home of Barnum and Bailey Circus. Settled about 1825.   p. 356.

Philadelphia (40°N/75°W) (fihl uh DEL fee uh).   City in Pennsylvania. Located at the point where the Delaware and Schuylkill rivers join. One of eight cities in the United States with more than 1,000,000 people. Settled in 1682.   p. 355.

Pittsburgh (40°N/80°W).   Second most populated city in Pennsylvania. Located at point where the Allegheny and Monongahela rivers join. Incorporated in 1794.   p. 355.

Portland (40°N/85°W).   County seat of Jay County. Located in eastern Indiana.   p. 356.

Posey County.   A county in southwest Indiana and location of the lowest land in the state.   p. 37.

Prime Meridian (prym muh RIHD ee un).   0° line of longitude. It divides the earth into the Eastern Hemisphere and the Western Hemisphere.   p. 18.

R

Richmond (40°N/85°W).   County seat of Wayne County. Located on the East Fork of the Whitewater River. Settled in 1806.   p. 356.

S

St. Joseph River.   Begins in southern Michigan, then flows west and southwest past Elkhart and South Bend, then northwest back into Michigan, and then flows into Lake Michigan.   p. 20.

St. Lawrence River.   A waterway that connects the Great Lakes to the Atlantic Ocean.   p. 355.

St. Meinrad (38°N/87°W) (saynt MYN rad).   A town surrounded by Spencer County in Indiana and location of the oldest seminary in the United States.   p. 356.

Seymour (39°N/86°W) (SEE mor).   An industrial city in Jackson County. It is the birthplace of rock artist John Cougar Mellencamp.   p. 356.

South America.   The earth's fourth largest continent.   p. 7.

South Bend (42°N/86°W).   County seat of St. Joseph County. It is the fifth most populated city in Indiana. Located on a bend in the St. Joseph River. The University of Notre Dame is in South Bend. Settled in 1820.   p. 39.

South Pole.   The most southern place on the earth.   p. 17.

South Whitley (41°N/86°W).   A city in Whitley County in northeastern Indiana. It is well known for the manufacturing of bassoons.   p. 356.

Southern Hemisphere.   The half of the earth that is south of the Equator.   p. 17.

Southern Hills and Lowlands.   One of three regions in Indiana. Located south of the Till Plains. The fertile Wabash lowland is in this region.   p. 47.

Spring Mill (39°N/86°W).   Restored pioneer village near Mitchell. It is a park owned by the state of Indiana.   p. 164.

Springfield (40°N/90°W).   Capital of Illinois. Located in the central part of the state.   p. 355.

T

Terre Haute (39°N/87°W) (ter uh HOHT).   County seat of Vigo County. It is the ninth most populated city in Indiana. Located on the Wabash River. Indiana State University is located here. Settled about 1811.   p. 39.

Till Plains.   One of three regions of Indiana. Located between the Great Lakes Plains and the Southern Hills and Lowlands. It is an important farming area. Indianapolis lies in the middle of the Till Plains.   p. 47.

Tippecanoe River.   Starts in Tippecanoe Lake in Kosciusko County. Flows into the Wabash River near Lafayette. General William Harrison defeated the Shawnee near this river in the Battle of Tippecanoe in 1811.   p. 164.

V

Valparaiso (41°N/87°W).   County seat of Porter County in northwestern Indiana. Orville Redenbacher popcorn is made here. p. 356.

Vanderburgh County.   A county in southwest Indiana and location of the lowest land in the state.   p. 37.

Vincennes (39°N/88°W).   County seat of Knox County. It was the first capital of the Indiana Territory. One of the oldest settlements in Indiana. First settled by the French in 1702. p. 20.

W

Wabash (41°N/86°W).   County seat of Wabash County. Located on the Wabash. Settled in 1835.   p. 356.

Wabash River.   One of the two longest rivers in Indiana. It rises in western Ohio, flows southwest across Indiana, and empties into the Ohio River at the southwest corner of the state.   p. 47.

Washington, D.C. (39°N/77°W).   Capital of the United States. Located on the Potomac River.   p. 355.

Wayne County.   A county in eastern Indiana. Location of the highest point of elevation in the state.   p. 37.

Western Hemisphere.   The half of the earth west of the Prime Meridian. Includes all of North America and South America.   p. 18.

White River.   One of the two longest rivers in Indiana. It begins near Petersburg and flows southwest to join the Wabash.   p. 20.

Wisconsin.   Located to the northwest of Indiana. One of the six states that made up the Northwest Territory.   p. 355.

Glossary

The page references tell where each entry first appears in the text.

A

acid rain. Rain containing gases or other particles of air pollution. p. 294.

ambassador. A person who represents the United States in another country. p. 325.

amend. To change, usually for the better. p. 145.

amendment. A change to a set of laws. p. 145.

ancestor (AN ses tur). A family member of the past. p. 182.

archaeologist (ahr kee AHL uh jist). A person who studies the times of people who lived long ago. An archaeologist digs up artifacts and ancient places. p. 71.

architect. A person who plans and helps build places to work, live, and play. p. 88.

artifact (AHRT uh fakt). An object, such as a weapon or tool, that was made and left behind by people. p. 71.

assassinate (uh SAS un ayt). To murder by a secret attack. p. 209.

B

bar graph. A graph that shows information by means of bars. p. 37.

barracks. A building or group of buildings where soldiers live. p. 175.

blab school. A school in which students studied out loud while the teacher listened for mistakes. p. 161.

blast furnace. A furnace used to melt iron out of iron ore. p. 287.

blockhouse. A fort made out of logs. p. 174.

boundary. A line that separates one state or country from another; a border. p. 11.

buhr (BUR). A stone used for grinding. p. 162.

C

campaign. A series of activities by those who hope to be elected to an office. p. 316.

canal (kuh NAL). A narrow waterway dug across land for ships or small boats to go through. p. 231.

candidate. A person who is running for an office or position. p. 316.

cannon. A large gun fixed to the ground or mounted on wheels. p. 118.

capital. A city where government leaders meet to make laws. p. 132.

capitol. A building in which government leaders meet. p. 301.

census. A government count of the number of people in a place. p. 141.

civil war. A war between groups of people in the same country. p. 203.

climate. The kind of weather a place has over a long period of time, as shown by such things as temperature and precipitation. p. 55.

coke. A fuel made from coal. p. 285.

communal (KAHM yoo nul) **living.** The condition of a group of people living together in a community. p. 190.

compass. A tool for finding directions. p. 12.

compass rose. A drawing that shows where north, south, east, and west are on a map. p. 12.

compete. To try to win. p. 94.

component (kum POH nunt). A part used in making something else. p. 280.

Confederacy (kun FED ur uh see). The union of the 11 Southern states that withdrew from the United States in 1860 and 1861. p. 204.

Congress. The group of men and women chosen by the people to speak for the people and to make the laws for the United States. p. 129.

conservation • evergreen

conservation (kahn sur VAY shun). The use of natural resources in such a way as to prevent their waste or complete destruction. p. 267.

constitution (kahn stuh TOO shun). A set of laws by which a state or country is governed. p. 141.

continent. A very large body of land on the earth. p. 7.

contour line. A line on a map drawn through all places having the same height. p. 44.

corduroy (KOR duh roi) **road.** A road constructed of logs laid crosswise. p. 225.

correspondent. A person employed by a newspaper, magazine, or radio or TV station to find and report the latest news from a certain place. p. 326.

council. A group that meets to discuss important subjects. p. 99.

councilor. A member of a council. p. 306.

county. The largest territorial division of local government within a state. p. 36.

cultivate (KUL tuh vayt). To prepare the land for growing crops. p. 256.

culture. The traditions, beliefs, and way of living of a group of people. p. 86.

custom. The special way a group of people does something. p. 182.

D

daub. Sticky mud pressed onto branches, creating a type of plaster that Indians used to build walls of forts. p. 79.

deciduous (dee SIHJ oo us). Shedding leaves each year. p. 265.

Declaration of Independence. The document that gave the reasons why the American colonies wanted to be free of British control. p. 119.

defeat. A loss of a conflict or contest. p. 137.

delegate (DEL uh gut). A person who has the right to act or speak for others. p. 141.

delta. Deposits of mud at the mouth of a river. p. 53.

democracy. A government that is run by the people who live under it. p. 309.

deposit. Material that has been laid down by water, ice, or wind. p. 48.

depression. A time of little work and little money. p. 211.

diagram. A special kind of drawing used to explain how something works or why something happens. p. 55.

discrimination (dih skrihm ih NAY shun). The unfair or unequal treatment of certain groups of people. p. 210.

E

elect. To choose or select by voting. p. 299.

election. The choosing of a person for a job by vote. p. 316.

elevation. Distance or height above sea level. p. 43.

energy. Power that can be used to make people or machines work. p. 290.

engineer. A person who knows about or studies the use of energy and the planning and building of engines, roads, canals, buildings, and bridges. p. 337.

Equator. The imaginary line on the earth that is halfway between the North Pole and the South Pole. It is shown on a map or globe by the latitude line numbered 0°. p. 16.

erosion (ee ROH zhun). The loss of soil due to its being washed away by rain or blown away by wind. p. 258.

estimate. To figure out *about* where a place is. p. 19.

evergreen. A tree that has green leaves or needles all year round. p. 265.

executive. Refers to the branch of government that makes sure laws are carried out. p. 314.

experiment. A test to find out facts. p. 338.

explorer. A person who travels in search of new lands. p. 69.

F

factory. A building in which goods are made. p. 274.

fairness. The equal treatment of others. p. 210.

federal. Another name for national. p. 299.

federation (fed ur AY shun). A union of separate states. p. 312.

fell. To cut down trees. p. 159.

fertile. Able to produce crops easily and plentifully. p. 256.

festival. A time of special celebrating and feasting. p. 198.

flatboat. A large, flat boxlike boat that can only float downstream. p. 230.

flute. A groove cut into a stone. p. 73.

free state. A state in the United States in which slavery was not allowed. p. 203.

freight. Goods or cargo transported by means of land, air, or water. p. 230.

frontier. The outer edge of a settled area. p. 107.

G

gallery. A room or building used to show collections of pictures and statues. p. 330.

general store. A store that sells many different things. p. 165.

geography. The study of the earth and how people use it. p. 9.

girdle. To cut a deep ring around the trunk of a tree in order to kill the tree to allow sunlight to come through. p. 159.

glaciation (glay shee AY shun). The covering of a land area by large sheets of ice. p. 48.

globe. A model of the earth. p. 6.

goods. Things that are made or grown to be sold. p. 274.

granary. A building used to store grain. p. 191.

granny cure. A home remedy. p. 170.

gravel. Material made up of small stones. p. 49.

greenhouse. A building with a glass roof and glass sides used for growing plants. p. 191.

grid. A system of crossing lines or boxes on a map or globe. Crossing latitude and longitude lines form a grid. p. 19.

gunport. An opening in a wall through which a gun or cannon can be fired. p. 118.

H

harmony. An agreement of feelings or ideas. p. 190.

hemisphere. Half of a sphere, or ball. Half of the earth. p. 16.

heritage. Customs and beliefs handed down from one generation to the next. p. 70.

history. The study of the past. History is filled with interesting stories about people and events. p. 9.

homestead. To build homes, live in the homes, and improve the land the homes are built on. p. 176.

horsepower. In pioneer times, a horse pulled a pole attached to a round grinding stone. Today, it is a unit for measuring the power of an engine or motor. p. 162.

house-raising. The gathering of neighbors to help build a new home. p. 159.

hydroelectric (hy droh ee LEK trihk) *power.* Power from running water, used to make electricity. p. 291.

immigrant • mine

I

immigrant.   A person of one country who moves to another country to live.   p. 196.

independent.   Able to think for oneself.   p. 108.

industry.   A business or trade that provides goods or services.   p. 273.

interdependent.   Dependent upon each other.   p. 215.

international (ihn tur NASH uh nul).   Between nations.   p. 239.

interstate.   Between states.   p. 226.

irrigation (ihr uh GAY shun).   A way of bringing water to fields through pipes and canals.   p. 260.

J

journal.   A daily record of events. It is also called a diary.   p. 96.

judicial.   Refers to the branch of the federal government that explains laws and judges cases that are brought before it.   p. 315.

K

keelboat.   Long, narrow boat that moves downstream but can travel upstream if helped by sails and poles.   p. 230.

key.   The place on a map where symbols are explained.   p. 26.

L

laboratory.   A place where medicines are made.   p. 287.

latitude.   Distance north or south of the earth's Equator; measured in degrees. The lines that measure latitude run east-west across a map or globe.   p. 17.

legend.   A story that may or may not be true but is usually based on some facts.   p. 138.

legislative.   Refers to the branch of the federal government that makes laws.   p. 312.

lifestyle.   Way of living.   p. 90.

line graph.   A graph used to show change over a period of time.   p. 41.

location.   Where a place is compared to other places.   p. 5.

lock.   A gate that controls a part of a canal so that the water level can be changed.   p. 232.

logrolling.   A part of a house-raising when the men formed teams to cut down trees and roll the logs to where a cabin was to be built.   p. 159.

longhouse.   A large wigwam in which many families lived together.   p. 90.

longitude.   The lines on a map or globe that run up and down from the North Pole to the South Pole. Lines of longitude represent the distance east or west of the Prime Meridian.   p. 18.

M

majority.   The larger group of people.   p. 187.

mammoth.   A large animal that looked like a hairy elephant.   p. 73.

manufacturing (man yoo FAK chur ing).   Making things by hand or by machine.   p. 274.

map.   A special kind of drawing used to show what the earth or a part of the earth looks like if viewed from overhead.   p. 5.

maritime.   Having to do with the sea.   p. 240.

mass-produce.   To make goods in large quantities, usually by machine.   p. 280.

memorial.   A way of remembering and honoring an important person or people.   p. 120.

migrate (MYE grayt).   To move from one place to another.   p. 266.

mine.   A tunnel or pit that goes deep into the earth.   p. 262.

minority. A group that is smaller and also different in some way from most people around it. p. 187.

moraine (muh RAYN). A sand and gravel heap or ridge left by glaciers. p. 49.

museum. A place in which rare and valuable objects are kept. p. 330.

N

Native American. One of any group of American Indians; people whose ancestors came to America long before anyone else. p. 70.

natural resource. A thing made by nature that is useful to people. Natural resources are such things as forests, water, land, and minerals. p. 255.

nuclear (NOO klee ur) *power.* Power generated from heat made as substances break up. p. 291.

O

ocean. A large body of salt water. There are four oceans—the Atlantic, Pacific, Indian, and Arctic. p. 7.

ordinance (ORD un uns). A law. p. 129.

ore. A natural resource from which we get metals such as iron and copper. p. 285.

organic (or GAN ihk). Relating to a natural substance, such as plant waste. p. 256.

P

petroleum (puh TROH lee um). An oily substance that is pumped from the ground and used as energy. Gasoline and fuel oil are made from petroleum. p. 290.

pharmacist. A person who works with medicine. p. 337.

pictograph. A graph that uses pictures to represent something. p. 40.

pie graph. A graph that shows parts of a whole. p. 41.

plank road. A road made of flat split logs. p. 225.

plantation (plan TAY shun). A very large farm or estate. p. 203.

plaza. A public square in a town or city. p. 79.

policy. The actions that a candidate will take if elected. p. 317.

poll. A place where one votes. p. 318.

pollute (puh LOOT). To dirty the environment with waste material. p. 293.

population density. The number of people per unit of area, as a square mile or square kilometer. p. 38.

portage. Overland route over which supplies can be carried. p. 97.

power station. A building in which fuel is burned to make energy. p. 290.

precipitation (pree sihp uh TAY shun). The moisture that falls on the earth's surface. It includes rain, snow, sleet, and hail. p. 57.

prehistoric (pre hihs TOR ihk). Having to do with the time in history before written records were kept. p. 70.

preserve. To keep from harm or change. To keep from spoiling. p. 109.

Prime Meridian. The line of longitude from which the other lines of longitude are measured. The Prime Meridian is numbered 0°. p. 19.

proclamation (prahk luh MAY shun). A law. p. 102.

Q

quarry. A large pit in the earth. p. 264.

rapids • *till*

R

rapids. Part of a river's course where the water rushes quickly, often over rocks near the surface. p. 113.

recreation. The activities that people choose for fun and rest. p. 339.

refine. To turn petroleum into gasoline and fuel oil. p. 291.

register. To have one's name put on the list of people eligible to vote in an election. p. 317.

relief map. A map that shows how high or low places are. p. 43.

representative. A person chosen to act or speak for others. p. 168.

research. A careful hunting for facts or truths. p. 338.

reservoir (REZ ur vwahr). A place where water is collected and stored for future use. p. 261.

rotate. To turn. p. 15.

route center. A place where roads and railroads come together. p. 51.

rural. A kind of area made up of farms and very small communities. p. 40.

S

scale. The size of a map or model compared with what it represents. p. 26.

scenic. Having beautiful scenery. p. 339.

seam. A level band of coal under the earth. p. 262.

secede (sih SEED). To pull away or leave. p. 203.

seminary. A place where priests or other religious leaders are trained. p. 341.

services. Work that people do for other people. p. 274.

sharecropper. A person who farms for the land's owner and in return receives part of the crops. p. 211.

shun. To leave alone or stay away from. p. 184.

silt. Fine mud picked up by a river and carried toward the sea. Some is deposited and makes very good soil. p. 51.

slavery. The practice of owning other people. p. 203.

smelting. The process of melting iron out of iron ore. p. 287.

Society of Friends. Another name for Quakers. p. 195.

solar energy. Energy from the sun. p. 293.

sphere. An object that is round like a ball. The earth is a sphere. p. 6.

squatter. A person who lives on land without owning it or paying any rent. p. 130.

stereotype (STER ee uh typ). An idea, not based on truth, about an entire group of people. p. 85.

stockade. A wall of a fort. p. 79.

suffrage (SUF rihj). The right to vote. p. 215.

surface mining. A way of mining in which large power shovels remove soil and dig out coal that lies close to the surface. p. 262.

surrender. The act of giving up. p. 118.

survey. To measure and map land so that boundaries can be set up. p. 112.

symbol. Something used on a map that stands for a real thing. p. 26.

T

temperature. Degree of hot or cold, such as of the air. p. 56.

term. The period of time for which a person is elected. p. 300.

territory. An area of land. p. 121.

thermometer. An instrument that is used to measure temperature. p. 56.

till. The name of the soft deposit left by ice from glaciers after they melted; also called boulder clay. p. 51.

time line. A visual tool that shows when and in what order certain things happened. p. 73.

time zone. Any of the regions into which the earth is divided for measuring standard time. p. 23.

tipi (TEE pee). Any of the homes of Native Americans that were made with trees and animal skins and were shaped like upside-down ice cream cones. p. 88.

toll. A fee, tax, or charge to use certain services. p. 226.

touring. Traveling for pleasure. p. 339.

tow. To pull. p. 232.

township. Part of a county having certain powers of government. p. 130.

trace. A narrow land trail. p. 223.

trading post. A store where things could be bought, sold, or traded. p. 96.

transportation (trans pur TAY shun). Ways of travel. p. 223.

treaty. An agreement between two or more persons or groups. p. 121.

tribe. A group of families who share the same way of life. p. 70.

U

UNIGOV (YOO nuh guv). The united government of city and county. p. 308.

Union. Another name for the early United States. p. 203.

urban. Of or relating to cities and towns. p. 40.

V

veterinarian. A doctor who takes care of animals. p. 337.

victory garden. A small vegetable garden raised by a family during wartime. p. 216.

W

water power. A form of energy created by water turning a wheel. p. 163.

wattle. Branches woven around posts to make walls of forts. p. 79.

weather. The changes in the air that occur from day to day or even from hour to hour. p. 55.

wigwam. A Native American home made from trees and bark, hides, or mats of woven grass. p. 89.

wilderness. Wild land. p. 94.

GEOGRAPHICAL DICTIONARY

1. Canyon

Grand Canyon
Arizona

A **canyon** is a deep valley with very steep sides. The best-known canyon in the United States is the Grand Canyon in Arizona.

2. Coast

Coast — Indiana Dunes
National Lakeshore

A **coast** is land next to a large body of water. The United States has thousands of miles of coasts. Indiana's only coast is on Lake Michigan, one of the Great Lakes.

3. Delta

Mississippi River Delta
Louisiana

A **delta** is a piece of land formed by mud and sand that settle from water flowing out of the place where a river ends. The soil of a delta usually makes rich farmland.

2
Coast

1
Canyon

5
Hawaiian Islands

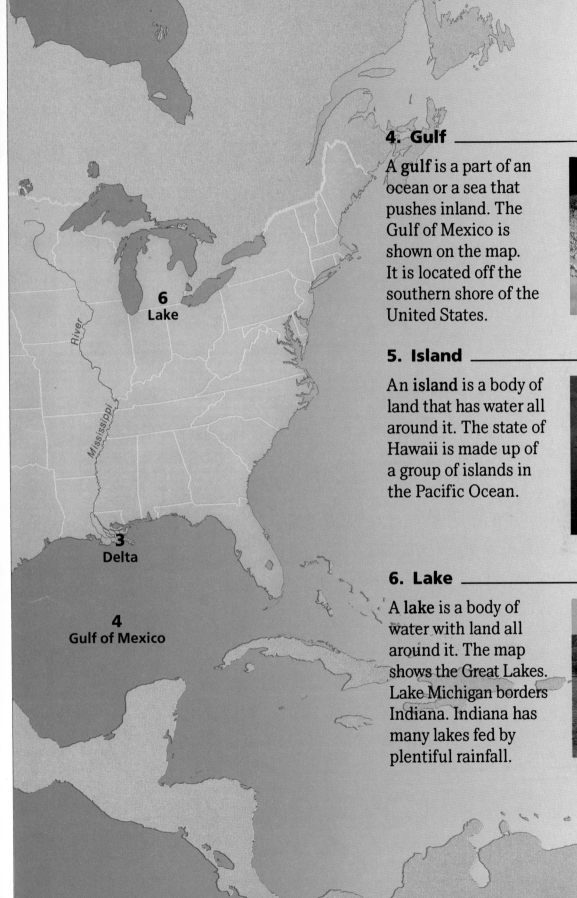

6
Lake

River

Mississippi

3
Delta

4
Gulf of Mexico

4. Gulf _____

A **gulf** is a part of an ocean or a sea that pushes inland. The Gulf of Mexico is shown on the map. It is located off the southern shore of the United States.

Gulf of Mexico

5. Island _____

An **island** is a body of land that has water all around it. The state of Hawaii is made up of a group of islands in the Pacific Ocean.

Island — Maine

6. Lake _____

A **lake** is a body of water with land all around it. The map shows the Great Lakes. Lake Michigan borders Indiana. Indiana has many lakes fed by plentiful rainfall.

Crooked Lake
Indiana

GEOGRAPHICAL DICTIONARY

7. Mountain _____

Red Mountain
Colorado

A **mountain** is a piece of land that rises sharply from the land that is around it. The top of a mountain is usually peaked or rounded. Indiana has no mountains.

8. Peninsula _____

Peninsula — Cape Cod
Massachusetts

A **peninsula** is a strip of land with water nearly all the way around it. It is connected to a larger body of land. The state of Florida is a peninsula.

9. Plain _____

Plains — Kansas

A **plain** is an almost level, often treeless piece of land that stretches for miles and miles.

10
Plateau

9
Plain

7
Mountain

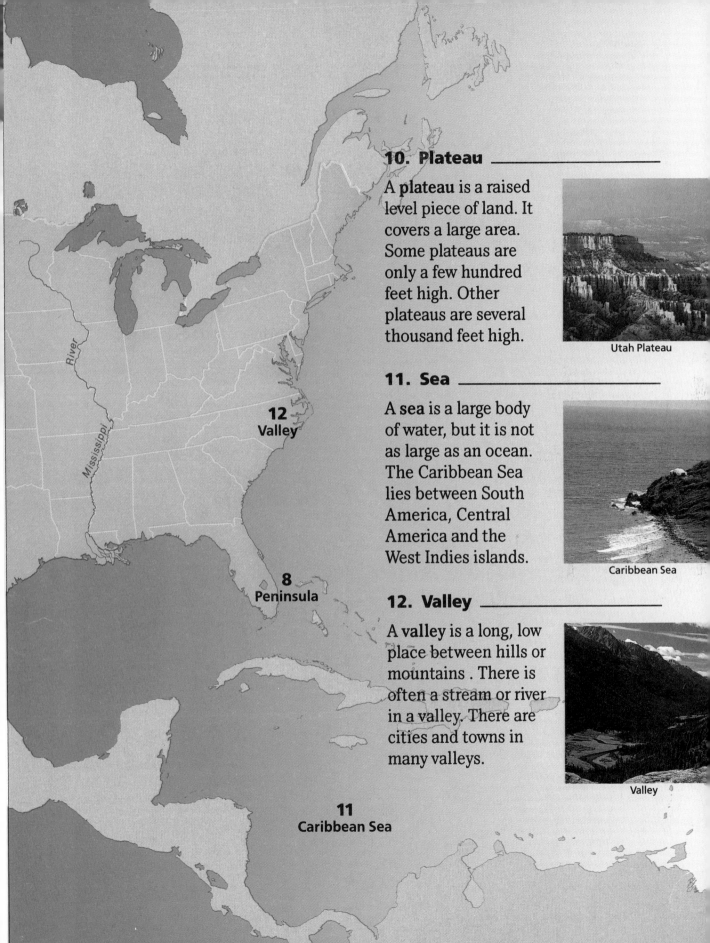

10. Plateau _____

A **plateau** is a raised level piece of land. It covers a large area. Some plateaus are only a few hundred feet high. Other plateaus are several thousand feet high.

Utah Plateau

11. Sea _____

A **sea** is a large body of water, but it is not as large as an ocean. The Caribbean Sea lies between South America, Central America and the West Indies islands.

Caribbean Sea

12. Valley _____

A **valley** is a long, low place between hills or mountains . There is often a stream or river in a valley. There are cities and towns in many valleys.

Valley

12
Valley

8
Peninsula

11
Caribbean Sea

River

Mississippi

SOME IMPORTANT INDIANA FARM PRODUCTS

Corn and Popcorn

Soybeans and Soy Products

SOY MEAL

Animal Feed

Wheat

Hay

Hogs

Cattle and Dairy Products

Chickens and Eggs

SOME IMPORTANT PRODUCTS MANUFACTURED IN INDIANA

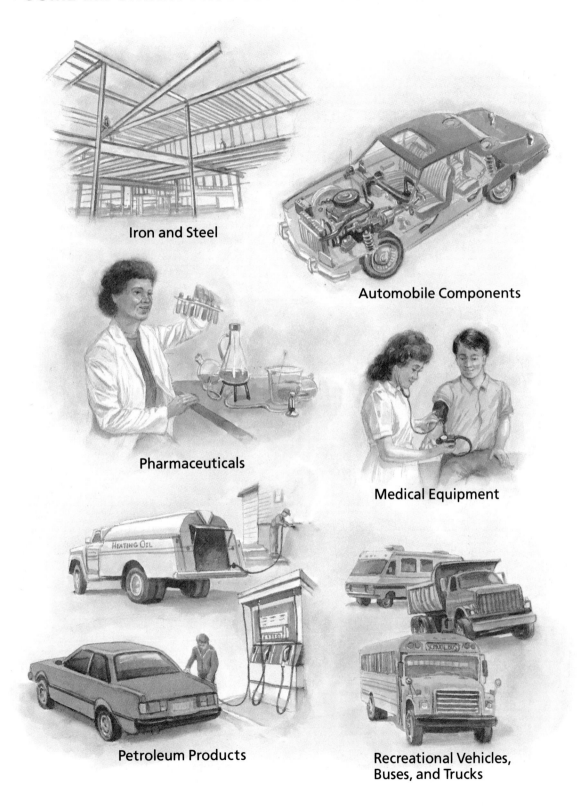

Iron and Steel

Automobile Components

Pharmaceuticals

Medical Equipment

Petroleum Products

Recreational Vehicles, Buses, and Trucks

GRAPH APPENDIX

AVERAGE MONTHLY PRECIPITATION

EVANSVILLE

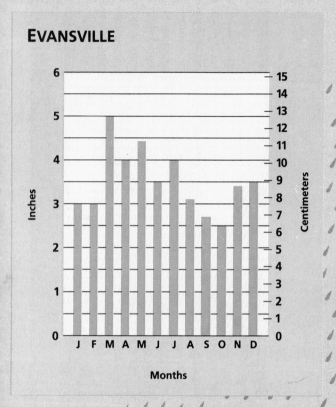

FORT WAYNE

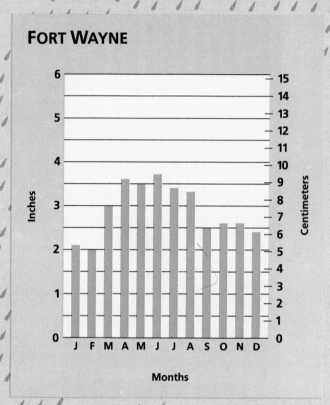

INDIANAPOLIS

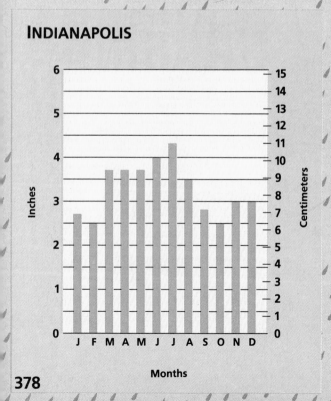

SOUTH BEND

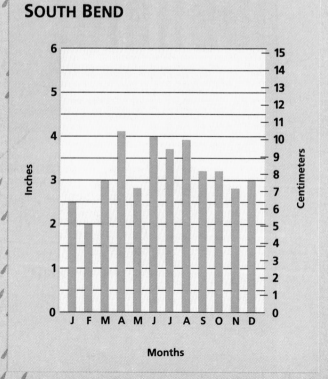

Average Monthly Temperatures

Evansville

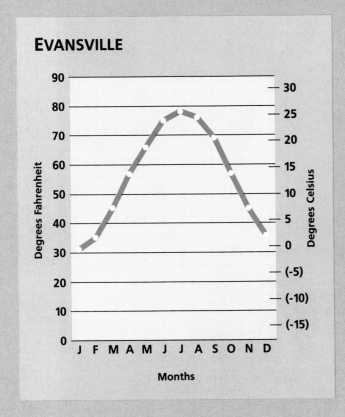

Fort Wayne

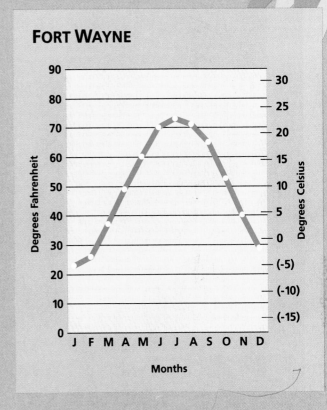

Indianapolis

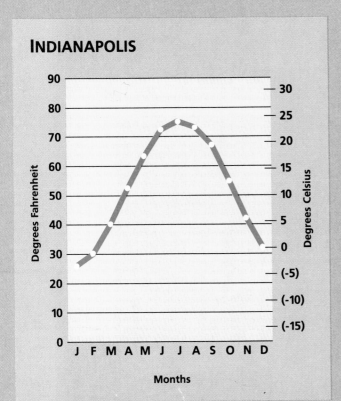

South Bend

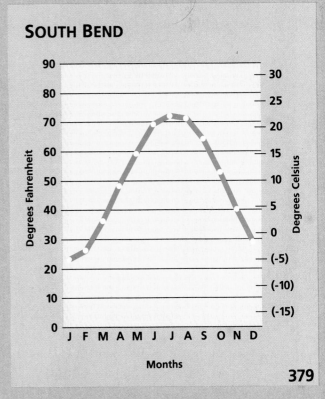

379

State Seal

State Bird — *Cardinal*

State Tree — *Tulip Tree*

State Flower — *Peony*

State Flag

Facts About Indiana Counties

County Name	County Seat	County Population	Population Rank	Area in Square Miles (Square Kilometers)		Area Rank	Became a County
Adams	Decatur	30,300	46	340	(880)	72	1836
Allen	Fort Wayne	295,300	3	659	(1,706)	1	1824
Bartholomew	Columbus	64,500	21	409	(1,059)	34	1821
Benton	Fowler	9,800	88	407	(1,053)	40	1840
Blackford	Hartford City	15,000	81	166	(429)	89	1839
Boone	Lebanon	38,400	33	423	(1,096)	28	1830
Brown	Nashville	12,800	85	312	(807)	76	1836
Carroll	Delphi	19,100	72	372	(964)	62	1828
Cass	Logansport	39,700	31	414	(1,073)	31	1828
Clark	Jeffersonville	88,800	15	376	(974)	60	1801
Clay	Brazil	24,700	59	360	(933)	70	1825
Clinton	Frankfort	31,100	44	405	(1,049)	41	1830
Crawford	English	10,300	87	307	(795)	79	1818
Daviess	Washington	28,700	50	432	(1,120)	26	1817
Dearborn	Lawrenceburg	37,200	36	307	(795)	79	1803
Decatur	Greensburg	23,500	61	373	(965)	61	1822
De Kalb	Auburn	33,800	42	364	(942)	68	1837
Delaware	Muncie	120,900	10	392	(1,015)	51	1827
Dubois	Jasper	36,000	38	429	(1,112)	27	1818
Elkhart	Goshen	146,400	6	466	(1,207)	16	1830
Fayette	Connersville	27,500	53	215	(558)	87	1817
Floyd	New Albany	63,000	23	150	(388)	91	1819
Fountain	Covington	18,600	76	398	(1,030)	46	1826
Franklin	Brookville	20,100	70	385	(998)	54	1811
Fulton	Rochester	18,700	75	369	(956)	64	1836
Gibson	Princeton	33,500	43	490	(1,268)	13	1813
Grant	Marion	77,100	18	415	(1,075)	30	1831
Greene	Bloomfield	30,400	45	546	(1,414)	4	1821
Hamilton	Noblesville	94,200	14	398	(1,030)	46	1823
Hancock	Greenfield	44,900	26	307	(795)	79	1828
Harrison	Corydon	29,100	49	486	(1,259)	14	1808
Hendricks	Danville	74,500	19	409	(1,059)	34	1824
Henry	New Castle	50,100	25	394	(1,020)	50	1822
Howard	Kokomo	85,200	16	293	(759)	82	1844
Huntington	Huntington	35,500	39	366	(948)	66	1834
Jackson	Brownstown	37,100	37	513	(1,329)	8	1816
Jasper	Rensselaer	26,300	56	561	(1,454)	3	1838
Jay	Portland	21,800	65	384	(995)	56	1836
Jefferson	Madison	29,300	48	363	(939)	69	1811
Jennings	Vernon	22,800	63	378	(980)	59	1817
Johnson	Franklin	83,200	17	321	(832)	75	1823
Knox	Vincennes	41,400	29	520	(1,346)	6	1790
Kosciusko	Warsaw	63,600	22	540	(1,398)	5	1836
Lagrange	Lagrange	28,000	52	380	(984)	58	1832
Lake	Crown Point	491,700	2	501	(1,297)	12	1837
La Porte	La Porte	106,100	12	600	(1,555)	2	1832

Facts About Indiana Counties

County Name	County Seat	County Population	Population Rank	Area in Square Miles (Square Kilometers)		Area Rank	Became a County
Lawrence	Bedford	42,400	28	452	(1,171)	20	1818
Madison	Anderson	132,700	7	453	(1,173)	19	1823
Marion	Indianapolis	785,000	1	396	(1,026)	49	1822
Marshall	Plymouth	41,300	30	444	(1,151)	23	1836
Martin	Shoals	11,000	86	339	(877)	73	1820
Miami	Peru	38,000	34	369	(956)	64	1834
Monroe	Bloomington	101,700	13	385	(996)	54	1818
Montgomery	Crawfordsville	35,300	40	505	(1,308)	10	1823
Morgan	Martinsville	53,000	24	409	(1,060)	34	1822
Newton	Kentland	13,900	82	401	(1,038)	44	1860
Noble	Albion	37,200	35	413	(1,069)	32	1836
Ohio	Rising Sun	5,300	92	87	(226)	92	1844
Orange	Paoli	19,300	71	408	(1,057)	38	1816
Owen	Spencer	16,900	77	386	(1,001)	53	1819
Parke	Rockville	15,900	80	444	(1,149)	23	1821
Perry	Cannelton	19,000	73	382	(989)	57	1814
Pike	Petersburg	13,200	83	341	(883)	71	1817
Porter	Valparaiso	123,100	9	418	(1,083)	29	1836
Posey	Mount Vernon	25,800	57	409	(1,059)	34	1814
Pulaski	Winamac	13,200	84	435	(1,126)	25	1839
Putnam	Greencastle	30,000	47	482	(1,248)	15	1822
Randolph	Winchester	28,000	51	454	(1,175)	18	1818
Ripley	Versailles	25,400	58	447	(1,158)	22	1818
Rush	Rushville	18,800	74	408	(1,057)	38	1822
St. Joseph	South Bend	241,400	4	459	(1,189)	17	1830
Scott	Scottsburg	20,400	68	191	(495)	88	1820
Shelby	Shelbyville	39,500	32	413	(1,070)	32	1822
Spencer	Rockport	20,300	69	400	(1,036)	45	1818
Starke	Knox	21,400	66	309	(801)	77	1850
Steuben	Angola	26,500	55	308	(798)	78	1837
Sullivan	Sullivan	20,600	67	452	(1,171)	20	1817
Switzerland	Vevay	7,300	90	223	(578)	86	1814
Tippecanoe	Lafayette	124,400	8	502	(1,299)	11	1826
Tipton	Tipton	16,200	79	260	(673)	83	1844
Union	Liberty	7,000	91	162	(420)	90	1821
Vanderburgl	Evansville	167,600	5	236	(611)	85	1818
Vermillion	Newport	17,600	78	260	(674)	83	1824
Vigo	Terre Haute	109,500	11	405	(1,049)	42	1818
Wabash	Wabash	35,200	41	398	(1,032)	48	1835
Warren	Williamsport	8,500	89	366	(949)	66	1827
Warrick	Boonville	45,400	27	391	(1,013)	52	1813
Washington	Salem	22,500	64	516	(1,336)	7	1814
Wayne	Richmond	72,200	20	404	(1,046)	43	1811
Wells	Bluffton	24,400	60	370	(959)	63	1837
White	Monticello	23,300	62	506	(1,311)	9	1834
Whitley	Columbia City	27,000	54	336	(870)	74	1838

The 50 Most Populated Cities

City Name	City Population	Population Rank	City Name	City Population	Population Rank
Indianapolis	719,820	1	Valparaiso	22,280	26
Fort Wayne	172,900	2	Noblesville	22,180	27
Gary	136,790	3	Hobart	22,140	28
Evansville	129,480	4	La Porte	21,720	29
South Bend	107,190	5	Goshen	21,370	30
Hammond	86,380	6	Jeffersonville	21,330	31
Muncie	72,600	7	West Lafayette	21,110	32
Anderson	61,020	8	Carmel	20,820	33
Terre Haute	57,920	9	Vincennes	20,550	34
Bloomington	52,500	10	Munster	20,010	35
Kokomo	45,610	11	New Castle	18,370	36
Lafayette	44,240	12	Logansport	17,270	37
Elkhart	44,180	13	Huntington	16,810	38
Mishawaka	41,400	14	Crown Point	16,490	39
Richmond	39,030	15	Connersville	16,470	40
New Albany	37,260	16	Griffith	16,110	41
East Chicago	36,950	17	Seymour	15,350	42
Marion	35,810	18	Frankfort	15,120	43
Michigan City	35,600	19	Clarksville	14,480	44
Columbus	30,890	20	Shelbyville	14,390	45
Portage	28,420	21	Schererville	14,310	46
Merrillville	26,530	22	Lake Station	14,170	47
Lawrence	26,480	23	Bedford	13,740	48
Highland	24,160	24	Crawfordsville	13,610	49
Greenwood	22,880	25	Peru	13,250	50

Governors of Indiana

	Name of Governor	Residence Before Appointment or Election	Term
Territorial Governors	1. William Henry Harrison	Vincennes	1800–1812
	2. John Gibson	Lancaster, PA	1812–1813
	3. Thomas Posey	Eastern Virginia	1813–1816
State Governors	1. Jonathan Jennings	Charlestown	1816–1822
	2. Ratliff Boon	Boonville	1822
	3. William Hendricks	Madison	1822–1825
	4. James B. Ray	Brookville	1825–1831
	5. Noah Noble	Indianapolis	1831–1837
	6. David Wallace	Covington	1837–1840
	7. Samuel Bigger	Rushville	1840–1843
	8. James Whitcomb	Bloomington	1843–1848
	9. Paris C. Dunning	Bloomington	1848–1849
	10. Joseph A. Wright	Rockville	1849–1857
	11. Ashbel P. Willard	New Albany	1857–1860
	12. Abram A. Hammond	Indianapolis	1860–1861
	13. Henry Smith Lane	Crawfordsville	1861
	14. Oliver P. Morton	Centerville	1861–1867
	15. Conrad Baker	Evansville	1867–1873
	16. Thomas A. Hendricks	Shelbyville	1873–1877
	17. James D. Williams	Knox County	1877–1880
	18. Isaac P. Gray	Union City	1880–1881
	19. Albert G. Porter	Indianapolis	1881–1885
	20. Isaac P. Gray	Union City	1885–1889
	21. Alvin P. Hovey	Mount Vernon	1889–1891
	22. Ira Joy Chase	Danville	1891–1983
	23. Claude Matthews	Vermillion County	1893–1897
	24. James A. Mount	Montgomery County	1897–1901
	25. Winfield T. Durbin	Anderson	1901–1905
	26. J. Frank Hanly	Warren County	1905–1909
	27. Thomas R. Marshall	Columbia City	1909–1913
	28. Samuel M. Ralston	Lebanon	1913–1917
	29. James P. Goodrich	Winchester	1917–1921
	30. Warren T. McCray	Kentland	1921–1924
	31. Emmett Forest Branch	Martinsville	1924–1925
	32. Ed Jackson	Indianapolis	1925–1929
	33. Harry G. Leslie	Lafayette	1929–1933
	34. Paul V. McNutt	Bloomington	1933–1937
	35. M. Clifford Townsend	Grant County	1937–1941
	36. Henry F. Schricker	Knox	1941–1945
	37. Ralph F. Gates	Columbia City	1945–1949
	38. Henry F. Schricker	Knox	1949–1953
	39. George N. Craig	Brazil	1953–1957
	40. Harold W. Handley	La Porte	1957–1961
	41. Matthew E. Welsh	Vincennes	1961–1965
	42. Roger D. Branigin	Lafayette	1965–1969
	43. Edgar D. Whitcomb	Seymour	1969–1973
	44. Dr. Otis R. Bowen	Bremen	1973–1981
	45. Robert D. Orr	Evansville	1981–1989
	46. Birch Evans Bayh III	Terre Haute	1989–

Indianapolis 500 Winners

Year	Winner	Year	Winner
1911	Ray Harroun	1954	Bill Vukovich
1912	Joe Dawson	1955	Bob Sweikert
1913	Jules Goux	1956	Pat Flaherty
1914	Rene Thomas	1957	Sam Hanks
1915	Ralph De Palma	1958	Jimmy Bryan
1916	Dario Resta	1959	Rodger Ward
1919	Howdy Wilcox	1960	Jim Rathmann
1920	Gaston Chevrolet	1961	A.J. Foyt
1921	Tommy Milton	1962	Rodger Ward
1922	Jimmy Murphy	1963	Parnelli Jones
1923	Tommy Milton	1964	A.J. Foyt
1924	L.L. Corum and Joe Boyer	1965	Jim Clark
1925	Peter De Paolo	1966	Graham Hill
1926	Frank Lockhart	1967	A.J. Foyt
1927	George Souders	1968	Bobby Unser
1928	Louis Meyer	1969	Mario Andretti
1929	Ray Keech	1970	Al Unser
1930	Billy Arnold	1971	Al Unser
1931	Louis Schneider	1972	Mark Donohue
1932	Frederick Frame	1973	Gordon Johncock
1933	Louis Meyer	1974	Johnny Rutherford
1934	Bill Cummings	1975	Bobby Unser
1935	Kelly Petillo	1976	Johnny Rutherford
1936	Louis Meyer	1977	A.J. Foyt
1937	Wilbur Shaw	1978	Al Unser
1938	Floyd Roberts	1979	Rick Mears
1939	Wilbur Shaw	1980	Johnny Rutherford
1940	Wilbur Shaw	1981	Bobby Unser
1941	Mauri Rose and Floyd Davis	1982	Gordon Johncock
1946	George Robson	1983	Tom Sneva
1947	Mauri Rose	1984	Rick Mears
1948	Mauri Rose	1985	Danny Sullivan
1949	William Holland	1986	Bobby Rahal
1950	Johnny Parsons	1987	Al Unser
1951	Lee Wallard	1988	Rick Mears
1952	Troy Ruttman	1989	Emerson Fittipaldi
1953	Bill Vukovich	**1990**	**Arie Luyendyk**

ates in Indiana's History

1609 Northwest country is given to Virginia by charter.

1679 LaSalle enters Indiana and camps in the river bend of the St. Joseph River.

1681 LaSalle holds a meeting with Indian chiefs of several tribes under the Council Oak Tree.

1720 The French build forts near Lafayette and Fort Wayne.

1732 The first permanent settlement is founded at Vincennes.

1749 Vincennes Roman Catholic Church, the first church in Indiana, is built.

1754 War breaks out between England and France. It is called the French and Indian War.

1763 The French and English sign a treaty of peace. Indiana is given to England. The French and Indian War ends.
Land west of the Alleghenies becomes an Indian reserve.
Pontiac leads tribes in war against settlers.

1774 The Quebec Act gives all lands in the northwest to the British province of Quebec.

1778 George Rogers Clark makes surprise attacks on Kaskaskia and Vincennes. The English later recapture Vincennes.

1779 Clark retakes Vincennes.

1783 The American Revolutionary War ends.

1785 The Land Ordinance of 1785 sets aside land for free schools in the Northwest Territory.

1787 Indiana becomes part of the Northwest Territory. Congress passes the Ordinance of 1787 to govern the territory.

1800 The Indiana Territory is established by Congress.
William Henry Harrison is appointed governor of the Indiana Territory. Vincennes is the capital.

1802 William Henry Harrison makes first treaties in which the Indians give up their land.

1803 Colonists from Switzerland settle in Switzerland County.

1804 The first newspaper in Indiana, the *Indiana Gazette*, appears.

1806 The first university is founded at Vincennes.

1811 General William Henry Harrison defeats the Indians at the battle of Tippecanoe.

1812 The War of 1812 begins.

1813 Corydon becomes the capital of the Indiana Territory.

1816 Indiana becomes the nineteenth state to enter the Union.
Seven-year-old Abraham Lincoln moves with his family from Kentucky to Indiana.

1824 The first mail is delivered between Vincennes and Louisville.

1825 Indianapolis becomes the state capital.
New Harmony is founded by Robert Owen.

1826 The Indians, by signing the Treaty of Wabash, give most of the land north and west of the Wabash River to the United States.

1831 The Underground Railroad begins in Randolph County.

1834 The first railroad track is laid in Shelbyville.

1840 William Henry Harrison is elected President.

1842 The Wabash and Erie Canal opens.

1851 Indiana's second constitution is adopted.

1852 The first state fair opens.

1859 The first air mail is carried by balloon from Lafayette to Crawfordsville.

1865 Abraham Lincoln's body lies in state in the capitol building in Indianapolis.

1880 Lew Wallace's *Ben Hur* is published.

1883 "The Old Swimmin' Hole" by James Whitcomb Riley is published.

1894 Elwood Haynes's first clutch auto runs at a speed of 8 miles per hour.

1911 The first 500-mile race is held at Motor Speedway in Indianapolis.

1928 The *Indiana Times* receives the Pulitzer Prize for its story about the Ku Klux Klan.

1956 The Northern Indiana Toll Road is finished.

1967 Richard Hatcher becomes Gary's first black mayor and the first black mayor of a northern city.

1970 Indianapolis and Marion County adopt a unified metropolitan government, called UNIGOV.

1979 A commission is created to develop Indiana's seventeenth state park. The White River Park is planned to be in Indianapolis.

1980 The official census ranks Indiana thirteenth in population among the 50 states.

1986 Union Station is renovated and reopened as a shopping center.

1988 J. Danforth Quayle is elected Vice President of the United States.

Index

county and city, 307–308
federal (U.S.), 299, 304–
    305, 312–315, 340
Indiana leaders in, 323–
    324
levels of, 308–309
local, 305–308
need for, 130
services, 308
state, 300–305, 314, 315,
    339
women in, 314
Governor, 315
    of Northwest Territory,
    131, 132–133
    See also names of specific
    governors
Governor's Circle, 169, 171
Granny cures, 170
Grant Line Road, 120
Graphs, 37–38, 40–42
Gravel roads, 225
Great Lakes, 49, 121, 217
Great Lakes Plains, 47, 48,
    49–50
Great War, changes brought
    by, 215–217
Greenfield, 324
Greenhouses, 191
Greenland, 47–48
Greenville, Treaty of
    (1795), 124
Greenwich, England, 19
Grid, 168
    example of (map), 20
    using a, 19–21
    See also Latitude;
    Longitude
Grissom, Virgil Ivan (Gus),
    241–243
Grouseland (house), 133,
    135
Gruelle, Johnny, 326

H
Hail, 57
Halleck, Charles A., 323
Hamer, Hugh and Thomas,
    165
Hamersley, George, 163,
    165
Hamilton, Henry, 112, 116,
    118
Hammond, George, 276–
    277
Hammond (town), 277, 337
Hanover (college), 338
Harbors, 240
Hardwoods, 265
Harmonie, 190–191
Harmonie State Park, 193
Harmonists (Rappites),
    190–191, 192
Harrison, Benjamin, 323
Harrison, William Henry,
    132, 135, 323
Hatcher, Richard, 324

Hay crop, 257
Haynes, Elwood, 229, 277–
    278
Hemisphere, 16
Hennepin, Father Louis, 97
Henry, Patrick, 113, 119
Heritage, 70
    See also Hoosier heritage
Higher education, 336–338
High schools, 335–336
Highway, interstate, 226,
    239
Highway 421, 227
Historic Indiana, 340–341
    map of, 164
History, defined, 9
Hogs, 259
Home front
    during Civil War, 206–
    207
    during world wars, 216–
    217
Home remedies, 170
Homestead Act (1862), 177
Homesteading, 176–177
Hoosier Dome, 332
Hoosier heritage, 180–199
    immigrants and, 196–197
    living with differences,
    181–187
    Owenites and, 192–193
    Rappites and, 190–191,
    192
    Society of Friends and,
    195–196
    Underground Railroad
    and, 194–195
Hoosier Hysteria, 330
Hoosier National Forest,
    266
Hoosier nickname, origin
    of, 35–36
Hoosier Schoolmaster, The
    (Eggleston), 325
Horseless carriage, 229,
    277, 278
Horsepower, 162
House of Representatives,
    state, 326
House of Representatives,
    U.S., 313–314, 316,
    323
House-raising, 159
Howard Steamboat
    Museum, 236
Hydroelectric power, 291

I
Ice Age, 47–49
Illinois, 132, 185
Illinois River, 98
Immigration and
    immigrants, 196–198
    Amish, 185
    German, 196
    Irish, 196

KKK and, 212
Independence, 108
    defined, 109
Indiana
    aerial photograph of, 30–
    31
    birth date of, 142
    first history of, 97–98
    foreign place names in
    (map), 197
    growth from 1785–1851
    (graph), 146
    location of, 36
    map of, 20
    maps at three different
    scales, 29–30
    time zones (map), 22
Indiana, meaning of, 69–
    70
Indiana, Robert, 329–330
Indiana Dunes National
    Lakeshore, 197, 240,
    340
Indiana Dunes State Park,
    340
Indiana Harbor, 286, 287
Indiana Natural Heritage
    Program, 267
Indianapolis, 58, 168–170,
    198, 216, 217, 236,
    307–308, 334, 336,
    337
    growth of, 172
    industry in, 287, 289
    land sale in, 170–171
    meaning of word, 145
    as route center, 51
    state government in, 300
    touring, 342–343
    as transportation hub,
    239
Indianapolis Colts, 332
Indianapolis Motor
    Speedway, 279
Indianapolis Museum of
    Art, 330
Indianapolis Zoo, 12, 13,
    343
Indiana State Museum, 330
Indiana State University,
    331
Indiana Territory, 129–133
    capital of, 140, 141
    in 1809 (map), 140
    growth of, 140
    map of, 133
Indiana University, 325,
    328, 330, 332, 333,
    336, 338
Indiana University-Purdue
    University at
    Indianapolis (IUPUI),
    337
Indian Creek, 141
Indians. *See* Native
    Americans
Indies, 69
Industry, 272–297

automobile, 229, 277–
    281, 284
defined, 273–274
early, 273–283
energy, need for, 290–
    293
farm equipment, 275–
    276
farm-related, 276–277
iron and steel, 218, 285–
    287, 288
medicine manufacturing,
    287–289
musical instruments,
    281–283
pollution from, 293–295
prefabricated homes, 283
problems of modern,
    290–295
service, 289
Indy 500 (race), 279, 333
International airport, 239
Interpreting map symbols,
    64–65
Interstate highway, 226,
    239
Iowa, 185
Irish immigrants, 196
Iron ore, 285
    making steel from, 287,
    288
Iroquois Indians, 86–87
Irrigation, 260

J
Jackson, Michael, 328
Jackson County, 219
James, Elijah, 211
Jasper County, 323
Jeffersonville, 235, 236
Jennings, Jonathan, 141,
    142
John Dillinger Historical
    Museum, 340
Johnson, H.D., 279
Johnston, Sarah Bush, 161
Judicial branch, 315
Justice. *See* Civil rights;
    Equality

K
Kankakee River, 98
Kaskaskia, Fort, 113, 116
Keelboats, 231
Kentucky, 52, 53
Kitty Hawk, North
    Carolina, 241
Kjellberg family, 196
Knight, Bobby, 330–331
Kokomo, 229, 278, 336
Ku Klux Klan (KKK), 211–
    212

L
Laboratory, defined, 287
Lafayette, 137, 337

Picture Index

CREDITS

B C D E F G H I J—VH—96 95 94 93 92 91 90